A SELECTIVE BIBLIOGRAPHY
OF CALIFORNIA LABOR HISTORY

A SELECTIVE BIBLIOGRAPHY OF CALIFORNIA LABOR HISTORY

By Mitchell Slobodek

Institute of Industrial Relations
UNIVERSITY OF CALIFORNIA, LOS ANGELES

Copyright, 1964, *by*

The Regents of the University of California

LIBRARY

AUG 26 1969

UNIVERSITY OF THE PACIFIC

204638

Western
American-

Z
7164
T7
863
copy 2

Copies of this publication may be purchased for $4.00 each from the

INSTITUTE OF INDUSTRIAL RELATIONS

Social Sciences Building
University of California
Los Angeles, California 90024

FOREWORD

The labor movement in California has had a long, distinctive, and colorful history. It began during the Gold Rush. In November 1849, for example, the carpenters of San Francisco struck to raise their daily wage from $12 to $16. San Francisco's reputation as a center of union strength goes back more than a century.

California, historically remote from the nation's centers of population and gifted with great natural resources, including climate, has graced her people, her economy, and her unions with a special quality found in no other part of the United States. One has difficulty putting this exactly into words, but the "feeling" is surely there. The doubting reader need only page casually through this volume for confirmation.

California's labor history has been rich in dramatic incidents: the Gold Rush, the Chinese exclusion movement, the bombing of the Los Angeles *Times* in 1910, the Preparedness Day bombing in San Francisco in 1916, the San Francisco general strike of 1934, the North American Aviation strike of 1941, the Hollywood jurisdictional strike of 1946. California labor has produced such colorful figures as the gold miner, the Chinese coolie, the seaman, the fruit tramp, the singing Wobbly, the Okie, the wetback and the bracero, the longshoreman, the logger, the over-the-road truck-driver, and the movie star. Several notable trials of labor and radical leaders have taken place in the state—the McNamara case, the Mooney–Billings case, the deportation proceedings against Harry Bridges. California has produced unusual labor leaders, among them Frank Roney, Denis Kearney, Andrew Furuseth, P. H. ("Pinhead") McCarthy, Tom Mooney, Mike Casey, Harry Bridges, Harry Lundeberg.

There is, as one might expect, an abundant literature devoted to these dramatic events and figures as well as to the more prosaic aspects of California's labor history. It was hardly surprising, therefore, that Mitchell Slobodek should come to the Institute of Industrial Relations almost a decade ago to say that he hoped to do an annotated bibliography of this material. The idea, certainly, was a good one and Mr. Slobodek brought a special combination of talents to the task. For one thing, he was a former seaman and a working dock clerk on the San Francisco waterfront who had himself participated in union affairs for many years. For another, he was a devoted bibliophile, a man who loved, read, and owned books. He had within his limited means put together respectable private collections of both Whitmaniana and labor history. Finally, his mind was keen and his style spare, suggesting that his annotations would be exact, unencumbered with extravagance, and useful. The Institute, therefore, assumed sponsorship for the undertaking and supplied assistance to the compiler within the resources at its disposal. The Institute lacked sufficient funds to finance the project, however, and these were generously supplied by the Louis M. Rabinowitz Foundation.

A Selective Bibliography of California Labor History should be of help to scholars working in both California and labor history. Its value to those working on broader topics should not be ignored, for it is suggestive of much that relates to the nation as a whole.

BENJAMIN AARON, *Director*
Institute of Industrial Relations
University of California, Los Angeles

PREFACE

The beginnings of this bibliography go back almost ten years. A casual interest at that time in a long forgotten labor-related incident on the San Francisco waterfront had led me on a quest for a bibliography of California labor materials. A thorough but unsuccessful search convinced me that none existed. The episode was soon forgotten but it was recalled later in conversations with friends. It was after one of these conversations, if memory serves me right, that I decided to compile this bibliography.

The decision was casually made and was unaccompanied by any urgency. But in time the work of compilation did get started, and continued for some years as an unhurried and rather pleasant week-end interest. Eventual outside assistance made it possible to plan completion of the bibliography for 1962, but unforeseen personal difficulties forced a change in schedule and it is only now complete.

The bibliography aims to meet the needs of the student and of those with interests in the labor movement and in related fields. This aim was the primary consideration in the choice of classifications, in their arrangement, and in the selection of the materials.

Two of the classifications require clarification. "Labor and Labor-Related Press" contains only noncurrent publications and is the only classification to include some items accepted from secondary sources. These consist of newspapers discussed by Ira B. Cross and Grace Heilman Stimson in their published work. I have included these newspapers with the hope that they may be found in collections other than those I have been able to examine. "Miscellaneous" includes items which refer to groups of workers or to subjects that do not readily fit into the selected classifications.

The literature of California labor history is of an unusual character. Only a small number of books deal wholly with the subject. Most of the material consists of pamphlets, articles in a great variety of periodicals, parts of books, parts of federal and state documents, and manuscript materials. The literature is scattered and some of it is of an ephemeral and fugitive nature, but only a small portion of it is scarce or rare.

With the exception of a few newspaper items, all the materials of the bibliography have been located and examined by me in accessible library collections, all of them located in the San Francisco Bay Area or on the

Stanford University campus. The complex of libraries at the University of California in Berkeley will yield all the literature with but few exceptions. The same is true of Stanford University but to a lesser degree. Most of the materials on the maritime industry are to be found in the Research Library of the International Longshoremen's and Warehousemen's Union in San Francisco. An excellent source for California state documents is the library of the California Division of Labor Statistics, also in San Francisco. The scarcer items can be located in the Bancroft Library, the California Room of the Oakland Public Library, the Hoover Institution Library at Stanford University, and in the special collections of the San Francisco Public Library. Public libraries should not be overlooked. Though they may lack many items, their collections will still include a considerable number of them. I made only token use of the collections of the California Historical Society, the California Pioneer Society, and the library of the University of California, Los Angeles.

Many friends of the bibliography helped me in its preparation. Bibliographers, professors of bibliography, and librarians willingly offered valuable suggestions and advice; librarians shared with me the labor of locating thousands of titles for examination. Because they are so numerous it would be difficult to acknowledge their individual contributions. I must express my indebtedness to them collectively.

I am grateful to the Institute of Industrial Relations of the University of California, Los Angeles for its sponsorship of the bibliography. I am particularly grateful to Professor Irving Bernstein, Associate Director of the Institute, for patiently guiding the project almost from its inception. I wish to express my thanks and appreciation to the Louis M. Rabinowitz Foundation for its financial assistance, which in great part made the completion of the bibliography possible. My thanks are due to Joan London for preparing the index.

MITCHELL SLOBODEK

April, 1964

CONTENTS

SPANISH AND MEXICAN BACKGROUND

Adam, Rev. J. "A Defense of the Missionary Establishments of Alta California," Historical Society of Southern California, *Annual Publications,* vol. 3, 1896, pp. 35–39.

Comments on some of the critical references made by Alexander Forbes on the treatment of the mission Indians by the mission fathers.

Bancroft, Hubert Howe. *History of the Pacific States of North America.* Vol. 29, *California Pastoral, 1769–1848.* San Francisco: The History Co., 1888. Chaps. 5–6, "Opposing Forces," "Golden Age of California," pp. 151–247.

A commentary on the California Indian's relationship to the mission system. The following excerpt is representative: "It is quite possible that the founders at first purposed not merely to convert the natives to Christianity, but to teach them the arts of civilized life. But be it as it may, they were taught what was barely necessary to utilize their labor."

Bolton, Herbert E. "The Mission as a Frontier Institution in the Spanish-American Colonies," *American Historical Review,* vol. 23, Oct. 1917, pp. 42–61.

Maintains that the basic motives responsible for the mission system are often overlooked. "Of the missions of Spanish America, particularly those in California, much has been written. But most that has been produced consists of chronicles of the deeds of the Fathers, polemic discussions by sectarian partisans or sentimental effusions. ... " The aims of the Spanish sovereigns, however, are shown to have been more realistic. As Spain herself did not have the population to colonize the conquered territories, the missions were used to hold and extend the Spanish frontiers. "The central interest around which the mission was built was the Indian. In respect to the native, the Spanish sovereigns from the outset, had three fundamental purposes. They desired to convert him, to civilize him and to exploit him."

Coman, Katharine. *Economic Beginnings of the Far West.* New York: Macmillan, 1912. 2 vols. "California," vol. 1, pp. 118–89.

Seeks an explanation for the failure of Spanish and Mexican colonization in California. A possible reason for the failure of the pueblos is suggested by the attitude of the San Jose colonists: "Proud of their Spanish name and lineage, they regarded labor as degrading, and managed to hire neophytes from the missions for such work as might not be avoided." As for the ranchos: "The encomienda was intended to prevent the enslavement of the Indians, but it led to peonage, a form of slavery which gave the proprietor all its profits with none of its responsibilities." And the missions: "With the achievement of success and the attainment of material comfort, missionary ardor languished."

1

Cook, Sherburne Friend. *The Conflict Between the California Indian and White Civilization. I: The Indian Versus the Spanish Mission*. Ibero-Americana: 21. Berkeley: University of California Press, 1943. "Labor," pp. 91–101.

In examining the factors that were responsible for the disintegration of the California Indian when he came under the influence of Spanish and American culture, the writer considers the factor of forced labor in the missions as being a major one. He maintains that the Indian was totally unprepared for such labor, that "the mental and bodily exertion of the type demanded by white civilization was completely new to him."

———. *Population Trends Among the California Mission Indians*. Ibero-Americana: 17. Berkeley: University of California Press, 1940. 48 pp.

An examination of the effect of the conditions of mission life and the mission system on the population patterns of the California mission Indians.

Cross, Ira B. *A History of the Labor Movement in California*. Berkeley: University of California Press, 1935. Chap. 1, "The Mission Era," pp. 1–9.

Writing of the California Indian's relationship to the missions, the author observes: "Virtually all the manual labor in and about the mission was carried on by the neophytes, the Padres busying themselves chiefly with supervision and religious instruction." He indicates the significance of the mission period to California labor history by pointing out that "For more than half a century (1776–1835) the life of the inhabitants of California centered around these outposts of Christianity, and in the Mission system we encounter the first labor problem in California."

Dana, Richard Henry. *Two Years Before the Mast*. New York: Harper, 1840. 483 pp.

The story of a two-year trip as a seaman on the sailing ship *Pilgrim* by a nineteen-year-old New England youth of patrician background. Since the greater part of the two years, 1835 and 1836, was spent on the California coast, the story includes a description of the daily life of contemporary California, with special emphasis on the hide trade, a major activity of the mission, rancho, and presidio Indians.

Engelhardt, Fr. Zephyrin. *The Missions and Missionaries of California*. San Francisco: James H. Barry, 1912. Vol. 2, chaps. 14–16, "The Aborigines: Their Habits," "The Mission System," "Mission System Vindicated," pp. 224–78.

Chap. 14 is an extremely unflattering description of the California aborigine and his way of life. Chaps. 15 and 16 in part describe the organization and daily routine of the mission but in the main serve as a fervent defense of the missionaries in their treatment of the Indians against what the author terms "their traducers." Particularly singled out are Hubert Howe Bancroft, Theodore Henry Hittell, and, to a lesser degree, Alexander Forbes.

Forbes, Alexander. *California: A History of Upper and Lower California*. London: Smith, Elder and Co., 1839; San Francisco: John Henry Nash,

1937. Chap. 5, "Account of the Missionary Establishments; Present State of the Indians in Them; Remarks on the Missionary System Generally, and on the Conversion of Infidels," pp. 124–52.

Pays tribute to the motives and intentions of the padres but questions the gains to the natives of California from their labors, stating: "They have transformed the aborigines of a beautiful country from free savages, into pusillanimous, superstitious slaves, they have taken from them the enjoyment of the natural productions of a delicious country, and administered to them the bare necessities of life, and that on the condition of being bondsmen forever."

Hansen, Woodrow James. *The Search for Authority in California*. Oakland: Biobooks, 1960. Chaps. 3–5, "Growth of the Secular Spirit," "A New Governor and the Emergence of Private Ownership of Land," "The Demise of the Missions and the Birth of a New Class System," pp. 12–22.

Reviews the rule of the Mexican governors who had the difficult task of secularizing the missions within the framework of California's conflicting interest groups. The missions were in time secularized, but the avowed aim of secularization—the distribution of the mission lands among the neophytes—was not realized. Instead, it is noted, a ranchero economy with wealthy ranch owners and a work force of ex-neophytes and gentile Indians came into being, an economy which "developed a social order that was virtually feudal."

Hart, James D. *American Images of Spanish California*. Published by the Friends of the Bancroft Library. Berkeley: Howell-North Press, 1960. 39 pp.

Observations on some of the literature that shaped the American image of Spanish California, especially stressing the period from 1830 to 1846. Among the authors discussed are Washington Irving, Richard Henry Dana, Helen Hunt Jackson, Alfred Robinson, Bret Harte, Robert Louis Stevenson, and Gertrude Atherton.

Hill, Joseph J. *History of Warner's Ranch and Its Environs*. Los Angeles: Privately printed, 1927. Chap. 5, "Secularization of the Missions," pp. 47–61.

Considers the purpose of the secularization decree and the more favorable conditions for its fulfillment in the Mexican missions as contrasted with those in the California missions.

Hittell, Theodore H. *History of California*. San Francisco: N. J. Stone & Co., 1897. Vol. 1, Book 3, chap. 12, "President Lasuen . . . ," pp. 452–72; Book 4, chap. 3, "Borica," pp. 558–73; chap. 12, "The Indians," pp. 728–44.

Book 3, chap. 12, includes an account of the visits of La Perouse and Vancouver to California and their observations on the conditions of the Indians at the missions. Book 4, chap. 3, includes a discussion of Governor Borica's disputes with the missionaries over the treatment of the mission Indians. Book 4, chap. 12, discusses the general characteristics of the California Indians and aims to determine how they would have developed under different treatment than they received under the Spanish and Mexican occupation.

Kroeber, Alfred L. "The Indians of California," *in* Zoeth Skinner Eldredge, ed., *History of California, Special Articles*. New York: Century History Co., 1914. Pp. 119–38.

The noted anthropologist describes the civilization of the California Indians and contends that it was too low in the scale of advancement to make possible a rapid adjustment to a civilized community. He notes that the Franciscans were aware of this and states: "They gathered no profits themselves from their converts' labors. The mission lands and improvements were merely held in trust for the Indians, as they might be for children or wards."

McGowan, Joseph A. "An Interpretation of Mission-Indian Relationships in Spanish California," *Proceedings,* First Annual Meeting of the Conference of California Historical Societies, June 24–25, 1955. Sonora, Calif.: Mother Lode Press, 1955. Pp. 7–17.

Contends that it is difficult to make a valid interpretation because "It is possible to find an eye-witness account for any viewpoint that anyone would care to take in regard to this subject." The author examines a number of such viewpoints by writers, including the romantic pro-clerical, the humanitarian liberal anti-clerical, and the debunking type. Concludes with observations on a more accurate approach to the problem.

Mora, Jo. *Californios: The Saga of the Hard Riding Vaqueros, America's First Cowboys*. Illustrated by the author. New York: Doubleday, 1949. 179 pp.

A somewhat romanticized account by a cowboy-artist of the California Indian vaquero who tended the vast herds of the missions and ranchos in Spanish and Mexican California. The description of the training and daily routine of the vaquero, the rodeos, the extraction of tallow, and the preparation of the hides for export provides an effective picture of the cattle industry.

Pourade, Richard F. *The History of San Diego: Time of the Bells*. San Diego: Union-Tribune Publishing Co., 1961. Chap. 3, "The Test by Fire," pp. 21–31.

An account of an uprising by Christianized and gentile Indians at the San Diego Mission in 1775.

Robinson, Alfred. *Life in California*. During a residence of several years in that territory.... New York: Wiley & Putnam, 1846. 341 pp. (Also: The Private Press of Thomas C. Russel, San Francisco, 1925. 316 pp.)

Referring to Mission San Luis Rey, the author writes: "At this time (1829) its population was about three thousand Indians, who were all employed in various occupations. Some were engaged in agriculture, while others attended to the management of over sixty thousand head of cattle. Many were carpenters, masons, coopers, saddlers, shoemakers, weavers, etc., while the females were employed in spinning...." The text includes many similar observations, many of them referring to the secularization of the missions.

Soulé, Frank, John H. Gihon, and James Nisbet. *The Annals of San Francisco*. New York: Appleton, 1854. Part 1, chap. 4, "Conduct of the Fathers Towards the Natives....," pp. 56–66.

A description of the wealth of the California missions and its dissipation after secularization; and a less than friendly description of how the mission fathers treated and employed the native Indians.

Webb, Edith Buckland. *Indian Life at the Old Missions*. Los Angeles: Warren F. Lewis, 1952. 326 pp.

A most painstaking and intimate record of the daily life and the daily routines at the California missions when Spain and Mexico ruled California. It describes in minute detail how the neophytes were taught the agricultural and vinicultural arts and the various manual trades, and how they were put to build aqueducts, dams, and reservoirs. One chapter is devoted to the California vaquero and his part in developing the hide and tallow industry and its by-products. The book is profusely illustrated, and photographs of miniatures depicting the numerous activities of the neophytes at the missions add to the realism of the record. A final chapter tells of the fate of the Indians after the secularization of the missions.

Young, John P. *San Francisco: A History of the Pacific Coast Metropolis*. San Francisco: S. J. Clarke Publishing Co., 1912. 2 vols.

Vol. 1, chap. 4, "Result of the Labors of the Missionaries," pp. 23–28.

Observes that the aims of the Spanish authorities and the mission padres concerning the California Indians were at variance. The authorities, it is maintained, regarded the missions as temporary establishments to exist only long enough to prepare the Indians for citizenship, while the padres aimed to save the souls of the Indians and considered the missions as permanent. But the padres found that the Indian would not work for wages, and "As their Catholic majesties, Ferdinand and Isabella, and their successors would not countenance nominal slavery, a method was devised which had many of the features of the feudal system of the middle ages...."

Vol. 1, chap. 12, "Labor Problems before American Occupation," pp. 77–82.

Observing that the Californians' only interest in the native Indian was the use they could make of him to relieve themselves of the drudgery of work, but that the Indian, especially after his treatment at the hands of the white man, could not be made to serve as a reliable labor supply, the author speculates that had gold not been discovered, California would have remained a backward agricultural area.

Barber, Ruth Kerns. "Indian Labor in the Spanish Colonies." Unpublished M.A. thesis. University of New Mexico, 1931. 135 pp.

Bowman, J. N. "The Resident Neophytes (Existentes) of the California Missions, 1769–1834," *Historical Society of Southern California Quarterly*, vol. 40, June 1958, pp. 138–48.

Casey, Jack Tull. "The Indians in the Settlement of California (1769–1869)." Unpublished M.A. thesis. University of California, Berkeley, 1946. 78 pp.

Clarke, E. P. "The Decline of the Mission Indians: Is the Gringo to Blame?" *Overland,* vol. 25, Jan. 1895, pp. 89–92.

De La Perouse, Jean Francois. "A Visit to Monterey in 1786 and a Description of the Indian of California," *California Historical Society Quarterly,* vol. 15, Sept. 1936, pp. 216–23.

Francis, Jessie Davies. "An Economic and Social History of Mexican California, 1822–1846." Unpublished Ph.D. dissertation. University of California, Berkeley, 1936. 2 vols. 805 pp.

Fuller, Varden. "The Supply of Agricultural Labor as a Factor in the Evolution of Farm Organization in California." Unpublished Ph.D. dissertation. University of California, Berkeley, 1939. Chap. 2, "Spanish and Mexican Colonial Agriculture and Impressed Indian Labor," pp. 16–54.

Geary, Rev. Gerald. *The Secularization of the California Missions (1810–1846).* Published Ph.D. dissertation. Washington, D.C.: Catholic University of America, 1934. 204 pp.

Kroeber, A. L. *Handbook of the Indians of California.* Berkeley: California Book Co., 1953. Chap. 57, "Population," pp. 880–91.

Langston, Kathryn Lee. "The Secularization of the California Missions, 1813–1846." Unpublished M.A. thesis. University of California, Berkeley, 1925. 291 pp.

Lowenstein, Norman. "Strikes and Strike Tactics in California Agriculture." Unpublished M.A. thesis. University of California, Berkeley, 1940. Chap. 1, "The Mission Indian Period," pp. 3–9.

Reid, Hugo. *The Indians of Los Angeles County.* Los Angeles: Privately printed, 1926. Letters nos. 16–22, pp. 44–70.

Scanland, J. M. "The Decline of the Mission Indians: Was It the Fault of the Padres?" *Overland,* vol. 24, Dec. 1894, pp. 634–39.

"The Secularization of the Missions: A Newly Discovered Document," Historical Society of Southern California, *Annual Publications,* 1934, pp. 66–73. [With an introduction by Henry R. Wagner]

Shinn, Charles Howard. *Mining Camps: A Study in American Frontier Government.* New York: Knopf, 1948. Chap. 6, "The Missions of the Pacific Coast," pp. 56–67.

Simpson, Lesley Byrd, trans. *The Law of Burgos, 1512–1513: Royal Ordinances for the Good Government and Treatment of the Indians.* San Francisco: John Howell, 1960. 57 pp.

Tac, Pablo. *Indian Life and Customs at Mission San Luis Rey.* A record of California mission life by an Indian neophyte. Edited and translated by Minna and Gordon Hewes. San Luis Rey, Calif. 1958. 33 pp.

Taylor, Paul S. "Spanish Seamen in the New World during the Colonial Period," *Hispanic American Historical Review,* vol. 5, Nov. 1922, pp. 631–61.

Tays, George. "Revolutionary California: The Political History of California during the Mexican Period, 1822–1846." Unpublished Ph.D. dissertation. University of California, Berkeley, 1932. 806 pp.

Willard, C. D. "The Padres and the Indians," *Land of Sunshine,* vol. 1, Sept. 1894, pp. 73–75.

Willoughby, Nona Christensen. "Division of Labor among the Indians of California." Unpublished M.A. thesis. University of California, Berkeley, 1950. 94 pp.

GENERAL

Bennett, John E. *The California Manufacturer and Eastern Competition.* San Francisco: Business Men's Economic Association [1914?]. 35 pp.

Seeks to prove that artificially created high wages prevent the California manufacturer from successfully competing in national and international markets and recommends that he "eliminate the union from his establishment" as a cure.

Bonner, John. "The Labor Question of the Pacific Coast," *Claifornian Illustrated Magazine,* vol. 1, April 1892, pp. 410–19.

Maintains that labor organizations on the Pacific Coast have kept wages at double or treble the eastern or European level by guarding against "An influx of labor from the eastern states, a flood of labor from China and a fresh supply of labor from natural increase...."

Brace, Charles Loring. *The New West, or California in 1867–1868.* New York: Putnam, 1869. Chap. 5, "Building Association...," pp. 49–73.

Comments on some of the labor conditions in San Francisco. He further relates: "I witnessed a most imposing, well dressed, and orderly procession of mechanics and laborers who were combining to get ten hours wages for eight hours work."

Bridges, Harry, and W. P. Fuller, Jr. *Verbatim Report of Statements, and Questions and Answers by Representatives of the Committee for Industrial Organization (CIO) and the Committee of 43.* Town Hall Meeting, Civic Auditorium, San Francisco, June 3, 1938. San Francisco, 1938. 39 pp.

Stating that the purpose of the meeting is to reply to the stand of the Committee of 43 on San Francisco labor relations as formulated in a report issued by it, Bridges gives the position of the CIO on the open versus the closed shop and on sympathetic and jurisdictional strikes, and tells how the CIO proposes to solve these problems. Fuller, representing the Committee of 43, explains the reasons for the views on these questions the committee has already expressed. Among those participating during the question and answer period are Henry Schmidt and Louis Goldblatt for the CIO and Roger Lapham and Almon Roth for the Committee of 43 and the employers.

California. Bureau of Labor Statistics. *Fourth Biennial Report, 1889–1890.* Sacramento, 1890. Part 5, "Investigations," pp. 314–28.

The investigations involved San Francisco and Oakland laundries, Chinese cigar factories, a Napa woolen mill, and a stonecutters' strike.

——. ——. *Statistical Report of Unions Represented in the Council of Federated Trades and Labor Organizations of the Pacific Coast*. Sacramento, 1887. 16 pp.

The report, compiled by V. Hoffmeyer, statistical secretary of the Council of Federated Trades, contains statistical summaries made by 21 unions including those of the bookbinders, cigar makers, seamen, and printers.

Carlson, Oliver. *A Mirror for Californians*. Indianapolis: Bobbs-Merrill, 1941. Chap 9, "Union Makers and Union Breakers," pp. 196–237.

A sketchy summary of the California labor movement from 1850 to 1940, told in a popular vein and liberally quoting from *A History of the Labor Movement in California* by Ira B. Cross.

Caughey, John Walton. *California*. New York: Prentice-Hall, 1940. Chap. 31, "Recent Political and Social Problems," pp. 562–87.

Includes brief but effective references to the intense agitation against the Japanese and their eventual exclusion, the measures taken at a later date against the Mexican agricultural worker, the McNamara case, the Wheatland riot, the Mooney case, the west coast maritime strikes of the 1930's, and the strikes of the migrant agricultural workers in 1933–34.

Cronin, Bernard Cornelius. *Father Yorke and the Labor Movement in San Francisco, 1900–1910*. Published Ph.D. dissertation. Studies in Economics, vol. 12. Washington, D.C.: Catholic University of America, 1943. 239 pp.

An account of Father Yorke's ten years of intense interest and activity in the labor movement of San Francisco. That activity included an active part in the 1901 teamster strike, participation in the stabilization of the labor movement after that strike, and a role in the streetcar strikes of 1906 and 1907. Particularly stressed is Father Yorke's contribution as a writer on labor questions and his considerable influence in the inner circle of San Francisco's trade-union leadership.

Cross, Ira B. *A History of the Labor Movement in California*. Berkeley: University of California Press, 1935. 354 pp.

Generally accepted as the pioneer effort in the field of California labor history, Professor Cross's study affords a comprehensive review of the development of the labor movement in California. A brief account of impressed Indian labor during the Spanish and Mexican periods is followed by a description of the beginnings of trade-union organization against the background of the gold rush, the ebb and flow of such organization through periods of depression and prosperity, the impact of Chinese and Japanese labor competition, the development of the labor press and of affiliated organizations on a local, state, and regional basis, the growth of employers' counterorganizations, and labor's involvement in political movements.

Dressmakers Union Local 22, ILGWU. *American Labor Faces the Future: The Problem of Trade Unionism in the Light of the San Francisco Gen-*

eral Strike. Letter of William Green to Charles S. Zimmerman; reply of Zimmerman to Green. New York, 1934. 18 pp.

An exchange of letters reflecting contrasting views on sympathetic and general strikes in general and on the San Francisco general strike of July 1934 in particular.

Eaves, Lucile. *A History of California Labor Legislation.* Berkeley: The University Press [1910]. Chap. 1, "The San Francisco Labor Movement," pp. 1–81.

Examines the factors that tended to make San Francisco a center not only for the California labor movement but often for that of the entire Pacific Coast, and reviews the three general forms that San Francisco's labor organizations assumed between 1850 and the turn of the century: trade unions, societies for the promotion of special causes, and labor parties. The trade unions are considered to have reached maturity with the organization of such permanent bodies as the Central Labor and Building Trades Councils; the anti-Chinese associations and the eight-hour leagues are treated among the special societies; and the Workingmen's Party of California is considered in some detail among the labor parties.

Industrial and Immigration Association of California. *Address and By-Laws.* San Francisco: Edward Bosqui and Co., 1867. 32 pp.

States that the Association aims to encourage immigration to California of the "European industrial classes" and to serve as adviser and aid to such immigrants in finding jobs and settling new land.

Kennedy, Van Dusen. *Nonfactory Unionism and Labor Relations.* Berkeley: Institute of Industrial Relations, University of California, 1955. 45 pp.

Maintains that American labor unions and labor relations may be divided into two broad forms: nonfactory and factory, the first being the characteristic form on the west coast and particularly in California. Nonfactory and factory unionism are held to differ in these major respects: emphasis on the local union as compared to centralization at the national level, stress on the business agent as opposed to the shop steward, multi-employer bargaining in contrast to single bargaining units, and marked differences in contract administration.

Kerr, Clark. "Collective Bargaining on the Pacific Coast," *Monthly Labor Review,* vol. 64, April 1947, pp. 650–74.

Discusses the organizational and collective bargaining history of the major industries on the Pacific Coast, including those of longshoring, maritime transportation, fishing, lumber, pulp and paper, motion picture production, aircraft, and teaming. A concluding section comments on the exceptionally developed multiple-employer bargaining procedures of the San Francisco area.

Kerr, Clark, and Lloyd H. Fisher. "Multiple-Employer Bargaining: The San Francisco Experience," *in* R. A. Lester and J. Shister, eds., *Insights into Labor Issues.* New York: Macmillan, 1948. Pp. 25–61.

The San Francisco–Oakland region, an area of medium and small-scale firms, has since 1934 seen the development of multiple-employer bargaining and the master agreement, features usually associated with large-scale industry. The authors examine the reasons for this development and its effect on the relative positions of the employers and the unions, and on the pattern of industrial relations in other areas.

Kerr, Clark, and Roger Randall. *Crown Zellerbach and the Pacific Coast Pulp and Paper Industry: A Case Study.* Case Study no. 1. Prepared for the National Planning Committee on the Causes of Industrial Peace under Collective Bargaining. Washington, D.C.: National Planning Association, 1948. 78 pp.

Examines the conditions and attitudes that have contributed to long-lasting peaceful industrial relations in the Pacific Coast pulp and paper industry. Among the factors cited are management's acceptance of the principle of unionization of its employees; industry consciousness rather than craft or class consciousness on the part of the unions; a high degree of respect for each other by representatives of both sides; assured good wages and security for the industry's workers; scrupulous observance of contracts by both sides; and enjoyment by management of good profits, high productivity, and a "neutral" and expanding market.

Knight, Robert Edward Lee. *Industrial Relations in the San Francisco Bay Area, 1900–1918.* Berkeley: University of California Press, 1960. 463 pp.

Writes of a period in the history of industrial relations in the San Francisco Bay Area when the organized labor movement had reached comparative maturity and when the employers were engaged in building organizations to counter the strength of labor. Among the significant events and characteristic features of the industrial relations of the period are the establishment of the dominance of the Building Trades Council; organization of the City Front Federation and its participation in the teamsters' strike in 1901; the capture of the San Francisco municipal administration by the Union Labor Party and the party's relationship to the Bay Area labor movement; the open-shop drives of the Citizens' Alliance; the Los Angeles *Times* bombing; the development of recognizable forms of collective bargaining; the longshore strike of 1916; the organization of the Waterfront Workers Federation; the assumption by the San Francisco Chamber of Commerce of an open-shop role; the Mooney-Billings case; and the history of San Francisco Bay Area labor during World War I.

Lang, Lucy Robins. *Tomorrow Is Beautiful.* New York: Macmillan, 1948. 303 pp.

An autobiography recalling four crowded decades of participation in the activities of the American labor movement. Often crossing ideological lines, Mrs. Lang associated with the leading figures influencing labor affairs in those years—Emma Goldman, Alexander Berkman, Jack London, Olaf Tweitmoe, Tom Mooney, Bill Haywood, Samuel Gompers, and William Green among them. Her main efforts were directed toward defending labor prisoners, and she was prominent in the defense of David Caplan, Matthew Schmidt, Mooney, and Eugene Debs.

London, Joan. *Jack London and His Times: An Unconventional Biography.* New York: Doubleday, Doran, 1939. 387 pp.

It has often been observed that Jack London among American writers was particularly representative of his time. Joan London, one of his daughters, gives substance to this observation in her critical biography of her father by weaving into a meaningful pattern the economic, social, and intellectual influences that shaped his writings, concepts, and actions. It is her view that these influences especially explain London's earnest participation in the labor and social movements of his time early in his career, and his later virtual abandonment of them.

McWilliams, Carey. *California: The Great Exception.* New York: A. A. Wyn, 1949. Chap. 8, "California Labor: Total Engagement," pp. 127–49.

Aims to demonstrate that the California labor movement has long occupied an exceptional position in the history of American labor. Particular reasons, it is suggested, account for this position: the deep-rooted native character of the California labor movement, its early political orientation, marked radicalism, early and continuous emphasis on joint action, and inclusion within its ranks of a large petty bourgeois element—all related to the distinctive social, geographic, and economic influences in California's development.

Perry, Louis B., and Richard S. Perry. *A History of the Los Angeles Labor Movement, 1911–1941.* Berkeley: University of California Press, 1963. 622 pp.

Records in broad chronological order the experiences of labor in Los Angeles, detailed to the local union level, during the years when that city was widely known as a citadel of the open-shop forces in the United States. Few groups of workers are excluded from the history, but the activities of those in the maritime, motion picture, and building industries and of the unemployed in the depression of the 1930's are stressed. The activities of the advocates of the open shop are especially emphasized.

Roney, Frank. *Irish Rebel and California Labor Leader: An Autobiography.* Edited by Ira B. Cross. Berkeley: University of California Press, 1931. 573 pp.

In his introduction to the autobiography, Cross states that one of the unique features of the history of the California labor movement is that each successive wave of trade-union organization, from the days of the gold rush to the early nineties, had been dominated, more or less completely, by some one personality. Frank Roney was one of these leaders, guiding the labor movement from 1881 to 1886. His autobiography affords an intimate picture of the California labor scene of that period and Roney's role in it, which was especially notable for his initiative in developing central labor organizations.

Soulé, Frank, John H. Gihon, and James Nisbet. *The Annals of San Francisco.* New York: Appleton, 1854. Part 2, chap. 9, "1849: Increase of Population . . . ," pp. 243–63.

Gives a picture of a "topsy-turvy" society in which "doctors and dentists become draymen, or barbers, or shoe-blacks . . . "; a society in which wages for both skilled and unskilled labor were high but little could be bought with them.

Stimson, Grace Heilman. *Rise of the Labor Movement in Los Angeles.* Berkeley: University of California Press, 1955. 529 pp.

A history of the development of the Los Angeles trade-union movement from 1875 to 1912. An introductory chapter traces the first faltering steps toward trade-union organization before 1875, beginning with the printers in 1859. A following chapter reviews the tendency of labor in the 1870's to seek reform through political action rather than through union organization. The history then follows the main-stream of the Los Angeles labor movement against the background of alternating booms and depressions, labor's occasional political involvements, the developing drive for the open shop culminating in the bombing of the Los Angeles *Times,* the aftermath of the bombing, and the victory of the open-shop elements.

Swift, Morrison I. *What a Tramp Learns in California.* Published for the Society of American Socialists. San Francisco: Chas. Wilson and Co., 1896. 26 pp.

Records his experiences during an extended trip through the counties adjacent to San Francisco and comments on unemployment, working conditions, and wages, particularly farm wages, he observed in that area.

U.S. Bureau of Labor Statistics. *Strikes in the United States, 1880–1936,* by Florence Peterson. Bull. no. 651. Washington, 1938. 183 pp.

A statistical study with the aim of recording not only the "gross number of strikes but also their causes and results....." Includes analytical tables on California strikes.

U.S. Congress. Senate. Commission on Industrial Relations. *Final Report and Testimony.* 64th Cong., 1st sess., S. Doc. 415. Washington, 1916. "Collective Bargaining in San Francisco," vol. 6, pp. 5169–401; "General Industrial Relations and Conditions in San Francisco," vol. 6, pp. 5421–72.

Testimony: Grant Fee, president, Building Trades Employers Association, pp. 5171–89; P. H. McCarthy, president, California Trades Council, pp. 5189–218; John A. O'Connell, secretary, San Francisco Labor Council, pp. 5278–83; J. D. Roantree, secretary, Franklin Printing Trades Association, pp. 5283–309; Robert Newton Lynch, manager, San Francisco Chamber of Commerce, pp. 5431–35; Fremont Older, editor, San Francisco *Bulletin,* pp. 5437–43; Andrew J. Gallagher, president, San Francisco Labor Council, pp. 5444–52.

Young, John P. *San Francisco: A History of the Pacific Coast Metropolis.* San Francisco: S. J. Clarke Publishing Co., 1912. 2 vols.

Vol. 1, chap. 39, "Labor Conditions and the Chinese Question," pp. 371–80.

Covers a decade of intense activity by San Francisco and California trade unions. The period, 1860–1870, was characterized by many pioneer efforts on the part of labor, including the organization of a Central Trades Assembly in 1863; initiation by the carpenters of an eight-hour league, which developed in 1867 into the Mechanics State Council; formation of the politically oriented Industrial League of California; the first agitation for participation in the national trade-union movement; and the beginning of San Francisco labor's preoccupation with the Chinese question.

Vol. 2, chap. 58, "Numerous and Serious Labor Troubles in the City," pp. 681–700.

Stating that San Francisco labor's activities took a new direction after it ended its preoccupation with the Chinese question, the author discusses the events which crowded the years 1883 to the re-election of Mayor Eugene Schmitz in 1903. Highlighted are the growth of the Knights of Labor, the organization and activities of the International Workingmen's Association, formation of the Federated Trades Council of the Pacific Coast, organization into trade unions of many unskilled groups, widespread strike activity including the strike of the City Front Federation in 1901, formation of the Union Labor Party, and Mayor Schmitz's first term in office under its banner.

Bernstein, Irving. "[West Coast] Trade Union Characteristics, Membership, and Influence," *Monthly Labor Review,* vol. 82, May 1959, pp. 530–35.

California State Federation of Labor. *Your State Federation of Labor.* San Francisco, 1951. 12 pp.

Coons, Arthur G., and Arjay R. Miller. "A Survey of the Economic Activities and Problems of the Los Angeles Industrial Area." Claremont, Calif., 1941. "Incomes and Planes of Living," pp. 86–116; "Influence of the Defense Program upon Labor," pp. 308–22. Typewritten.

Cross, Ira B. *Collective Bargaining and Trade Agreements in the Brewery, Metal, Teaming and Building Trades of San Francisco.* University of California Publications in Economics, vol. 4, no. 4. Berkeley: University of California Press, 1918. Chapter 1, "Historical Sketch of Trade Unionism in San Francisco," pp. 235–42.

———. "The Labor Movement in California," *in* International Typographical Union, *57th Convention, Official Souvenir.* San Francisco, 1911. Unpaged.

Dixon, Marion. "The History of the Los Angeles Central Labor Council." Unpublished M.A. thesis. University of California, Berkeley, 1929. 240 pp.

Flannery, Helen Ida. "The Labor Movement in Los Angeles, 1880–1903." Unpublished M.A. thesis. University of California, Berkeley, 1929. 103 pp.

General Campaign Strike Committee. *California Labor's Greatest Victory.* Final report of General Campaign Strike Committee for unionizing of

Los Angeles, embracing receipts and expenditures, June 1, 1910–April 1, 1912. [San Francisco? 1912?] 60 pp.

General Campaign Strike Committee of San Francisco. *Report on Strikes by Carmen, Telephone Operators, Laundry Workers and Iron Trades Unions, June 10, 1907 to December 30, 1907.* San Francisco, 1908. 62 pp.

Goldberger, Jack, and George W. Johns. "A Great Union Town: The San Francisco Story," *American Federationist,* vol. 58, June 1951, pp. 12–15.

Hurt, Elsey. *California State Government: An Outline of Its Administrative Organization from 1850 to 1936.* Sacramento: State Printing Office, 1937. "Department of Industrial Relations," pp. 89–100.

Jacobson, Pauline. *Struggles of Organized Labor in Los Angeles.* Compiled from special articles published in San Francisco *Bulletin.* Los Angeles: Central Labor and Building Trades Councils of Los Angeles, 1911. 42 pp.

"Labor Problems in California," *Transactions of the Commonwealth Club of California,* vol. 5, April 1910, pp. 15–164.

"Labor Relations in War and Peace," *Transactions of the Commonwealth Club of California,* vol. 38, Jan. 1944, pp. 47–98.

Lopez, Espiridion Barrientos. "The History of the California State Federation of Labor." Unpublished M.A. thesis. University of California, Berkeley, 1932. 121 pp.

Morgans, Robert DeWitt. "A History of Organized Labor in Long Beach, California." Unpublished M.A. thesis. University of California, Berkeley, 1939. 161 pp.

Mortenson, Clara Estelle. "Organized Labor in San Francisco from 1892 to 1902." Unpublished M.A. thesis. University of California, Berkeley, 1916. 116 pp.

"Municipal and County Labor Boards," *Transactions of the Commonwealth Club of California,* vol. 32, Dec. 1937, pp. 141–75.

"Oakland and the Working Man," *East Bay Labor Journal,* Labor Day Number, Aug. 30, 1929, pp. 10, 48.

Ohlson, Robert Verner. "The History of the San Francisco Labor Council, 1892–1939." Unpublished M.A. thesis. University of California, Berkeley, 1940. 195 pp.

Orcutt, Eddy, and Wells Toft. "The San Diego Story," *American Federationist,* vol. 58, Sept. 1951, pp. 26–27, 31–32.

[Osborne, J. W.] *Industrial Interests of California: By an Old Resident.* San Francisco: Towne and Bacon, 1862. "Our Labor Interests," pp. 41–50.

Peterson, Florence. *Handbook of Labor Unions.* Washington, D.C.: American Council on Public Affairs, 1944. 415 pp.

Rosenson, Alexander Moses. "Origin and Nature of the CIO Movement in Alameda, California." Unpublished M.A. thesis. University of California, Berkeley, 1938. 187 pp.

Russell, Phillips. "The Class Struggle on the Pacific Coast: An Interview with O. A. Tweitmoe," *International Socialist Review,* vol. 13, Sept. 1912, pp. 236–38.

Ryan, Frederick L. *A History of the San Diego Labor Movement.* San Diego: San Diego State College, 1959. 165 pp.

Sheetz, Carson P. "History of Labor Unions in Sacramento, 1849–1899." Unpublished M.A. thesis. University of California, Berkeley, 1933. 107 pp.

Shelley, John F. "This Is San Francisco," *American Federationist,* vol. 55, June 1958, pp. 20–22.

Tipton, Gene B. "The Labor Movement in the Los Angeles Area during the Nineteen-Forties." Unpublished Ph.D. dissertation. University of California, Los Angeles, 1953. 395 pp.

Troy, Leo. *Distribution of Union Membership among the States, 1939 and 1953.* New York: National Bureau of Economic Research, 1957. 32 pp.

"The World in California," *Hutchings California Magazine,* vol. 1, Feb. 1857, pp. 337–45; March 1857, pp. 385–93.

Wright, Doris Marion. "The Making of Cosmopolitan California—an Analysis of Immigration, 1848–1870," *California Historical Society Quarterly,* vol. 19, Dec. 1940, pp. 323–43; vol. 20, March 1941, pp. 65–79.

INDUSTRIES, CRAFTS, AND TRADES

AGRICULTURE

Adamic, Louis. "Cherries Are Red in San Joaquin," *Nation,* vol. 142, June 27, 1936, pp. 840–41.

Scenes in the San Joaquin Valley at cherry-picking time, with talk among the migratory workers of organization and expected trouble.

Anderson, Nels. *Men on the Move.* Chicago: University of Chicago Press, 1940. 357 pp.

Includes extended references to migrant agricultural workers in California.

Bancroft, Philip S. *The Farmer and the Communists.* An address by the president of the Associated Farmers of Contra Costa County before the Commonwealth Club of California, April 26, 1935. San Francisco: Associated Farmers of California, 1935. 13 pp. (Also published in *Daily Commercial News,* S.F., April 29 and 30, 1935.)

Describes the conditions which do not allow the California farmer to pay high wages and which determine his opposition to trade-union organization among agricultural workers. Contends, however, that the workers have been satisfied with their wages and that strikes and disturbances in the agricultural areas have been due to the activity of professional Communist agitators. Suggests measures to deal with the Communists, detailing the efforts of the Associated Farmers as examples.

Beals, Carleton. *American Earth: The Biography of a Nation.* New York: Lippincott, 1939. Chap. 21, "Migs: Shantytown on Wheels," pp. 393–408.

Notes that 80 per cent of the California migrants in the mid-1930's were from the drought areas, but maintains that although drought and depression were immediately responsible, the reason for their migration was more fundamental. It is seen as part of a trek from lands of declining soil fertility which had begun before the Civil War. These latter-day migrants, however, find no frontier waiting for them; they come into a highly developed, industrialized agricultural system, cannot regain their former relation to the soil, and can look forward only to a bare existence.

Bloch, Louis. "Report on the Mexican Labor Situation in the Imperial Valley," *in* California Bureau of Labor Statistics, *Twenty-second Biennial Report, 1925–1926.* Sacramento, 1926. Pp. 113–27.

Reports on claims of a labor shortage in the Imperial Valley in 1925 on the basis of which demands had been made by farm operators for the registration of additional Mexican agricultural workers. Indicates that an investigation did not reveal an actual labor shortage that year, but did show that growers had been compelled to pay higher wages and provide better housing and better working conditions to obtain sufficient labor.

California. Division of Labor Law Enforcement. *Farm Labor Contractors in California.* Draft for review, submitted by Alan Bruce. [San Francisco? 1948?] 183 pp.

A survey made to gather information which would aid in the enforcement of the Labor Code as it applied to farm labor contractors, and to serve as a basis for possible changes in the code. The information is based on interviews with labor contractors, foremen, agents, and group leaders, and covers farm operations in 1947 in the San Joaquin, Sacramento, Santa Clara, Salinas, and Imperial valleys. Among the subjects treated are: functions of contractors, analysis of contracts, and how contractors function. An appendix contains representative contracts.

————. Legislature. Joint Committee on Agriculture and Livestock Problems. Partial Report: Part 1, *Farm Labor Housing in California.* Sacramento, 1949. 128 pp.

Features a photographic display of farm labor housing in California, pp. 43–100.

California State Chamber of Commerce. *Migrants: A National Problem and Its Impact on California.* Report and recommendations of the Statewide Committee on the Migrant Problem. San Francisco, 1940. 51 pp.

Seeks to ascertain the factors in the states of origin which cause migration and the factors in California which attract migrants. Pointing to the need for prompt action, the Chamber recommends measures to retard out-migration and to care for migrants already in California.

Caughey, John W. "Current Discussion of California's Migrant Labor Problem," *Pacific Historical Review,* vol. 8, Sept. 1939, pp. 347–54.

Chiefly a review of John Steinbeck's *The Grapes of Wrath* and Carey McWilliams' *Factories in the Fields.*

Central Labor Council, Santa Clara County. *Labor in Field and Orchard! A Call to Organize.* [Santa Clara? 1936?] 15 pp.

Discusses the living and working conditions of the field workers and their families, the methods used by the ranchers to keep wages low, and their failure to supply proper housing, sanitary facilities, and transportation for the field workers or proper schooling for their children. Urges them to organize into trade unions, pointing to other groups of agricultural workers who have improved their conditions by organization.

"Discussion on the Labor Question," *Proceedings,* 27th Convention of the California Fruit Growers, San Francisco, Dec. 2–5, 1902. Pp. 272–81, 395–98.

Stresses the need to amend the Chinese Exclusion Act so as to allow a limited number of Chinese to come to the United States for field work.

"Discussion on Labor Resolution No. 110," *Monthly Bulletin,* California State Commission on Horticulture, vol. 7, Jan.–Feb. 1918, pp. 102–9.

The resolution concerned shortages of agricultural labor in California during World War I.

"Farm Labor," *Transactions of the Commonwealth Club of California,* vol. 13, May 1918, pp. 73–122.

Partial contents: R. L. Adams, University of California, "The Existing Labor Situation," pp. 74–83; George W. Pierce, California Almond Growers Association, "Farm Labor from an Orchardist Point of View," pp. 84–94.

Fisher, Lloyd H. *The Harvest Labor Market in California.* Cambridge: Harvard University Press, 1953. 183 pp.

Considers the character of California's agriculture to be directly related to the volume and nature of its labor supply. As the major labor-consuming operation on the farm is the harvest, its characteristics are analyzed in detail, including a study of the labor-contractor system and of wage-fixing practices by employers' associations and government agencies, especially as these practices operated during World War II. An appendix contains a number of representative labor contracts.

Fuller, Varden. "Farm Labor: Supply, Policies, and Practices," *Monthly Labor Review,* vol. 82, May 1959, pp. 518–23.

"As in the nation at large, one of the most outstanding changes affecting farm manpower in the Pacific Coast States during the past decade has been a sharp decline in agricultural employment," due in the main to mechanization. However, it is pointed out that the peaks of seasonal labor need still remain, that there is the contradiction of a "coexistence of a labor surplus and a labor shortage," and that agriculture uses five times as many alien laborers as it did during the second world war. The author examines the causes of these conditions and suggests possible remedies.

———. *Labor Relations in Agriculture.* Berkeley: Institute of Industrial Relations, University of California, 1955. 46 pp.

Seeks the reasons for the almost total absence of collective bargaining in agriculture. Some of the possible reasons examined are the special nature of the industry and its labor force, the failure to apply federal labor laws to agriculture, and, in recent years, the influence of the bracero program and continuing mechanization of harvesting operations.

Galarza, Ernesto. "Big Farm Strike: A Report on the Labor Dispute at the Di Giorgio's," *Commonweal,* vol. 48, June 4, 1948, pp. 178–82.

"In California's central valley the homesteader and the family farm are yielding to the assembly line methods of corporations like Di Giorgio's." The strike at the 12,000-acre ranch in Kern County had been in progress for eight months, and the author tells of the methods used by the corporation during that time to break the strike: violence, imported and smuggled Mexican nationals, legislative lobbying, wild charges of Communism, and expensive publicity, to name but a few.

Gardner, Virginia. "Back to the Cotton Patch," *Masses & Mainstream,* vol. 3, Jan. 1950, pp. 23–36.

Describes a trip by truck from Los Angeles to a cotton patch near Bakersfield, California, and a day's cotton picking. The cotton pickers on the trip are mostly Los Angeles unemployed Negro and Mexican industrial workers who have exhausted their unemployment compensation benefits.

Goldschmidt, Walter. *As You Sow.* New York: Harcourt, Brace, 1947. 288 pp.

"From industrialized sowing of the soil is reaped an urbanized rural society." Studies of Wasco and the neighboring towns of Dinuba and Arvin are case histories to illustrate the basic structure of California agriculture. As large-scale farming in California depends on an abundant supply of low-paid labor, considerable attention is given to the social and economic status of the "lower" or "outside" group in the communities, comprised of whites ("Okies"), Mexicans, and Negroes.

Hartranft, Marshall V. *Grapes of Gladness: California's Refreshing and Inspiring Answer to John Steinbeck's "Grapes of Wrath."* Los Angeles: De Vorss & Co., 1939. 127 pp.

An introductory statement by the author, boxed for emphasis, reflects his approach to the problems raised in Steinbeck's novel: "You are not broke, though you have no money. You are worth $1000 in California land values just because you sit in that auto. Los Angeles has many skyscrapers worth a million dollars each, only because a million law-abiding refined people dwell there. California still has room for any who can feed themselves from our endless chain-gardens instead of from the state treasury."

Hewes, Laurence. *Boxcar in the Sand.* New York: Knopf, 1957. 262 pp.

Reminiscences of twenty-five years of federal government service. After a term as an assistant to Under Secretary of Agriculture Tugwell, the author served as western regional director of the Farm Security Administration, which at that time had the welfare of the agricultural migrant worker as one of its main responsibilities. The coming of the second world war temporarily solved the problem of the migrants, and the FSA was given the task of evacuating the Japanese to resettlement camps and later of recruiting thousands of braceros to fill the wartime need for farm labor.

Hibbs, Ben. "Footloose Army," *Country Gentleman,* vol. 110, Feb. 1940, pp. 7–8, 42–44.

Deals with Madera County's experience with migrant agricultural workers.

The Imperial Valley Farm Labor Situation. Report of the Special Investigating Committee appointed at the request of the California State Board of Agriculture, the California Farm Bureau Federation, and the Agricultural Department of the California Chamber of Commerce. San Francisco: Associated Farmers of California, 1934. 16 pp.

The committee—C. B. Hutchison, W. C. Jacobsen, and John Phillips—reports by answering three key questions: What is the situation in the Imperial Valley? Is there immediate danger of a strike or serious trouble? Is the situation localized, or is it related to labor disturbances in other agricultural areas of the state? The answers, in the main, are: Wages in the valley are fair when related to returns; the workers are satisfied and there is no danger of a strike or of any disturbance; activities of the Cannery and Agricultural Workers Industrial Union are part of a statewide conspiracy by Communist elements. Recommends minimum improvements for the field workers and measures to cope with labor disturbances.

Jackson, Joseph Henry. *Why Steinbeck Wrote the Grapes of Wrath, and Other Essays*. Lithographs by Thomas Hart Benton. New York: Limited Editions Club, 1940. 30 pp.

Discusses the circumstances, both in Steinbeck's literary life and in the agricultural areas of California, that inspired him to write *The Grapes of Wrath*. Comments especially on the wide sympathetic public response to the novel.

Jamieson, Stuart. *Labor Unionism in American Agriculture*. U.S. Bureau of Labor Statistics, Bull. no. 836. Washington, 1945. 457 pp.

A history of trade-union activities of American agricultural workers with considerable emphasis on California. The writer sees this emphasis as inevitable for a number of reasons: large-scale farming is dominant in the state; the IWW, TUUL, AFL, and Teamsters Union had concentrated their organizational activities on California farms; the La Follette Committee hearings in the late 1930's had made available extensive information on the trade-union movement in California agriculture. Treats also of the special role of racial minorities in the history of trade unionism in agriculture.

Kantor, Harry S. *Problems Involved in Applying a Federal Minimum Wage to Agricultural Workers*. Washington: U.S. Dept. of Labor, 1960. 2 vols. 272 and 253 pp.

A study, national in scope, whose purpose is to determine whether a federal minimum wage in agriculture is practicable and desirable.

Lamb, Helen Boyden. "Industrial Relations in the Western Lettuce Industry." Unpublished Ph.D. dissertation, Radcliffe College, 1942. 545 pp.

Chaps. 7–14, pp. 185–513, deal with the history of labor relations in the California lettuce industry.

Lange, Dorothea, and Paul S. Taylor. *An American Exodus: A Record of Human Erosion*. New York: Reynal & Hitchcock, 1939. 158 pp.

Using the camera as a tool of research, a social scientist and a photographer join to sketch a vivid outline of the migrant agricultural problem of the 1930's. Photographs, captions, and text trace the migrants' origins in the "Old South," "Mid-Continent," "Plains," and "Dust Bowl," and follow them to their ultimate destination, "Last West."

Luck, Mary Gorringe. "Labor Contractors," *in* Emily H. Huntington, *Doors to Jobs*. Berkeley: University of California Press, 1942. Chap. 8, pp. 306–44.

Evaluates the information gathered in 1938 in a field investigation of the labor contractor system used to supply labor to California farmers. The investigation revealed a diversity of contractors as well as a diversity of modes of operation, abuses, and advantages, with the abuses overweighing the benefits; the reasons for the support of the contractor system by most medium-sized farmers and other elements among the employer groups; and the inadequacy of measures to regulate the system. Concludes with a discussion of the possibility of eliminating the labor contractor from California agriculture.

McWilliams, Carey. *California: The Great Exception*. New York: A. A. Wyn, 1949. Chap. 9, "California's Peculiar Institution," pp. 150–70.

Traces the course of California's migratory farm labor cycle which began with the change-over from cattle raising to wheat culture, when the first large-scale use of migratory labor was introduced, consisting mostly of Indians and Chinese. The expansion of irrigation systems resulted in a marked increase in orchard acreage and wider use of Chinese labor, and the eventual trebling of acreage under irrigation and the vast growth in specialty crops made possible the employment of hundreds of thousands of migratory workers—at one period Japanese and at others Hindus, Mexicans, and "dust bowl" migrants.

————. *Factories in the Field: The Story of Migratory Labor in California*. Boston: Little, Brown, 1939. 334 pp.

A study of California's agricultural industry and its workers, tracing in varied detail the historical background of California's giant farm factories of today. A description of the acquisition of vast land holdings by a small group through fraudulent Mexican and questionable railroad grants and outright brigandage is followed by the story of the intensive exploitation of both these land empires and the labor of masses of successive racial minorities—Chinese, Japanese, Mexican, Filipino, and others. Suppression, it is shown, was the usual response to any organized attempt on the part of these workers to improve their lot, suppression that reached its extreme form of vigilante terrorism in the 1930's when the California agricultural areas witnessed widespread trade-union and strike activity. Concludes with observations on the significance of the emergence of the native American migrant as the dominant factor on California farms.

————. *Ill Fares the Land: Migrants and Migratory Labor in the United States*. Boston: Little, Brown, 1942. Book 1, chaps. 1–2, "Senator La Follette in California," "The Messengers Arrive," pp. 13–50.

Observes that although the La Follette Committee had come to California in 1939 only to investigate violations and denial of civil liberties to agricultural workers, it found itself inevitably investigating the industrial revolution in California agriculture. This revolution was characterized by large-scale land ownership, shipper-grower leasing of extensive acreage, and shipper-grower-canner financing and contracting to purchase the produce of entire areas. The committee found that this dominance of industry in agriculture determined the nature of the labor policy of California agriculture.

Reichard, Alice. "California's Adult Children," *Country Gentleman,* vol. 110, Feb. 1940, pp. 9, 34–35.

A less than friendly view of migrant agricultural workers.

Roe, Wellington. *Juggernaut: American Labor in Action.* New York: Lippincott, 1948. Chap. 17, "Mr. Green's Success Story," pp. 220–35.

Part of the chapter (pp. 231–35) deals with the Salinas lettuce strike of 1936 and contends that it represented a retreat, typical of Green's leadership of the AFL.

Rowell, Edward J. "Drought Refugee and Labor Migration to California in 1936," *Monthly Labor Review,* vol. 43, Dec. 1936, pp. 1355–63.

Attempts to determine the relationship between the flight of refugees from the drought area of the Great Plains and labor migration into California in 1936. The figures used as a basis for the estimates were collected at California plant quarantine points and are included in statistical tables.

Schwartz, Harry. *Seasonal Farm Labor in the United States.* With special reference to hired workers in fruit and vegetable and sugar-beet production. New York: Columbia University Press, 1945. 172 pp.

California figures prominently in this study as fruit and vegetable production is most typical of California farming. Chaps. 2 and 3, in particular, have reference to California's seasonal farm labor, the latter part of chap. 2 considering migrant labor and the latter part of chap. 3 providing some history of trade-union organization among agricultural workers in the state.

Shotwell, Louisa Rossiter. *The Harvesters: The Story of the Migrant People.* Garden City: Doubleday, 1961. 242 pp.

Fiction and commentary dramatize the issues that the migratory workers raise for themselves and for the communities and states that recruit their labor. Chap. 16, "The Man and the Machine," pp. 189–207, deals with recent advances in the mechanization of operations normally performed by migrant workers, and the most recent attempt (1959–1961) to organize migrant agricultural workers in California.

Spector, Frank. *Story of the Imperial Valley.* With an introduction by John Dos Passos. Pamphlet no. 3. New York: International Labor Defense [1932?] 31 pp.

Gives a damning description of working and living conditions of the agricultural workers of the Imperial Valley and the difficulties encountered by those attempting to improve those conditions by organization.

Steinbeck, John. *Their Blood Is Strong.* San Francisco: Simon Lubin Society of California, 1938. 33 pp.

Driven from the land by the midwestern drought in the mid-thirties, thousands of small farmers and independent farm hands and their families crowded the agricultural areas of California in search of work. John Steinbeck paints a vivid and frightening picture of the living and working conditions of these migrants and points to the need for measures to prevent the big farm interests from turning these people into a native peon class as they had done in the past with imported foreign labor. To this end he proposes specific measures calling for initiative by state and national authorities.

Stone, Lee Alexander. *Migrant Situation in Madera County*. Feb. 2, 1940. 15 pp.

Attempts to answer some of the questions raised by the California State Chamber of Commerce in its study of the migrant problem in the San Joaquin Valley.

Strong, John L. "Labor in Cotton Culture," *Overland,* vol. 13, July 1874, pp. 18–25.

As a cotton grower, the author disagrees with the contention that cotton culture, to be profitable, requires cheap labor, thus necessitating the use of Chinese labor in large numbers.

Taylor, Frank J. *California's Grapes of Wrath*. Fresno, Calif.: Associated Farmers of Fresno County [1939?] [11] pp.

Seeks to refute the charges implicit in John Steinbeck's *Grapes of Wrath* that California farmers were cruel in their treatment of "dust bowl" refugees and that the real and sinister power in California agriculture was the Bank of America and the Associated Farmers.

Taylor, Paul S. "Migratory Agricultural Workers on the Pacific Coast," *American Sociological Review,* vol. 3, April 1938, pp. 225–32.

Points out that, unlike other parts of the country, the Pacific Coast states have long depended on a mobile work force to harvest their crops and that this work force has problems not common to other agricultural workers, such as child labor, health, unemployment relief, social security, difficult labor relations, and a constantly changing agricultural structure. States that despite efforts to deal with these problems, they remain largely unsolved.

Taylor, Paul S., and Clark Kerr. "Uprisings on the Farms," *Survey Graphic,* vol. 25, Jan. 1935, pp. 19–22, 44.

Discusses trade-union organization among agricultural workers with emphasis on California.

Taylor, Paul S., and Edward J. Rowell. "Patterns of Agricultural Labor Migration within California," *Monthly Labor Review,* vol. 47, Nov. 1938, pp. 980–90.

The patterns of California agricultural labor migration are shown to be both statewide and within certain areas. These migrations are determined by the shifting seasonal and area labor peaks. Statistical tables, maps, and graphs accompany the text.

————. "Refugee Labor Migration to California, 1937," *Monthly Labor Review,* vol. 47, Aug. 1938, pp. 240–50.

An estimate of refugee labor migration to California in 1937, based, as in previous similar studies, on data obtained at California border plant quarantine check points. It is stated, however, that a closer study of the data for this estimate and also for that of 1936 shows a need for a broader interpretation of the causes of migration to California. Among the new factors noted are the general agricultural depression in some states and mechanization in the cotton belt.

Taylor, Paul S., and Tom Vasey. "Drought Refugee and Labor Migration to California," *Monthly Labor Review,* vol. 42, Feb. 1936, pp. 312–18.

Estimates the number of refugees from the Great Plains drought area who entered California in the last six months of 1935. Statistical tables, compiled from data collected at border plant quarantine points, are interpreted to obtain the necessary estimates and are included in the text.

————. "Historical Background of California Farm Labor," *Rural Sociology,* vol. 1, Sept. 1936, pp. 281–95.

Describes the changes in the form of land use in California since Spain first colonized it and the adjustment of farm labor to these changes. This labor has been successively performed by ranch hands, farm hands, and a semi-industrialized proletariat. Statistical tables and graphs illustrate the changes in crops, the increased use of irrigation, and the resulting effects on the type of labor used.

U.S. Congress. Senate. Committee on Education and Labor. *Violations of Free Speech and Rights of Labor.* Hearings.

76th Cong., 2d sess. Washington, 1940.

Part 47

Testimony: Paul S. Taylor on the conflict between employee and employer in agriculture, pp. 17214–36, 17239–42, 17266–86; R. L. Adams on the nature of California crops, the labor required in harvesting and marketing them, and the extent of the demand for seasonal labor, pp. 17287–96; Varden Fuller on the economic and social characteristics of the California agricultural labor force, pp. 17307–16.

Part 48

Testimony: Joseph Di Giorgio on his connections with the Associated Farmers, pp. 17643–58; Emily H. Huntington on migratory labor, pp. 17669–74.

Part 50

Testimony: Paul S. Taylor with statistical information on California agricultural labor, pp. 18198–202; Murray R. Benedict on some of the relationships between different groups in California agriculture, pp. 18324–38.

Part 51

Testimony: Richard L. Adams on wage relationships the subcommittee was considering, pp. 18709–12; Carey McWilliams on wage-rate determination, pp. 18712–24.

76th Cong., 3d sess. Washington, 1940.

Part 54

Testimony: Varden Fuller on "The Supply of Agricultural Labor as a Factor in the Evolution of Farm Organization in California," pp. 19778–898; Paul S. Taylor and Clark Kerr on "Documentary History of the Strike of the Cotton Pickers in California, 1933," pp. 19947–20036.

Part 55

Testimony on the Imperial Valley strike: Pelham D. Glassford, pp. 20135–53; Joseph M. Casey, pp. 20194–200.

Part 59

Testimony: Harrison S. Robinson on California's migrant problem, pp. 21731–41; Carey McWilliams on housing conditions among agricultural workers in California, pp. 21768–78; Laurence I. Hewes on the Farm Security Administration in relation to migratory labor in Region 9, pp. 21778–91.

Part 62

Testimony: Paul S. Taylor on "Factors Which Underlie the Infringement of Civil Rights in Industrialized Agriculture," pp. 22488–514; Stuart M. Jamieson on "The Origins and Present Structure of Labor Unions in Agriculture and Allied Industries of California," pp. 22531–40.

U.S. Congress. Senate. Committee on Education and Labor. *Violations of Free Speech and Rights of Labor.* Report of the Committee. 77th Cong., 2d sess., S. Rept. 1150. Washington, 1942. Part 3. "The Disadvantaged Status of Unorganized Labor in California's Industrialized Agriculture," pp. 153–399.

Analyzes the agricultural labor market and some of its problems, describes its unorganized status, and tells of some of the attempts on the part of agricultural workers to organize during the years 1900–1940, attempts that were met by hostility and interference from the employers.

———. ———. Committee on Labor and Welfare. *The Migrant Farm Worker in America.* Background data on the migrant worker situation in the U.S. today. Prepared by Daniel H. Pollitt and Selma M. Levine for the Subcommittee on Migratory Labor. 86th Cong., 2d sess. Washington, 1961. 79 pp.

Tells of the developments in American agriculture that brought the migrant into being, his characteristic division into domestic and foreign patterns of migration, where and under what conditions he works, and what his future prospects are.

U.S. Farm Security Administration, Region IX. *A Study of 6655 Migrant Households Receiving Emergency Grants, Farm Security Administration, California, 1938.* San Francisco, 1939. 69 pp. and [55] pp. of appendix tables.

Included in the findings are the states of origin of the households, their occupations prior to migration, and their employment in 1937.

U.S. Federal Writers' Project. "A History of the Cannery and Agricultural Workers Union," by Porter M. Chaffee. [Oakland? 1937?] Vol. 2. Various pagings. Typewritten.

Stresses the high points in the history of the C&AWIU: the hard-fought cotton strike of 1933 which raged along a 500-mile front, lasted 23 days, and involved some 20,000 cotton pickers, and the lettuce strike in the Imperial Valley in 1934 which experienced large-scale vigilante activity. Also discussed are the lesser strikes led by the C&AWIU in 1934 and the concentrated drive against the union by the Associated Farmers, climaxing in the trial of the union's leaders on charges of criminal syndicalism in 1935.

———. "Unionization of Agricultural Labor in California." [Oakland? 1938?] 23 pp. Typewritten.

Reviews the changes in California agriculture during the second half of the nineteenth century that called for an ever-increasing use of casual labor; describes some of the spontaneous strike actions by farm workers to improve their working conditions in the early part of the twentieth century, and the later organized efforts of the IWW, the Communists, and the AFL to unionize agricultural workers.

Adams, R. L. *Common Labor Needs of California Crops*. Berkeley: College of Agriculture, University of California, 1930. 46 pp.

———. *Seasonal Labor Needs for California Crops*. Mimeograph Report no. 53, issued as progress reports for individual counties. Berkeley: Giannini Foundation of Agricultural Economics, University of California, 1936 and 1937. Various pagings.

Adams, R. L., and T. R. Kelly. *A Study of Farm Labor in California*. Circular no. 193. Berkeley: College of Agriculture, University of California, 1918. 75 pp.

Aiken, G. W. "The Labor Question in Vineyard and Orchard," *Proceedings, 27th Convention of the California Fruit Growers*, San Francisco, Dec. 2–5, 1902. Pp. 392–95.

American Civil Liberties Union. *The Struggle for Civil Liberty on the Land*. New York [1935?] "The Farm Workers: Imperial Valley, San Joaquin Valley and the Sacramento Prosecution," pp. 16–25.

Bailey, Stanley. Series of articles on migratory workers in California, San Francisco *Chronicle*, Feb. 11–16, 1940.

Bauers, Ulla Edwin. "The Di Giorgio Strike." Unpublished M.A. thesis. University of California, Berkeley, 1949. 140 pp.

Beals, Carleton. "Migs," *Forum*, vol. 99, Jan. 1938, pp. 10–15.

Benedict, M. R. "The Problem of Stabilizing the Migrant Farm Laborer of California," *Rural Sociology*, vol. 3, June 1938, pp. 188–94.

California. Bureau of Labor Statistics. *Tenth Biennial Report, 1901–1902.* Sacramento, 1902. "Agricultural Labor in the State of California," pp. 10–15.

California. Department of Employment. *Labor Requirements for California Crops, Major Seasonal Operations, Based on Estimated Acreages and Production for 1947,* by Margot W. Lenhart. Report 882, No. 1. Sacramento, 1948. 19 pp.

——. *. . . Based on Estimated Acreages and Production for 1948.* Report 882, No. 2. Sacramento, 1949. 27 pp.

——. *. . . Based on Acreages and Production for 1949.* Report 882, No. 3. Sacramento, 1952. 28 pp.

——. *. . . Based on Acreages and Production for 1950.* Report 882, No. 4. Sacramento, 1953. 35 pp.

——. Governor's Committee to Survey the Agricultural Labor Resources of the San Joaquin Valley. *Agricultural Labor in the San Joaquin Valley: Final Report and Recommendations.* Sacramento, 1951. Part 3, sec. 5, "Farm Labor and Mechanization," pp. 136–55.

——. Industrial Welfare Commission. *Report and Recommendations of the Wage Board for Agricultural Occupations.* [San Francisco?] 1960. Various pagings.

——. Legislature. Joint Committee on Agriculture and Livestock Problems. *Information on Various Farm Labor Camps,* by R. J. Welch. Partial Reports, Parts 2 and 3. Sacramento, Jan. 1949. 79 pp. and 242 pp.

——. Joint Interim Committee on Agriculture and Livestock Problems. *The Recruitment of Farm Laborers and Their Appropriate Placement to Meet in Full the Labor Supply Requirements of California Agriculture.* Sacramento, 1949. 165 pp.

——. Joint Legislative Committee on Agriculture and Livestock Problems. *The Recruitment and Placement of Farm Laborers in California, 1950: With Special Consideration and Recommendations Concerning Proposals for Extension of Unemployment Insurance.* Special and Partial Report. Sacramento, 1951. 376 pp.

——. Joint Legislative Fact-Finding Committee on Agricultural and Industrial Labor. *Final Report.* Sacramento, 1945. 80 pp.

——. State Relief Administration. *Migratory Labor in California.* San Francisco, 1936. 224 pp.

California State Chamber of Commerce. *Recommendations for Improvement in Statistics Relating to Farm Labor.* Prepared by the Farm Labor

Statistics Committee of the Statewide Agricultural Committee. [San Francisco?] 1940. 34 pp.

"California's Farm Labor Problems," *Transactions of the Commonwealth Club of California,* vol. 30, April 1936, pp. 153–96.

Cross, William T. "The Poor Migrant in California," *Social Forces,* vol. 15, March 1937, pp. 423–27.

Darnton, Byron. Series of articles on migratory workers in California, New York *Times,* March 4–9, 11, 1940.

Dawber, Mark A. *Our Shifting Populations.* Frontiers of American Life, no. 2. New York: Home Missions Council and Council of Women for Home Missions. [1941?] Chap. 3, "Migrants and the Grapes of Wrath," pp. 14–18.

Devlin, Robert. "The Compulsory Labor Laws of Maryland and West Virginia and Their Application to California Conditions," *Monthly Bulletin,* California State Commission on Horticulture, vol. 7, Jan.–Feb. 1918, pp. 95–100.

Ducoff, Louis J. "Migratory Farm Workers: A Problem in Migration Analysis," *Rural Sociology,* vol. 16, Sept. 1951, pp. 217–24.

"A Farm Labor Disputes Board," *Transactions of the Commonwealth Club of California,* vol. 31, Dec. 1936, pp. 221–55.

Feder, Ernest. "'Hot Milk' in California," *Farm Policy Forum,* vol. 3, Dec. 1950, pp. 9–13.

———. "The Milkers' Unions of the San Francisco and Los Angeles Milksheds," *Journal of Farm Economics,* vol. 32, Aug. 1950, pp. 458–77.

Fry, C. L. "Migratory Workers of Our Industries," *World's Work,* vol. 40, Oct. 1920, pp. 600–11. Illustrated.

Fuller, Varden. *The California Labor Situation.* Berkeley: U.S. Bureau of Agricultural Economics, 1941. 10 pp.

———. "The Development and Prospects of California's Agriculture," *in* Warren S. Thompson, *Growth and Changes in California's Population.* Los Angeles: Haynes Foundation, 1955. Chap. 18, pp. 273–93.

———. "The Supply of Agricultural Labor as a Factor in the Evolution of Farm Organization in California." Unpublished Ph.D. dissertation. University of California, Berkeley, 1939. 345 pp.

———. "Wage Rates and Expenditures for Labor, California Agriculture, 1909–1935." Berkeley: U.S. Bureau of Agricultural Economics, 1937. 121 pp. Typewritten.

Fuller, Varden, and Seymour J. Janow. "Jobs on Farms in California," *Land Policy Review,* vol. 3, March–April 1940, pp. 34–43.

Fuller, Varden, John W. Mamer, and George L. Viles. *Domestic and Imported Workers in the Harvest Labor Market, Santa Clara County, California, 1954.* Report no. 184. Berkeley: Agricultural Experiment Station, University of California, 1956. 52 pp.

Galarza, Ernesto. *American and Foreign Farm Workers in California.* Statement to the President's Commission on Migratory Labor. Washington, D.C.: National Agricultural Union, 1950. 30 pp.

George, Harrison. "Class Forces in California Agriculture," *Communist,* vol. 18, Feb. 1939, pp. 156–62; March 1939, pp. 269–73.

Gleason, George. *The Fifth Migration: A Report on the California Migratory Agricultural Workers Situation.* Prepared for Los Angeles County Committee for Church and Community Cooperation. Los Angeles, 1940. 29 pp.

Greenfield, Margaret. *Unemployment Insurance for Farm Workers.* 1953 Legislative Problems, no. 8. Berkeley: Bureau of Public Administration, University of California, 1953. 49 pp.

Hewes, Laurence Ilsley, Jr. "Some Migratory Labor Problems in California's Specialized Agriculture." Unpublished Ph.D. dissertation. George Washington University, 1945. 295 pp.

Hyacinth, Socrates. "A Flock of Wool," *Overland,* vol. 4, Feb. 1870, pp. 141–46. [About shepherds and sheep herding]

"Immigration and Farm Labor," *Proceedings,* 56th Convention of the California Fruit-Growers and Farmers, Santa Ana, Dec. 6–7, 1923. Discussion by R. W. Kearney, George C. Roeding, and George W. Pearce, pp. 35–46.

Jamieson, Stuart M. "A Settlement of Rural Migrant Families in the Sacramento Valley, California," *Rural Sociology,* vol. 7, March 1942, pp. 49–61.

Janow, Seymour. "Migration Westward: Summary of a Decade," *Land Policy Review,* vol. 4, Oct. 1941, pp. 10–14.

Janow, Seymour, and Davis McEntire. "Migration to California," *Land Policy Review,* vol. 3, July–Aug. 1940, pp. 24–36.

Johns, Bryan Theodore. "Field Workers in California Cotton." Unpublished M.A. thesis. University of California, Berkeley, 1948. 177 pp.

Jones, Victor. *Transients and Migrants.* Berkeley: Bureau of Public Administration, University of California, 1939. 67 pp.

Jones, William O. "The Salinas Valley: Its Agricultural Development, 1920–1940." Unpublished Ph.D. dissertation. Stanford University, 1947. 404 pp.

Kerr, Clark. "Industrial Relations in Large-Scale Cotton Farming," *Proceedings,* 19th Annual Conference of the Pacific Coast Economic Association, 1940. Pp. 62–69.

Krysto, Christiana. "California's Labor Camps," *Survey,* vol. 43, Nov. 8, 1919, pp. 70–78.

Landis, Paul H. "Social Aspects of Farm Labor in the Pacific States," *Rural Sociology,* vol. 3, Dec. 1938, pp. 421–33.

Lenhart, Margot W. "Analyzing Labor Requirements for California's Major Seasonal Operations," *Journal of Farm Economics,* vol. 27, Nov. 1945, pp. 963–75.

————. *Labor Requirements for California Crops.* Major seasonal operations, based on estimated acreages and production for 1944. Emergency Farm Labor Project. Berkeley: Agricultural Extension Service, University of California, 1945. 14 pp.

Lively, D. O. "Agricultural Labor Problems during the Past Season," *Monthly Bulletin,* California State Commission on Horticulture, vol. 7, Jan.–Feb. 1918, pp. 71–73.

Lowenstein, Norman. "Strikes and Strike Tactics in California Agriculture: A History." Unpublished M.A. thesis. University of California, Berkeley, 1940. 124 pp.

McEntire, Davis. "Characteristics of California's Migrant Population," *Occidental College Bulletin,* n.s., vol. 26, Nov. 1948, pp. 20–41.

McEntire, Davis, and N. L. Whetten. "Recent Migration to the Pacific Coast," *Land Policy Review,* vol. 2, Sept.–Oct. 1939, pp. 7–17.

McWilliams, Carey. "California Pastoral," *Antioch Review,* vol. 2, March 1942, pp. 103–21.

————. "Farms into Factories: Our Agricultural Revolution," *Antioch Review,* vol. 1, Dec. 1941, pp. 406–31.

————. "Glory, Glory, California," *in* Warren French, ed., *A Companion to the Grapes of Wrath.* New York: Viking, 1963. Pp. 140–43. [Review of *Of Human Kindness* by Ruth Comfort Mitchell]

Mainwaring, Daniel. "Fruit Tramp," *Harper's,* vol. 169, July 1934, pp. 235–42.

Metzler, William H. *Analysis of the Operation of the Wage Ceiling in the Asparagus Industry, Sacramento–San Joaquin Delta, 1943.* Berkeley: U.S. Bureau of Agricultural Economics, 1943. 56 pp.

————. *Analysis of the Operation of the Wage Ceiling on the Picking of Sun Dried Raisin Grapes, California, 1943.* Berkeley: U.S. Bureau of Agricultural Economics, 1944. 46 pp.

————. *Analysis of the Operation of the Wage Ceiling Order for Harvesting Cannery Tomatoes, California, 1943.* Berkeley: U.S. Bureau of Agricultural Economics, 1944. 45 pp.

————. *Operation of the Wage Ceiling on Picking Cotton, California, 1943.* Berkeley: U.S. Bureau of Agricultural Economics, 1944. 62 pp.

————. *Two Years of Farm Wage Stabilization in California.* Berkeley: U.S. Bureau of Agricultural Economics, 1946. 65 pp.

————. *Surveys of Wages and Wage Rates in Agriculture.* Washington: U.S. Bureau of Agricultural Economics, 1945 and 1946. Report no. 5—*Farm Workers in the Citrus Harvest, Los Angeles Area, California, April–June, 1945.* 21 pp. No. 6—*Seasonal Farm Workers in USDA Labor Supply Centers at Arvin, Linnell and Shafter, California, June 1945.* 19 pp. No. 9—*Seasonal Farm Workers at Selected USDA Labor Supply Centers in North Central California, August–October, 1945.* 21 pp. No. 10—*Seasonal Farm Workers in the Harvest of Selected Truck Crops, California, 1945.* 31 pp. No. 12—*Seasonal Farm Workers in the Harvest of Selected Deciduous Fruits, California, May–September, 1945.* 34 pp. No. 13—*Seasonal Farm Workers in USDA Labor Supply Centers at Arvin, Woodville, and Firebaugh, California, 1945.* 18 pp. No. 14—*Farm Workers in the Potato, Sugar Beet and Cotton Harvests in California, 1945.* 34 pp.

Metzler, William H., and Afife F. Sayin. *The Agricultural Labor Force in the San Joaquin Valley, California: Characteristics, Employment, Mobility, 1948.* Washington: U.S. Bureau of Agricultural Economics, 1950. 73 pp.

Milne, Robert D. "Hoodlums on a Hop Ranch," *Californian,* vol. 1, Feb. 1880, pp. 171–76.

————. "Shepherds and Sheep Herding," *Californian,* vol. 1, March 1880, pp. 224–28; April 1880, pp. 321–26.

Perry, Pettis. "The Farm Question in California," *Political Affairs,* vol. 30, July 1951, pp. 50–65.

Reagan, B. B., and W. H. Metzler. *Wages and Wage Rates of Seasonal Farm Workers in Maricopa County, Arizona, and Imperial County, California, February–March, 1945.* Report no. 2, Surveys of Wages and Wage Rates in Agriculture. Washington: U.S. Bureau of Agricultural Economics, 1945. 21 pp.

Rorty, James. "Lettuce—with American Dressing," *Nation,* vol. 140, May 15, 1935, pp. 575–76.

Russell, J. H. *Cattle on the Conejo.* Los Angeles: Ward Ritchie Press, 1957. Chaps. 4–5, "Tramps—Blanket Stiffs and Hobos," "Mexican Labor," pp. 16–24.

Schwartz, Harry. "Organizational Problems of Agricultural Unions," *Journal of Farm Economics,* vol. 23, May 1941, pp. 456–66; Nov. 1941, pp. 833–42.

Smith, Roy James. "An Economic Analysis of the California State Land Settlements at Durham and Delhi." Unpublished Ph.D. dissertation. University of California, Berkeley, 1938. Chap. 11, "Farm Laborers' Allotments," pp. 356–99.

Speth, Frank A. "A History of Agricultural Labor in Sonoma County, California." Unpublished M.A. thesis. University of California, Berkeley, 1938. 109 pp.

Spivak, Joseph. "Measure of Recovery," *Ken,* vol. 1, May 19, 1938, pp. 74–77; June 2, 1938, pp. 9–12.

Steinbeck, John. "The Harvest Gypsies." Series of articles in San Francisco *News,* Oct. 5–10, 12, 1936.

Sufrin, Sidney C. "Labor Organization in Agricultural America, 1930–1935," *American Journal of Sociology,* vol. 43, Jan. 1938, pp. 544–59.

Tarpey, M. F. "Some Possibilities of the Development of New Labor during the War," *Monthly Bulletin,* California State Commission on Horticulture, vol. 7, Jan.–Feb. 1918, pp. 74–79.

Taylor, Paul S. *Adrift on the Land.* New York: Public Affairs Committee, 1940. 32 pp.

Teague, Charles C. *Fifty Years a Rancher.* Los Angeles: Ward Ritchie Press, 1943. Chap. 15, "Labor in Agriculture," pp. 141–50.

Tetreau, E. D. "Profile of Farm Wage Rates in the Southwest," *Rural Sociology,* vol. 4, March 1939, pp. 36–42.

Thompson, Alvin H. "Aspects of the Social History of California Agriculture, 1885–1902." Unpublished M.A. thesis. University of California, Berkeley, 1953. Part 2, "Labor," pp. 234–321.

Tugwell, Rexford G., Philip Bancroft, Carey McWilliams, and Hugh Bennett. "What Should America Do for the Joads," *Bulletin of America's Town Meeting of the Air,* vol. 5, March 11, 1940, pp. 3–30.

U.S. Bureau of Agricultural Economics. *Labor and Other Factors Influencing Dairy Production in the Los Angeles Milksheds, November, 1942.* Washington, Feb. 1943. 46 pp.

U.S. Congress. Senate. Special Committee to Investigate Unemployment and Relief. Hearings, 75th Cong., 3d sess. Washington, 1938. Testimony of Paul S. Taylor, Appendix 7, pp. 1157–70.

U.S. Farm Security Administration. *Migrant Farm Labor: The Problem and Ways of Meeting It.* Washington, 1940. 14 pp.

U.S. Federal Writers' Project. "The Contract Labor System in California Agriculture." [Oakland? 1938?] 200 pp. Typewritten.

———. "History of Living Conditions among Migratory Laborers in California." [Oakland? 1938?] 192 pp. Typewritten.

———. "Influence of Employment Agencies on California Farm Labor." [Oakland? 1939?] 38 pp. Typewritten.

———. "Labor in California Cotton Fields." [Oakland? 1938?] 84 pp. Typewritten.

———. "The Migratory Agricultural Worker and the American Federation of Labor to 1938 Inclusive." [Oakland? 1939?] 55 pp. Typewritten.

———. "Proposed Remedies for Migratory Labor Problems." [Oakland? 1939?] 136 pp. Typewritten.

———. "The Social Security Act in Respect to Agricultural Labor." [Oakland? 1938?] 18 pp. Typewritten.

———. "Unionization of Migratory Labor, 1903–1930." [Oakland? 1938?] 22 pp. Typewritten.

———. "Wage Chart by Crops, State of California, 1865–1938." [Oakland? 1939?] [182] pp. Typewritten.

U.S. President's Commission on Migratory Labor. *Report on Migratory Labor in American Agriculture.* Washington, 1951. 188 pp.

Warkentin, Joel. "A Decade of Migratory Labor in the San Joaquin Valley, 1940–1950." Unpublished M.A. thesis. University of California, Berkeley, 1952. 142 pp.

Willi, Ottilia. "Hop-picking in the Pleasanton Valley," *Out West,* vol. 19, Aug. 1903, pp. 155–63.

Williamson, Paul Garland. "Labor in the California Citrus Industry." Unpublished M.A. thesis. University of California, Berkeley, 1947. 182 pp.

Wisker, L. A. "How the Army Draft Affects the Farm Labor Situation," *Monthly Bulletin,* California State Commission on Horticulture, vol. 7, Jan.–Feb. 1918, pp. 79–88.

Wood, Samuel E. "California Migrants," *Sociology and Social Research,* vol. 24, Jan.–Feb. 1940, pp. 248–61.

———. "Wine from the 'Grapes of Wrath,'" *National Municipal Review,* vol. 28, Sept. 1939, pp. 611–18.

MARITIME

GENERAL

Adamic, Louis. "Harry Bridges: Rank-and-File Leader," *Nation,* vol. 142, May 6, 1936, pp. 576–80.

Less a portrait of Harry Bridges than a description of relations between the maritime workers and the maritime employers at a tense moment.

American Federation of Labor Rank and File Committee of Oakland, California. *The Lessons of the Bay District 1934 General Strike.* [Oakland? 1934?] [14] pp.

Examines the factors that prevented the San Francisco Bay Area general strike of July 1934 from being completely effective, listing, among others, such general factors as the craft structure of the American Federation of Labor and the traditional opposition of top union officials to sympathetic strikes. Discusses the particular weaknesses evident in the conduct of the strike in the East Bay area.

Berry, Charles F. "The Gentleman from Stanford: How a 'Tough' College Professor Brought Industrial Peace to San Francisco's Waterfront," *Forbes Magazine,* Feb. 15, 1941, pp. 13–15, 35.

The gentleman from Stanford is Almon E. Roth.

Brier, Royce. "The Front Page: Bloody Thursday," *in* William Hogan and William German, eds., *The San Francisco Chronicle Reader.* New York: McGraw-Hill, 1962. Pp. 275–78.

An on-the-spot reporter's portrait of San Francisco's Bloody Thursday, July 5, 1934, the one-day war on the waterfront which raged from the Embarcadero to the top of Rincon Hill and from Rincon Hill to Market Street.

Camp, William Martin. *San Francisco: Port of Gold.* New York: Doubleday, 1947. Part 3, "Men and Ships," pp. 197–338. Part 4, "Water-Front Warfare," pp. 339–495.

The story, documented yet unencumbered by footnotes, of San Francisco's waterfront workers, with particular emphasis on its seamen. Part 3 describes the life of the seaman aboard ship and ashore, the crimps and shanghaiers who exploited him, the maritime laws that made him a virtual slave, the early unsuccessful and eventually successful attempts to form protective organizations, some of the strike action and legislative efforts that improved his conditions, and the men whom he accepted as his leaders. Part 4 reviews the sixty years of conflict on the waterfront from 1886 to 1946, which called for increasingly broader forms of organization and cooperation by both the waterfront workers and the waterfront employers and which culminated in the industry-wide Pacific Coast strikes of the 1930's.

Cannon, James P. *Notebook of an Agitator.* New York: Pioneer Publishers, 1958. "San Francisco: 1936–1937," pp. 97–124.

Deals with the maritime strike and with the Communist Party and the maritime unions.

Chambers, Walter. *Labor Unions and the Public.* New York: Coward-McCann, 1936. "Stevedores Go Back in Defeat," pp. 188–200.

An off-beat account of the 1934 Pacific Coast maritime strike. It contains statements which are not likely to be found elsewhere. The following are typical: "By June 19, 1934, 33,000 pier and maritime workers were out in San Francisco . . ."; ". . . raids began on the headquarters of the striking 120 unions." It may also be the only account of this strike in which the name of Harry Bridges does not appear.

Chaplin, Ralph. *Wobbly: The Rough-and-Tumble Story of an American Radical.* Chicago: University of Chicago Press, 1948. "Class War on the Waterfront," pp. 376–89.

Ralph Chaplin, a past editor of IWW publications, came to San Francisco in 1937 to edit the *Voice of the Federation* and to join Harry Lundeberg, secretary of the Sailors Union of the Pacific, in his opposition to Harry Bridges' leadership of the west coast waterfront. In this chapter Chaplin relates his experiences during his brief editorship of the *Voice.*

CIO Maritime Committee. *Minutes of the Meeting Held in Washington, March 12, 1947.* Washington, D.C.: Ward & Paul, 1947. 189 pp.

Meeting at which the International Longshoremen's and Warehousemen's Union broke with the CIO Maritime Committee.

Coast Committee for the Shipowners. *A.B.C.'s of the Maritime Strike: A Primer of Basic Facts.* San Francisco, 1936. 18 pp.

The Pacific Coast shipowners, by means of questions and answers, seek to acquaint the public with their position and attempt to interpret the position of the maritime unions on the basic issues of the 1936–37 strike—hiring control and arbitration.

―――. *The Pacific Maritime Crisis.* San Francisco, 1936. [12] pp.

The Pacific Coast shipowners appeal to the public to support their position on pending new agreements with the maritime unions. This position, stressing arbitration of unresolved issues and contract-performance guarantees, is brought out in an exchange of telegrams between the waterfront employers and the Maritime Commission.

Crook, Wilfrid H. *Communism and the General Strike.* Hamden, Conn.: Shoestring Press, 1960. Chaps. 8–9, "Job Control in San Francisco, 1934," "San Francisco: The Strike and Its Implications," pp. 107–48.

After a brief outline of past strife on the waterfront, analyzes the immediate events leading to the maritime strike of 1934, the strike itself as it developed in the direction of a general strike, and the planning and outbreak of the general strike. Examines the roles of a number of conflicting groups in the general strike and its settlement. These groups include the federal government, the employers, the press, the police and the National Guard, and particularly both the right and the left wings of labor, including the Communists.

Darcy, Sam. "The Great West Coast Maritime Strike," *Communist,* vol. 13, July 1934, pp. 664–86.

The California district organizer of the Communist Party critically reviews the prestrike period and the first phase of the maritime strike of 1934, reflecting a more than ordinary grasp of detail. Throughout is a running commentary on the role of the Communist Party in these events. Of particular interest are references to early organizational steps toward a general strike.

————. "The San Francisco Bay Area General Strike," *Communist,* vol. 13, Oct. 1934, pp. 985–1004.

An attempt at an exhaustive Marxist analysis of the preparation, course, and termination of the general strike of July 1934. Among the issues discussed are the objectives of the strike and the degree to which they were realized. The Communist Party is credited with a leading role in all phases of the strike.

Dunne, William F. *The Great San Francisco General Strike: The Story of the West Coast Strike—the Bay Counties General Strike and the Maritime Workers' Strike.* New York: Workers Library Publishers, 1934. 80 pp.

A day-to-day account of the general strike, with special emphasis on two aspects: The conduct of leading AFL officials who had decisive control of the strike committee is critically reviewed, and the contention made that they deliberately betrayed the strikers. The violent treatment accorded the Communist Party and organizations and individuals thought to be sympathetic to the party is condemned. A resolution of the Central Committee of the Communist Party, having reference to the strike, is appended.

Eliel, Paul. "Labor Problems in Our Steamship Business," *Yale Review,* vol. 26, March 1937, pp. 510–32.

Briefly sketches the history of maritime labor relations on the Pacific Coast for the twenty years preceding the 1934 and 1936–37 maritime strikes to show the inevitability of their occurrence and of the course they took. Maintains that neither the maritime employers nor the maritime workers are in a mood to live together and suggests that an outside agency similar to the railroad mediation service be created to keep the peace.

————. *The Waterfront and General Strikes, San Francisco, 1934.* San Francisco: Hooper Printing Co., 1934. 256 pp.

An account by the director of the Industrial Relations Department of the Industrial Association of San Francisco of the events leading up to the Pacific Coast maritime strike and the San Francisco Bay Area general strike, the course of these strikes, and their termination. Chronologically arranged, the account is based largely on newspaper sources and on the records of the Industrial Association. An appendix, pp. 183–243, contains numerous exhibits of related documentary material.

Foisie, F. P. "A Case Study in Labor Relationships," in *First Annual Stanford Industrial Relations Conference.* Division of Industrial Relations, Graduate School of Business, Stanford University, 1938. Pp. 97–103.

The Coast Coordinator of the Waterfront Employers Association of the Pacific Coast describes the intricate organization of the Pacific Coast maritime industry, the special nature of the seamen's mode of existence, and the peculiar problems of the longshore industry as he tries to account for the complicated nature of maritime industrial relations. Points to the improved methods being worked out to meet these special problems and predicts improved waterfront labor relations.

Gorter, Wytze, and George H. Hildebrand. *The Pacific Coast Maritime Shipping Industry, 1930–1948.* Berkeley: University of California Press, 1952 and 1954. 2 vols.

Vol. 2, chap. 7, "Wages and Productivity," pp. 129–51.

Contends that there is strong reason to believe that the rapid rise in maritime wages during the period 1935–1948 without a compensating rise in longshore productivity contributed importantly to the long-run decline in the tonnage carried by the industry, especially in the coastwise and intercoastal trades. Notes that the rise in railway and truck wage rates during the same period was only half that of the maritime rates.

Chap. 9, "Major Strikes," pp. 173–220.

Following a review of the decline of the maritime unions in 1919 and 1921 and their resurgence in 1933, discusses the maritime strikes and their issues in 1934, 1936–37, 1946, and 1948.

Chap. 10, "Job-Action Strikes and Other Issues," pp. 221–57.

Examines the issues of discipline, job action, productivity, and jurisdictional conflicts and their effects on the industry.

Chap. 11, "Underlying Causes of Conflict," pp. 258–85.

Analyzes the ideological basis of the conflict on the Pacific Coast waterfront, taking into account both the motivation of the shipowners and the clash between Harry Bridges and Harry Lundeberg.

Harrison, Gregory. *Maritime Strikes on the Pacific Coast: A Factual Account of Events Leading to the 1936 Strike of Marine and Longshore Unions.* Statement before the United States Maritime Commission, November 2, 1936. San Francisco: Waterfront Employers Association, 1936. 30 pp.

A review of the 1934 Pacific Coast maritime strike and its settlements is followed by charges of widespread violations of those settlements. Among the violations cited are practices connected with the longshoremen's and seamen's hiring halls and numerous "quickie," sympathetic, or "hot cargo" strikes. Concludes with a review of the adverse effects of these conditions on Pacific Coast shipping.

Hedley, George P. *The Strike As I Have Seen It.* An address before the Church Council for Social Education, Berkeley, California, July 19, 1934. 14 pp.

A Bay Area churchman joins the striking maritime workers on their picket line for two weeks and later recounts his impressions. He weighs the claims of the contending sides and concludes that those of the strikers are more valid. Particularly graphic is his description of police activity on July 5, 1934, still referred to as "Bloody Thursday."

Hudson, Roy. "The Lessons of the Maritime Strikes," *Communist,* vol. 16, March 1937, pp. 229–40.

An evaluation of the effectiveness of the aid afforded the Pacific Coast maritime workers during their 1936–37 strike by the supporting action of the seamen in Gulf and Atlantic ports.

International Longshoremen's Association, Local 38-79. *The Maritime Crisis: What It Is and What It Is Not.* San Francisco, 1936. 19 pp.

Addressing itself to the public, the International Longshoremen's Association explores the issues of the 1936–37 Pacific Coast maritime strike. It contends that the demands of the seamen and longshoremen are modest and would entail only minor modifications of the 1934 award, whereas the counterdemands of the shipowners would nullify the award. Arbitration, one of the major issues in the strike, is given particular consideration.

Kerr, Clark, and Lloyd Fisher. "Conflict on the Waterfront," *Atlantic Monthly,* vol. 184, Sept. 1949, pp. 17–23.

Views the conclusion of the 95-day Pacific Coast longshore strike of 1948 as marking the end of fourteen years of intensive warfare between the ILWU and the shipowners and as ushering in a period of peaceful industrial relations on the waterfront. Examines the probable factors which influenced the changed attitudes of both the employers and the union and the probable effect of the new contract on the shipping industry.

"The Maritime Strikes of 1936–37," *Monthly Labor Review,* vol. 44, April 1937, pp. 813–27.

Discusses the principal issues in the 1936–37 Pacific Coast maritime strike, which involved the longshoremen and all the seafaring groups, licensed and unlicensed, and the extent to which these issues were resolved. Outlines the demands of both the employers and the unions and the terms of the final settlement, and analyzes the changes in wage rates, working conditions, hiring procedures, and procedures to settle disputes. Includes a comment on a strike called by the Seamen's Defense Council, a group from the ranks of the International Seamen's Union, sympathetic to the west coast strikers.

National Convention of Maritime Unions (CMU). *Proceedings, May 6–11, 1946.* San Francisco, 1946. 274 pp.

The purpose of the convention was to organize the maritime unions into a single national organization. The unions participating were ACA, IBU, ILWU, MEBA, MFOW, NMU, and MCS. (Also typewritten transcript, 552 pp.)

National Union of Marine Cooks and Stewards, CIO. *The Strike as a Weapon of Labor.* San Francisco, 1946. [8] pp.

Treats of the strike in the experiences of maritime workers.

————. *Treacherous Passage*. The story of the maritime unions' twelve year fight against spies, goon squads, intrigue, murder and other shipowner devices of sabotage. San Francisco [1945?] 35 pp.

Examines the role of the labor spy in the seamen's unions, with special emphasis on the Marine Cooks and Stewards Union. The activities of many proven and suspected labor spies in the MCS, the Sailors Union of the Pacific, the Marine Firemen, Oilers, Watertenders and Wipers Association, and the National Maritime Union are described in varied detail.

Pacific American Shipowners Association and Waterfront Employers Association of California. *White Paper: West Coast Maritime Strike*. San Francisco, 1948. 15 pp.

Addressing themselves apparently to the public, the maritime employers contend that in the current waterfront strike the "issue is the communist party line leadership of the International Longshoremen's and Warehousemen's Union and of the National Union of Marine Cooks and Stewards," and seek to justify their refusal to negotiate with that leadership until it has disavowed communism.

Plant, Thomas G. *Statement to the National Longshoremen's Board, July 11, 1934*. San Francisco: Waterfront Employers Union, 1934. 43 pp.

The board appointed by President Roosevelt to mediate the 1934 Pacific Coast maritime strike is given an outline of the previous attempts made to bring about an agreement. The statement reflects sharp differences of interest and viewpoint between the opposing groups. An appendix contains material relative to the issues raised in the statement.

Quin, Mike. *The Big Strike*. Postscript by Harry Bridges. Olema, Calif.: Olema Publishing Co., 1949. 259 pp. Illustrated.

A panoramic treatment of the west coast maritime strikes of the mid-thirties, with particular emphasis on the San Francisco Bay Area general strike of July 1934. After rapidly sketching the growing dissatisfaction of the west coast maritime workers with their conditions and the unwillingness of the shipowners to agree to extensive changes, the account moves to a description of prestrike maneuvers, the beginning and course of the 1934 strike, the shipowners' attempt to open the port of San Francisco, "Bloody Thursday," and the climax of the general strike with all its impact and repercussions. Final chapters refer to the 1935 tanker and steam-schooner strikes and the second coast maritime strike of 1936–37. An appendix includes related documentary material.

Record, Jane Cassels. *The San Francisco Waterfront: Crucible of Labor Factionalism*. Berkeley: Institute of Industrial Relations, University of California [1953?] 111 pp.

An examination of factional strife among maritime unions, its origins, and its impact on the unions involved and on their relations with the maritime employers. An explanation is sought in the organizational traditions of the individual unions and the marked differences in skills, both tending to freeze their craft structure; the long-established economic rivalry between the sailors and the longshoremen; personality and ideological differences; and a desire to use factionalism as a weapon to gain economic advantage.

Riesenberg, Felix, Jr. *Golden Gate: The Story of San Francisco Harbor.* New York: Knopf, 1940. Chap. 23, "Bloody Thursday," pp. 308–27.

Affords vivid impressions of the rising tension on the San Francisco waterfront in 1933 and 1934, some of the events of the 1934 maritime strike, Harry Bridges as a leader of the longshoremen, and, most effectively, "Bloody Thursday" and the general strike, which are sketched in some detail.

Saxton, Alexander. *CMU Looks Ahead.* Photos by Morris Watson, Lou Pinson, and others. San Francisco: Committee for Maritime Unity, 1946. 31 pp.

A statement of the structural features and purposes of the CIO maritime unions' Committee for Maritime Unity and an account of its progress in the few months since its organization in May 1946. Cites in particular the successful conclusion in June 1946 of the first negotiations on a national scale in the maritime industry, and concludes with a statement of future aims.

Schneider, Betty V. H. *Industrial Relations in the West Coast Maritime Industry.* Berkeley: Institute of Industrial Relations, University of California, 1958. 83 pp.

A historical review with emphasis on the influence of interunion strife and rivalry, particularly between the longshoremen's and the sailors' unions, on west coast maritime industrial relations. The influence of friction and rivalry among the employers on those relations is also considered. The study attempts to answer such questions as: What has caused interunion tensions to remain unresolved for so long? Why have rivalries taken such extreme forms? Why have employers failed to deal more effectively with the situation?

———. "The Maritime Industry," *Monthly Labor Review,* vol. 82, May 1959, pp. 552–57.

Notes the improved labor-management relations in the Pacific Coast maritime industry in the fifties and attempts to find an explanation for the improvement by examining the factors that have influenced relations in the industry since 1934. Among the factors considered are resolution of the problem of job security, liquidation of many of the interunion conflicts, and the unqualified acceptance of the ILWU and its leadership by the employers after fourteen years of resistance.

Schneiderman, William. "The Pacific Coast Maritime Strike," *Communist,* vol. 16, April 1937, pp. 342–57.

Considers some of the important features of the recently concluded 1936–37 maritime strike, such as the objectives of both the unions and the shipowners, the tactics employed by both, and the strengths and weaknesses revealed within the ranks of the unions. Also examines the activity, successful or otherwise, of the Communist Party in the strike.

Taylor, Paul S., and Norman Leon Gold. "San Francisco and the General Strike," *Survey Graphic,* vol. 23, Sept. 1934, pp. 405–11.

Highlights of the San Francisco Bay Area general strike of July 1934; illustrated with contemporary photographs.

To Fink or Not to Fink: Facts Instead of Distortion for N.M.U. Members on the West Coast Strike. New York: Rank and File NMU Members [1948?] 14 pp.

A criticism of the official NMU attitude and actions in the west coast maritime strike of 1948.

U.S. Works Progress Administration. *The Law in Action during the San Francisco Longshore and Maritime Strikes of 1934.* Berkeley, 1936. 294 pp.

A three-part survey: the first part includes an outline of the strike, some of the encounters with the police, a statistical record of arrests, the role and attitude of the trial judges, the administration of bail, and the application of the antipicketing and handbill ordinances; the second reviews the legal implications of the actions of the police and the court procedures during the strike; the third consists of related supplementary materials.

Varney, Harold Lord. "Sovietizing Our Merchant Marine," *American Mercury,* vol. 44, May 1938, pp. 31–43.

Contends that the American merchant marine is the advance guard of Stalinism in the American labor movement and that it all started in San Francisco in 1932. Harry Bridges, Joseph Curran, and Roy Hudson are given considerable credit for bringing this condition about, with only Joseph Ryan, Harry Lundeberg, and Paul Scharrenberg opposing them.

Vorse, Mary Heaton. *Labor's New Millions.* New York: Modern Age Books, 1938. Chap. 21, "The West Coast," pp. 210–20.

Describes the attempt by the AFL to eliminate the CIO from the west coast (about 1937), with Dave Beck leading the attack. The fight centered on the longshoremen, the warehousemen, and the seamen.

"After the Battle," *Fortune,* vol. 31, Feb. 1945, pp. 176–9, 226–33.

Boyer, Richard, and Herbert M. Morris. *Labor's Untold Story.* New York: Cameron Associates, 1955. Chap. 9, "Solidarity on the Embarcadero," pp. 282–89.

Burke, Earl. "Dailies Helped Break General Strike," *Editor and Publisher,* vol. 67, July 28, 1934, p. 5.

California. Bureau of Labor Statistics. *Eleventh Biennial Report, 1903–1904.* Sacramento, 1904. "Maritime Labor Organizations of California," pp. 49–72.

Cantwell, Robert. "San Francisco: Act One," *New Republic,* vol. 79, July 25, 1934, pp. 280–82.

———. "War on the West Coast," *New Republic,* vol. 79, Aug. 1, 1934, pp. 308–10.

CIO Maritime Committee. *Minutes of Meeting Held in New York, June 15, 1947.* [New York, 1947?] 232 pp.

———. *The Post War Program of the C.I.O. Maritime Committee.* Washington, 1944. 31 pp.

Council of Marine Crafts of America. Organizational material. San Francisco, 1934 and 1935. Various pagings.

de Ford, Miriam Allen. "San Francisco: An Autopsy on the General Strike," *Nation,* vol. 139, Aug. 1, 1934, pp. 121–22.

Dimock, Marshall E., and Arthur Wubnig. "The Maritime Industry during World War II," *in* Institute of Labor Studies, *Year Book of American Labor.* New York: Philosophical Library, 1945. Vol. 1, chap. 16, pp. 304–23.

Francis, Robert Coleman. "A History of Labor on the San Francisco Waterfront." Unpublished Ph.D. dissertation. University of California, Berkeley, 1934. 230 pp.

Goldberg, Joseph P. "Collective Bargaining in the Maritime Shipping Industry," *Monthly Labor Review,* vol. 71, Sept. 1950, pp. 332–37.

Goldbloom, Maurice, and others. *Strikes Under the New Deal.* New York: League for Industrial Democracy [1936?] "The San Francisco General Strike," pp. 44–52.

Hamilton, Iris. "General Strike," *New Masses,* vol. 12, July 24, 1934, pp. 9–11.

Haskett, William. "Ideological Radicals, the American Federation of Labor and Federal Labor Policy in the Strikes of 1934." Unpublished Ph.D. dissertation. University of California, Los Angeles, 1957. Chap. 7, "West Coast Maritime Situation, 1934," pp. 237–86.

Jensen, George Charles. "The City Front Federation of San Francisco: A Study in Labor Organization." Unpublished M.A. thesis. University of California, Berkeley, 1912. 52 pp.

Joint Action Committee. *Joint Action in the 1948 West Coast Maritime Strike, Port of San Francisco.* San Francisco, 1948. 13 pp.

Kleiler, Franklin M. "Maritime Labor Grows Up," *Survey Graphic,* vol. 28, Jan. 1939, pp. 18–22.

Knies, Donald Arthur. "Labor Conflict on the San Francisco Waterfront, 1934–1948." Unpublished M.A. thesis. Stanford University, 1952. 116 pp.

Lampman, Robert J. "Rise and Fall of the Maritime Federation of the Pacific, 1935–1941," *Proceedings,* Western Economic Association, 1950. Pp. 64–67.

Lannon, Al. "The West Coast Maritime Strike: Showdown for Labor," *Political Affairs,* vol. 27, Nov. 1948, pp. 962–68.

Lapham, Roger D. *Maritime Employer-Employee Relations.* Address before the American Merchant Marine Conference, New Orleans, Dec. 10, 1940. [1940?] 14 pp.

———. "Pacific Coast Labor Conditions," *Nation's Business,* vol. 24, June 1936, pp. 75–77.

La Piere, Richard T. "The General Strike in San Francisco. A Study of the Revolutionary Pattern," *Sociology and Social Research,* vol. 19, March–April 1935, pp. 355–63.

Lerner, Tillie. "The Strike," *Partisan Review,* vol. 1, Sept.–Oct. 1934, pp. 3–9.

Levenson, Lew. "California Casualty List," *Nation,* vol. 139, Aug. 29, 1934, pp. 243–45.

Lucy, Rev. George E. "Group Employer-Employee Industrial Relations in the San Francisco Maritime Industry, 1888–1947." Unpublished Ph.D. dissertation. St. Louis University, 1948. 382 pp.

Lundeberg, Harry. *Labor Relations in the West Coast Maritime Industry.* Western Management Association and California Personnel Management Association. Management Report no. 204. Berkeley, n.d. 10 pp.

Marine Workers Industrial Union. *Centralized Shipping Bureaus; or Workers' Control of Hiring.* New York, 1934. 32 pp.

Maritime Federation of the Pacific Coast. *Men and Ships.* A pictorial of the maritime industry. San Francisco: District Council No. 2, MFP, 1937. 62 pp.

National Maritime Union. *Fight for Maritime Unity.* NMU Publication no. 11. [New York?] 1947. [76] pp.

Pacific American Shipowners Association and Waterfront Employers Association of the Pacific Coast. *A Report to the People from the Shipping Industry on the Pacific Coast.* San Francisco, 1946. 18 pp.

Palmer, Dwight L. "Pacific Coast Maritime Labor." Unpublished Ph.D. dissertation. Stanford University, 1935. 519 pp.

Raushenbush, Carl, and Emanuel Stein, eds. *Labor Cases and Materials: Readings on the Relation of Government to Labor.* New York: Crofts, 1941. "Events of San Francisco Longshore Strike," pp. 12–14; "The San Francisco General Strike," pp. 174–78.

Record, Jane Cassels. "Ideologies and Trade Union Leadership: The Case of Harry Bridges and Harry Lundeberg." Unpublished Ph.D. dissertation. University of California, Berkeley, 1954. 231 pp.

Robinson, Robert McClure. "A Study of Inter-Union and Employer-Union Relations on the San Francisco Waterfront, 1933–1937." Unpublished M.A. thesis. University of California, Berkeley, 1937. 182 pp.

San Francisco Bay Area Council. *A Recommended Program for Increasing Labor-Management Cooperation in the San Francisco Bay Area Shipping Industry*. San Francisco: McKinsey & Co., 1953. 2 vols. Various pagings.

San Francisco Junior Chamber of Commerce. *1936 Federal Legislation Affecting Maritime Shipping*. San Francisco, 1936. 26 pp.

Seeley, Evelyn. "Journalistic Strikebreakers," *New Republic,* vol. 79, Aug. 1, 1934, pp. 310–12.

———. "San Francisco's Labor War," *Nation,* vol. 138, June 13, 1934, pp. 672–74.

"Seven Seamen; The Maritime Unions," *Fortune,* vol. 16, Sept. 1937, pp. 121–37.

Simon Lubin Society of California. *San Francisco at Bay: To California Farmers*. San Francisco [1939?] 8 pp.

Steffens, Joseph Lincoln. *Lincoln Steffens Speaking*. New York: Harcourt, Brace, 1936. "I Cover the General Strike," pp. 199–202.

Sturm, Herman M. "Postwar Labor Relations in the Maritime Industry," *in* Colston E. Warne, ed., *Labor in Postwar America*. Brooklyn, N.Y.: Remsen Press, 1949. Chap. 21, pp. 461–87.

Taft, Philip. "Strife in the Maritime Industry," *Political Science Quarterly,* vol. 54, June 1939, pp. 216–36.

Taylor, Frank J. "Behind the S.F. Strike," *Nation's Business,* vol. 23, March 1935, pp. 25–27, 62–65.

U.S. Shipping Board. *Report on Marine and Dock Labor*. Work, wages and industrial relations during the period of the war. By Horace B. Drury. Washington, 1919. 203 pp.

West, George P. "California Sees Red," *Current History,* vol. 40, Sept. 1934, pp. 658–62.

Winter, Ella. "Stevedores on Strike," *New Republic,* vol. 79, June 13, 1934, pp. 120–22.

Wissmann, Rudolf Walter. *The Maritime Industry: Federal Regulation in Establishing Labor and Safety Standards*. New York: Cornell Maritime Press, 1942. 386 pp.

LONGSHOREMEN

Bridges, Harry R. *Remarks at Fiftieth Anniversary Convention, American Association of Port Authorities, Long Beach, California, September 28, 1961.* San Francisco: ILWU, 1961. 9 pp.

Reviews the technological changes in the maritime industry that made a new understanding between the longshoremen and the employers imperative, and tells of the realistic manner in which both the International Longshoremen's and Warehousemen's Union and the Pacific Maritime Association cooperated to reach an agreement. Characterizes the ILWU-PMA Mechanization and Modernization Agreement as superior to any other yet negotiated to meet the challenge of technological advancement in industry.

California. Bureau of Labor Statistics. *Investigation of Labor Matters on the City Front, Commencing July 6, 1887.* Sacramento, 1887. 57 pp.

Deals chiefly with the jurisdictional differences between the Stevedores Protective Association and its longer-established rival, the Riggers and Stevedores Union. Testimony by officials and members of both unions establishes discriminatory practices against the members of the younger union by the Riggers and Stevedores Union. The latter claims justification on the grounds that the Stevedores Protective Association is a dual organization and that its policies have been undercutting the existing working conditions of the stevedores.

Eliel, Paul. "Industrial Peace and Conflict: A Study of Two Pacific Coast Industries," *Industrial and Labor Relations Review,* vol. 2, July 1949, pp. 477–501.

The author finds basic differences in the histories of the labor relations of the two industries studied—pulp and paper and longshoring. To find an explanation for these differences he seeks to determine "what are the ingredients of employer-employee relations that make for labor peace or labor conflict?" These ingredients, he concludes, are the atmosphere of collective bargaining; direct collective bargaining instead of through a third party; the effect of violence; basic worker and employer attitudes; the motives behind collective bargaining; and the important role of ideology.

———. "Labor Peace in the Pacific Ports," *Harvard Business Review,* vol. 19, Summer 1941, pp. 429–37.

Cites some of the causes for the almost continuous warfare between the longshoremen and the waterfront employers in the years 1934–1940. These include the failure of many employers to realize that they no longer had complete control over conditions, their conviction that the program of the longshoremen's union was Communist-inspired, the longshoremen's belief that the agitation for the deportation of Harry Bridges was employer-inspired and was meant to weaken their union, and their use of the organized slowdown. The contract of 1940 is considered a departure in the direction of future peace for the Pacific waterfronts.

Fairley, Lincoln. "The ILWU–PMA Mechanization and Modernization Agreement," *Proceedings of the 1961 Spring Meeting,* Industrial Relations Research Association, Chicago, May 4–5, 1961. Pp. 664–80.

A review by the ILWU research director of the development of the ILWU-PMA Mechanization and Modernization Agreement and an analysis of its essential features. Surveys the degree of present and expected future mechanization in the handling of maritime cargoes and describes the successive steps since 1957 in the development and acceptance of the agreement, the groups in the ILWU and PMA it will involve, and the reciprocal benefits provided in it. Concludes with comments on some of the still unsolved problems, on the agreement as a partial solution of the general problem of unemployment, and on the possibilities of its application in other industries.

Glazier, William. "Automation and the Longshoremen: A West Coast Solution," *Atlantic Monthly,* vol. 206, Dec. 1960, pp. 57–61.

A review of the technological revolution that has swept American industry since World War II, the strains it has imposed upon labor-management relations, and the attempts which have been made to effect the necessary adjustments in these relations. Maintains that the mechanization programs of the meat-packing unions and the United Mine Workers are largely ineffective when compared to the ILWU-PMA approach. Speaking of the longshore plan, the author states that "the aim is to create a framework within which the industry can bring about an increase in productivity by introducing new methods and new machines, while at the same time guaranteeing the workers on the docks and in the ships' holds their job security, along with a share of the benefits from technical progress."

Hagel, Otto (photo story) and Louis Goldblatt (ed. and text). *Men and Machines.* San Francisco: International Longshoremen's and Warehousemen's Union, Pacific Maritime Association, 1963. 161 pp.

An impressive photographic record of the changing scene on the Pacific Coast waterfronts, reflecting the new methods being introduced in the movement and handling of cargoes and the development of new approaches to labor relations. The text includes a joint introduction by J. Paul St. Sure for the PMA and Harry Bridges for the ILWU, concluding statements by each, and a review by the secretary of the ILWU of the development of the Mechanization and Modernization Agreement between the ILWU and the PMA and a description of the agreement's features and their application in practice. This photo story contrasts in many ways with an earlier one, *Men and Ships,* composed by the noted photographer in 1937.

Hudson, Roy. "The I.L.W.U. Convention—A Victory for All Labor," *Political Affairs,* vol. 28, July 1949, pp. 45–57.

Critically reviews the issues dealt with by the 1949 convention of the International Longshoremen's and Warehousemen's Union. Special reference is made to the sharp conflict between two groups at the convention on the issues of local autonomy versus greater control by the national CIO and of continued membership in the World Federation of Trade Unions.

International Longshoremen's Association, Local 38-79. *The Truth About the Waterfront.* The I.L.A. states its case to the public. San Francisco [1935?] 19 pp.

Addressing itself to the public, the ILA maintains that the recent campaign against its membership and officials is prompted by a desire on the part of some shipowner groups to return to pre-1934 conditions on the waterfront. It describes these conditions and the improvements gained as a result of the 1934 west coast maritime strike and points to the many attempts to provoke another strike in an effort to nullify these gains.

International Longshoremen's and Warehousemen's Union. *The I.L.W.U. Story: Two Decades of Militant Unionism.* Illustrated with drawings by Rockwell Kent and photographs. San Francisco, 1955. 91 pp. 2d ed., revised to March 1963. 88 pp.

A history and description of the International Longshoremen's and Warehousemen's Union in capsule form. Describes its various departments and tells of its gains in improved working conditions and in the fields of welfare, health, and pensions. Concludes with a statement of principles.

————. *Why Not Longshore Wages and Hours on Steam Schooners? Why Not?* San Francisco [1938?] [6] pp.

Addressed to steam schooner sailors in the Sailors Union of the Pacific. Answers SUP secretary Harry Lundeberg's claim that the longshoremen are trying to steal their jobs and appeals to them to force Lundeberg to join the longshoremen in efforts to secure longshore rates and hours for the steam schooner men when they perform longshore work.

Kampelman, Max M. *The Communist Party vs. the C.I.O.: A Study in Power Politics.* New York: Praeger, 1957. "Harry Bridges and West Coast Shipping," pp. 199–215.

Contends that the general policy of the International Longshoremen's and Warehousemen's Union and the position of the Communist Party of the United States have followed a parallel course. Referring to materials related to the expulsion of the ILWU from the CIO, the author points to specific examples of such parallel policy positions or changes, cites policy statements from official ILWU publications, and particularly quotes from statements by Harry Bridges to prove his contention.

Killingsworth, Charles C. "The Modernization of West Coast Longshore Work Rules," *Industrial and Labor Relations Review,* vol. 15, April 1962, pp. 295–306.

Studies the factors originally responsible for the restrictive work rules and examines the means used to change them in the agreement of 1960 between the PMA and the ILWU.

Kossoris, Max D. "Working Rules in West Coast Longshoring," *Monthly Labor Review,* vol. 84, Jan. 1961, pp. 1–10.

The director of the Western Regional Office of the U.S. Bureau of Labor Statistics views the ILWU–PMA Mechanization and Modernization Agreement as a transaction in which the west coast shipping industry agreed to "... buying out the restrictive rules (including the resistance to mechanization) for a fixed sum...." He reviews the growth and nature of the restrictive working rules and their effect on the industry, considers the kind of changes their elimination may bring, and offers some observations on likely future developments in the relations between the longshoremen and the ship operators as the agreement becomes fully operative.

Malm, F. Theodore. "Wage Differentials in Pacific Coast Longshoring," *Industrial and Labor Relations Review,* vol. 5, Oct. 1951, pp. 33–49.

Traces the development of wage differentials based on skill classifications, penalty rates for special types of cargo, and overtime and night-time rates. Particularly stressed is the development of these differentials in the port of San Francisco.

Morris, George. *A Tale of Two Waterfronts.* Reprint of a series of four articles in *The Worker* (weekend edition of the New York *Daily Worker*) starting Jan. 18 [1953] New York [1953] 31 pp.

Contrasts the port of New York with that of San Francisco, citing differences in trade-union organization among the longshoremen of the two waterfronts, and in their working conditions, wages, and hiring practices. Concludes that the port of San Francisco has the advantage, because the longshoremen there long ago took steps to remove abuses still tolerated in the port of New York. Describes the racketeer-dominated nature of the New York waterfront and advises the eastern longshoremen to follow the example of San Francisco in order to realize basic changes in their conditions.

Neuberger, Richard L. "Labor's Overlords—Bridges and Beck," *American Magazine,* vol. 125, March 1938, pp. 16–17, 166–70.

Portrays Bridges and Beck as ideological opposites, out to eliminate each other. "Beck believes labor should show business how to make a profit"; "Bridges thinks labor should operate business on a non-profit basis."

Pacific American Shipowners and Waterfront Employers of San Francisco, Seattle, Portland, and San Pedro. *Hot Cargo: The Longshoremen's Alibi for Arbitration Award Violations.* San Francisco, 1935. 15 pp.

Denounces the refusal of Pacific Coast longshoremen to load and discharge cargoes associated with current labor disputes. Maintains that the position of District 38 of the International Longshoremen's Association is indefensible and, as proof, reproduces the award of federal arbitrator, Judge M. C. Sloss, a statement by Assistant Secretary of Labor E. F. McGrady, editorials from an official publication of the ILA, and a telegram from William Green, president of the AFL.

Phleger, Herman. *Pacific Coast Longshoremen's Strike of 1934.* Arbitration before National Longshoremen's Board. Oral argument of Herman Phleger, Esq., in behalf of Waterfront Employers, September 25, 1934. San Francisco, 1934. 71 pp.

The major issues to be arbitrated—wages, hours, and methods of hiring—are developed in detail from the point of view of the waterfront employers, and arguments are advanced to induce the Board to accept their position rather than that of the longshoremen, represented by the International Longshoremen's Association.

San Francisco Chamber of Commerce. *Law and Order in San Francisco: A Beginning.* San Francisco: H. S. Crocker Co., 1916. 41 pp.

Describes in some detail the organization of the Law and Order Committee of the San Francisco Chamber of Commerce and the part it played in the strikes of the longshoremen, culinary workers, bay and river boatmen, and structural steel workers. Special mention is made of the committee's efforts in the adoption of an antipicketing ordinance and the rousing of public sentiment following the Preparedness Day bombing, July 22, 1916.

Schneider, Betty V. H., and Abraham Siegel. *Industrial Relations in the Pacific Coast Longshore Industry.* Berkeley: Institute of Industrial Relations, University of California, 1956. 89 pp.

After examining the historical background, 1853–1947, of longshore employer-labor relations, the authors conclude that these relations cannot be fitted into the pattern of the development of industrial relations as an evolutionary process—periods of intense antagonism and sporadic negotiation evolving into a final state of cooperation, all within a short term. They state that the history of longshore industrial relations, in fact, showed a movement in the opposite direction, and undertake an examination of the factors which led to long-term conflict rather than peace and to the climactic 1948 strike and the "New Look" that followed it.

Swados, Harvey. *A Radical's America.* Boston: Little, Brown, 1962. Part 1, "West Coast Waterfront: End of an Era," pp. 45–64.

A novelist and essayist, familiar with waterfront labor problems, comments on some of the implications of the 1961 PMA-ILWU Agreement on Mechanization and Modernization. Disregarding the optimistic official pronouncements of both the longshoremen and the shipowners, he examines the seamier aspects of the contract, tries to fathom the motivations behind it, and speculates on what effect its application may have on the west coast longshoreman's job, which for many years has been considered almost ideal in its limited field.

U.S. Bureau of Labor Statistics. *Cargo Handling and Longshore Labor Conditions,* by Boris Stern. Productivity Series, Bull. no. 550. Washington, 1932. 559 pp.

Examines, by means of numerous statistical tables and interpretive text, the problems and methods of cargo handling, the productivity and cost of longshore labor, and longshore labor conditions in the coastal, intercoastal, and foreign trade in the major ports of the United States, including San Francisco and Los Angeles. The discussion of longshore labor conditions covers the nature of longshore work, hours and wages, conditions of employment, and problems of decasualization. The statistical material for San Francisco and Los Angeles deals with the late 1920's.

U.S. Congress. Senate. Committee on Labor and Public Welfare. *To Legalize Maritime Hiring Halls.* Hearings on S. 1044 before the Subcommittee on Labor and Labor Management Relations. 82d Cong., 1st sess. Washington, 1951.

Testimony of William Glazier on the position of the ILWU, pp. 4–50.

U.S. Works Progress Administration. *Decasualization of Longshore Work in San Francisco: Methods and Results of the Control of Dispatching and Hours Worked, 1935–1937.* Philadelphia, 1939. 157 pp.

Surveys, with the aid of many charts and tables, the longshore dispatching system in San Francisco, after briefly sketching previous attempts to decasualize longshore labor in various ports of Europe, Great Britain, and the United States. The main features of the survey are a description of the mechanics of dispatching, an analysis of the labor force and the labor demand, and the means used to achieve equalization of hours and earnings. An appendix refers to efforts to rotate longshore work in west and east coast ports prior to 1934 and contains documentary material on Pacific Coast maritime contracts.

Waterfront Employers Union. *"Full and By": A Message from the Waterfront Employers Union.* San Francisco, 1921. 22 pp.

Reviews the longshoremen's strikes of 1916 and 1919, the disintegration of the Riggers and Stevedores Union, and its displacement by the newly organized Longshoremen's Association of San Francisco which had the support of the waterfront employers.

Waterfront Workers Federation. *The Longshoremen's Strike.* A brief historical sketch of the strike inaugurated on June 1, 1916, in Pacific Coast ports of the United States. San Francisco, 1916. 30 pp.

The Federation, comprising fourteen San Francisco unions connected with the shipping industry, seeks to justify its failure to order sympathetic strike action by member unions during the strike of the longshoremen. It maintains that the longshore union was not entitled to such support because it had refused to follow the constitutional procedures of the Federation, had infringed on member unions' jurisdictions, and had frustrated the good offices of the Federation's committee. It contends that the virtual loss of the strike was due to the irresponsibility of the Pacific Coast ILA leadership, which it claims had come under control of IWW elements.

Wolfe, Burton H. "The Strange Twilight of Harry Bridges: A Labor Leader Turns Businessman," *Harper's,* vol. 228, March 1964, pp. 78–80, 83–84, 86.

A journalist's sketch of the west coast longshore leader as he appears today, with flashbacks to past phases of his 30-year leadership of the longshoremen. Touched on are Bridges' views on politics, civil rights, unemployment, the present top officials of the AFL and their policies, and particularly the ILWU-PMA Mechanization and Modernization Agreement.

"Arbitration Award—Ship Clerks' Union of San Francisco," *Monthly Labor Review,* vol. 51, Nov. 1940, pp. 1086–93.

Belman, Albert A. "Wage Chronology, No. 10: Pacific Longshore Industry, 1934–1950," *Monthly Labor Review,* vol. 70, May 1950, pp. 521–26.

Bridges, Harry. "Basic Report," *in* All Pacific & Asian Dockworkers Corresponding Committee, *Report of the First Pacific & Asian Dockworkers Conference.* [Tokyo? 1959?] Pp. 42–53.

Fairley, Lincoln. "Problems of the West Coast Longshore Mechanization Agreement," *Monthly Labor Review,* vol. 84, June 1961, pp. 597–600.

——. "Two Unions: ILWU and ILA," *March of Labor,* vol. 3, Feb. 1951, pp. 16–18.

Gilliam, Harold T. "Arbitration Procedures in the Pacific Coast Longshore Industry." Unpublished M.A. thesis. University of California, Berkeley, 1942. 130 pp.

Goodman, Jay Selvin. "One-Party Union Government: The ILWU Case." Unpublished M.A. thesis. Stanford University, 1963. 89 pp.

Hamilton, James W., and William J. Bolce. *Gateway to Victory.* Stanford: Stanford University Press, 1946. Chap. 10, "We Load the Ships," pp. 75–86. Illustrated.

"Harry Bridges and Joe Ryan," *Fortune,* vol. 39, Jan. 1949, pp. 152–54.

Hield, Wayne Wilbur. "Democracy and Oligarchy in the I.L.W.U." Unpublished M.A. thesis. University of California, Berkeley, 1950. 286 pp.

International Longshoremen's Association Committee. *Report and Recommendations of Committee Appointed by I.L.A. President, Captain William Bradley, to Visit the Pacific Coast to Observe the Operation of the Hiring and Dispatching Halls and Various Longshore Operations.* New York, 1957. 9 pp.

International Longshoremen's Association, District No. 38–Local 38-79. *April 21st Agreement Between Waterfront Employers Association of San Francisco and I.L.A., District No. 38–Local 38-79 with Transcript of Proceedings.* San Francisco [1936?] 32 pp.

International Longshoremen's and Warehousemen's Union. *Information and Union Comment on the 1960 Mechanization and Modernization Fund Agreement Between the Longshoremen of the Pacific Coast and the Steamship and Stevedoring Employers.* San Francisco, 1960. 12 pp.

International Longshoremen's and Warehousemen's Union–Pacific Maritime Association Welfare and Pension Funds. *Welfare and Pensions on the Docks of the Pacific Coast.* San Francisco, 1956. 22 pp.

Kraus, Henry. "Lessons from the Longshoremen," *Masses and Mainstream,* vol. 2, June 1949, pp. 42–52.

Liebes, Richard A. "Longshore Labor Relations on the Pacific Coast, 1934–1942." Unpublished Ph.D. dissertation. University of California, Berkeley, 1942. 391 pp.

Longshore Arbitration Awards, 10/12/1934 to 6/30/1953. San Francisco, 1953. 7 vols. + 1 vol. index. Various pagings. [Bound together by ILWU and presented to UC, Berkeley, Main Library]

"Longshore Labor Conditions in the United States," *Monthly Labor Review,* vol. 31, Nov. 1930. "San Francisco," "Los Angeles," pp. 19–25.

Longshore Lumbermen's Protective Association. *Constitution, By-Laws, Rules of Order and List of Members.* San Francisco: Munk's Printing House, 1885. 26 pp.

Madison, Charles A. *American Labor Leaders.* New York: Harper, 1950. Chap. 14, "Harry Bridges: The Militantly Left Wing I.L.W.U.," pp. 404–33.

Randolph, Robert E. "History of the International Longshoremen's and Warehousemen's Union." Unpublished M.A. thesis. University of California, Berkeley, 1952. 233 pp.

Riggers and Stevedores Union Association of San Francisco. *Constitution and By-Laws.* San Francisco: Women's Cooperative Print, 1878. 23 pp.

Thomas, C. "The West Coast Longshoremen and the 'Bridges Plan,'" *Fourth International,* vol. 3, Dec. 1942, pp. 362–70.

U.S. Congress. Senate. Committee on Labor and Public Welfare. *Communist Domination of Certain Unions.* Report of the Subcommittee on Labor and Labor Management Relations. 82d Cong., 1st sess., S. Doc. 89. Washington, 1951. "International Longshoremen's and Warehousemen's Union," pp. 79–96.

SEAFARING GROUPS

Asbury, Herbert. *The Barbary Coast: An Informal History of the San Francisco Underworld.* New York: Knopf, 1933. Chap. 9, "'God Help the Poor Sailor,'" pp. 198–231.

A chronicle of the misfortunes that awaited the sailor in the port of San Francisco in years past, stressing at times the exotic and bizarre. The author describes in some detail the role of the boardinghouse keepers and their runners in robbing the sailor of his wages, shanghaiing him, and sometimes even depriving him of his life. Of particular interest is the detailed description of the operations of the runners and the shanghaiing transactions.

Bailey, Hiram P. *Shanghaied Out of San Francisco in the 'Nineties.* Boston: Charles E. Lauriat Co. [1925?] 187 pp.

Shanghaied by the infamous Calico Jim, a young English engineer spent sixty-four days on the barque *General Gordon,* bound for Australia and South America, before he saw San Francisco again.

Bendich, Albert M. "The History of the Marine Cooks and Stewards Union." Unpublished M.A. thesis, University of California, Berkeley, 1953. 240 pp.

> Fifty years (1901–1951) of the MCS reviewed by a "trip-card member" of the union who "believes that the union is justifiably proud of its left-wing character and has written the present study from a point of view largely in agreement with that of the union." Highlighted among the activities of the union are its participation in a number of vital waterfront strikes, its relations with the Maritime Federation of the Pacific and the Committee for Maritime Unity (CMU), the fight against raiding efforts by the Sailors Union of the Pacific, expulsion from the CIO, and its reaction to the screening program during the Korean war. An added feature is an examination of the conditions which fostered radicalism and a left-wing leadership in the MCS.

Brown, Giles T. "The West Coast Phase of the Maritime Strike of 1921," *Pacific Historical Review,* vol. 19, Nov. 1950, pp. 385–96.

> Discusses the issues in the national strike of seamen and officers and describes the course and outcome of the strike in Pacific Coast ports.

Clark, George. *The Point Gorda Strike.* Report of Ship Delegate George Clark. New York: Marine Workers Industrial Union [1932?] 23 pp.

> Tells how the crew of an intercoastal freighter organized to carry on a fight, including strike action, against intolerable working and living conditions. The action, successful in the main and the first of such an organized nature to occur in seven years, takes place in the ports of Oakland, San Pedro, and New Orleans.

Dillon, Richard H. *Shanghaiing Days.* New York: Coward-McCann, 1961. 351 pp.

> A collection of tales of the brutality to which the American merchant seaman was subject during most of the nineteenth and in the early part of the twentieth centuries. Many famous shanghaiings and the almost unbelievable brutalities of numerous bunco mates and masters, including the infamous "Bully" Waterman, are repeated, in much the same form as when they first stirred San Francisco, the "Queen of America's shanghaiing cities," "her hoyden lady-in-waiting Portland," and other Pacific Coast ports. Chap. 8, "Tomorrow Is Also a Day," is both a thumbnail history of the Sailors Union of the Pacific and a sympathetic sketch of Andrew Furuseth.

Furuseth, Andrew. *Second Message to Seamen: His Relationship to the Harbor Workers and the Shipowners.* Chicago: International Seamen's Union of America, 1919. 29 pp.

> Part of the message, pp. 17–27, treats of the relations between seamen and long-shoremen on the Pacific Coast and particularly in California ports shortly after the seamen had organized into trade unions. These relations first involved the Wharf and Wave Union and later the City Front Federation. Furuseth contends that those experiences showed that cooperation with longshoremen always ends up with losses to the seamen.

————. *The Shipowners and the I.W.W.* San Francisco: James H. Barry, [1922] 15 pp.

A miscellany including comments on the contents of a pamphlet the shipowners had issued to introduce their new shipping offices and observations on the IWW constitution. Furuseth's comments have to do mainly with his claim that a collusive agreement, official or unofficial, was in existence between the shipowners and the IWW.

Goldberg, Joseph P. *The Maritime Story: A Study in Labor-Management Relations*. Cambridge: Harvard University Press, 1958. 361 pp.

An historical survey of the development of trade-union organization among American seamen and counterorganizations among shipowners, emphasizing the special role of the west coast seamen's unions, particularly the Sailors Union of the Pacific, in realizing a national organization of seamen. Among the themes developed are the efforts, under the leadership of Andrew Furuseth, to obtain legislation freeing the seamen of long-standing abuses, the special interests of the federal government in the economics and labor-management relations of the industry, the varying fortunes of IWW and Communist influence in the seamen's unions, and the struggle for stable organizations and full bargaining rights. The relationship of the organizational problems of the longshoremen to those of the seamen is given only incidental mention.

Hoffmeyer, V. *The Sailors' Cause*. A summary of the evidence given at an investigation held by the Commissioner of the California Bureau of Labor Statistics in conjunction with the Special Agent for the National Bureau of Labor Statistics. San Francisco: Peoples Publishing Co., 1887. 12 pp.

The summary by the chairman of the Advisory Committee of the Coast Seamen's Union maintains that the evidence proves the existence of a collusive agreement between ship captains and boardinghouse masters and clothiers to deprive the sailor of the better part of his wages by systems of advance payment of wages. Reference is also made to blacklisting practices by the shipowners and the inauguration of a discriminatory shipping office by the newly organized Shipowners Association.

Hohman, Elmo Paul. *History of American Merchant Seamen*. Hamden, Conn.: Shoestring Press, 1956. 125 pp.

A broad historical sketch of America's seagoing labor by a noted writer on maritime labor problems, whose stated aim is to fill the need for knowledge of the labor economics and labor history of the American merchant marine. Part 1 briefly reviews the development of world seamanship, noting in particular the changes in the conditions of seagoing life and in the position of the seamen which affected the American merchant seaman. Parts 2 and 3 cover the organizational and legislative history of the seamen from 1790 to 1952 and the role of the federal government in their affairs.

————. "Work and Wages of American Merchant Seamen," *Industrial and Labor Relations Review,* vol. 15, Jan. 1962, pp. 221–29.

Considers the nature of the merchant seaman's work, the wages he receives for it, and the effect on both of union affiliation.

Hopkins, William S. "Employment Exchanges for Seamen," *American Economic Review*, vol. 25, June 1935, pp. 250–58.

Describes the organization of the Marine Service Bureau as a device for providing strikebreakers in the 1919 west coast longshore strike and its later use for the same purpose in the 1921 seamen's strike and the 1934 west coast maritime strike. Described also is the hiring routine of the Bureau, including discriminatory practices and blacklisting features which resulted in court actions against it in the 1920's. Concludes with suggested alternatives to the Bureau.

International Seamen's Union of America. *Thirty-third Convention, Report of Secretary-Treasurer, Victor A. Olander, Washington, D.C., January 13, 1936.* [Chicago, 1936] 58 pp.

Includes references to the 1934 Pacific Coast maritime strike, the activities of the Marine Workers Industrial Union, and the expulsion of Paul Scharrenberg from the Sailors Union of the Pacific.

Kampelman, Max M. *The Communist Party vs. the C.I.O.: A Study in Power Politics.* New York: Praeger, 1957. "American Communications Association," pp. 195–98.

Outlines the history of the ACA as it related to Communist Party policy, and tells how and on what grounds the organization was expelled from the CIO in 1950 for pro-Communism.

Leiter, Robert David. *The Foreman in Industrial Relations.* New York: Columbia University Press, 1948. "Maritime," pp. 62–79.

Reviews some of the organizational history of the Marine Engineers Beneficial Association and the National Organization of Masters, Mates and Pilots, and analyzes their collective bargaining position in the maritime industry. Mention is also made of the chief steward as a supervisory employee.

Lundeberg, Harry. *S.I.U. of N.A., AFL-CIO: Facts about the Seamen's Trade Union Movement in the United States, 1885–1956.* San Francisco: SUP, 1956. 29 pp.

In reviewing seventy years of trade-union organization among American seamen, the head of the Sailors Union of the Pacific credits that union with the leading role in organizing not only the west coast seamen but also those of the Atlantic and Gulf coasts and the Great Lakes, as well as having been the parent organization of the seamen's movement of Europe. Especially stressed are the many difficulties the SUP, the International Seamen's Union, and the Seafarers' International Union had with the Communists on the American and Canadian waterfronts before finally defeating them. Only occasional mention is made of relations between the seamen and the longshoremen.

Marine Cooks and Stewards Association, CIO. *Twelve Thousand Marine Cooks and Stewards.* Designed and illustrated by Giacomo Patri. San Francisco [1944?] 19 pp.

"This is the story of one man and it is the story of the twelve thousand men who are the Marine Cooks and Stewards Association." The history is unfolded through the medium of the autobiography of an old-time member of the union and includes the first attempts at organization, the founding of the union in 1901, the strikes of 1906, 1921, and the 1930's, and the union's part in World War II.

Marine Workers Industrial Union. *Four Fighting Years: A Short History of the Marine Workers Industrial Union.* Also a letter to ship delegates. [New York? 1934?] 31 pp.

Sketches the steps leading to the organization of the MWIU and reviews its activities on the nation's waterfronts. Outlines its organizational structure and concludes with observations on the importance and functions of the ship's delegate in realizing the aims of the union.

National Union of Marine Cooks and Stewards. *The Rank and File Is on Trial: A Message to the Rank and File of All C.I.O. Unions.* San Francisco [1949?] [10] pp.

Refers to the impending trial of the MCS by the national CIO.

————. *Your Union and You.* San Francisco [1951?] [15] pp.

A thumbnail historical review of the MCS. Text, colored line drawings, and photographs briefly sketch highlights in its history and past and present working conditions, structural features, and policy aims.

Pacific American Shipowners Association and Waterfront Employers Association of the Pacific Coast. *Story of a Strike.* San Francisco, 1946. 20 pp.

Discusses the 1946 strike of ship's officers, organized into the Marine Engineers Beneficial Association and the National Organization of Masters, Mates and Pilots. Reviews the contract demands of the striking officers, maintains that the shipowners cannot and will not agree to the hiring practices proposed, and offers various reasons to justify that position.

Pacific Coast Marine Firemen, Oilers, Watertenders and Wipers Association. *So! You're in the Union!* San Francisco, 1943. 75 pp.

Written to introduce the MFOWW to its new members and permit men, the pamphlet tells the story of the union, sometimes in the colorful language of the sea. The account stresses its organization in 1883 and its participation in the strikes of 1906, 1921, and the mid-thirties. Final chapters cover the union's working rules, hiring practices, finances, seamen's legal rights, and the exploits of MFOWW members in the war zones of World War II.

Petersen, Walter J. *Marine Labor Union Leadership.* San Francisco: Employment Service Bureau, 1925. 56 pp.

Using the publication of *The Sailors' Union of the Pacific* by Paul S. Taylor as the occasion, the general manager of the Employment Service Bureau bitterly criticizes the officials of the seamen's unions, especially Andrew Furuseth. Attacking Taylor's work as biased and inaccurate, he offers his own version of the history of the SUP and other Pacific Coast seamen's unions. He defends the position of the shipowners in the 1921 seamen's strike, cites extensive benefits to the seamen under the open-shop conditions following the strike, and promises even greater future benefits.

Rank and File Members of the MCS. *What Course, Brother.* San Francisco, 1942. 22 pp.

Takes issue with the officials of the MCS, maintaining that their policies are leading toward disaffiliation with the CIO and affiliation with the SIU.

Rapoport, David Charles. "The Politics and Psychology of a Maritime Trade Union." Unpublished M.A. thesis, University of California, Berkeley, 1952. 172 pp.

The union dealt with is the Marine Cooks and Stewards.

Record, Jane Cassels. "The Rise and Fall of a Maritime Union," *Industrial and Labor Relations Review,* vol. 10, Oct. 1956, pp. 81–92.

Reviews the maneuvers that preceded the absorption of the MCS by Harry Lundeberg's SIU in 1955. Concludes with an examination of the union's positive features which explain its ability to withstand for a long time concerted attacks from many directions.

Riesenberg, Felix, Jr. *Golden Gate: The Story of San Francisco Harbor.* New York: Knopf, 1940. Chapter 16, "Red Record," pp. 218–33.

Sketches from the history of San Francisco's seamen during the years 1885–1921, touching on their first successful moves toward organization under the guidance of the International Workingmen's Association; Andrew Furuseth's activities; their participation in the strike action of the City Front Federation in 1901; and the successful passage of the Maguire, White, and Seamen's Acts. Included are excerpts from *Red Record,* a listing of unpunished acts of brutality committed against seamen.

Sailors Union of the Pacific, 1885–1950. San Francisco [1950] [15] pp.

The program for the dedication of the union's new headquarters, with a selection of highlights from the union's history and a statement by Harry Lundeberg.

Seamen's Advance Wages: Evils of the System. Proceedings in the trial of the "Eclipse" case in the United States District Court in San Francisco. Judge Morrow's Decision. Seamen's and boarding house masters' testimony before the State Labor Commissioner. San Francisco: Coast Seamen's Journal Print, 1893. 60 pp.

The specific issue in the trial was the payment of seamen's wages by Andrew Anderson, managing owner of the *Eclipse,* to John Savory, agent for certain boardinghouse masters, as part of an agreement to furnish him with a crew. The court ruled that such payments were in violation of federal statutes. Andrew Furuseth, secretary of the Sailors Union of the Pacific, participated in both the trial and the hearing before the Labor Commissioner.

"The Slaves of the Sea," *Oakland Monthly Review,* vol. 1, Dec. 1873, pp. 23–30.

"It is a common occurrence, almost a weekly occurrence, for the captains and officers of American vessels arriving in San Francisco to be charged with the commission of the most brutal atrocities upon their seamen. . . ." In this instance the reference is to Captain Robert K. Clarke of the ship *Sunrise,* who was convicted of such atrocities by a trial jury in San Francisco in 1873.

Standard, William L. *Merchant Seamen: A Short History of Their Struggles.* New York: International Publishers, 1947. 224 pp.

An account of the organizational history of American seamen, with emphasis on the problems of the Atlantic and Gulf Coast seamen. The Pacific Coast is given only minor attention. The activities of the Marine Workers Industrial Union, on both the east and west coasts, are sketched in greater detail than may be found in other sources.

Stimson, Grace Heilman. *Rise of the Labor Movement in Los Angeles.* Berkeley: University of California Press, 1955. Chap. 7, "Trouble on the Waterfront," pp. 81–87.

Describes the organization of the San Pedro branch of the Coast Seamen's Union in 1885, its relationship to the trade-union movement in Los Angeles, and the part played by the Knights of Labor in its activities. Especially stressed is the joint strike of the San Pedro seamen, longshoremen, and lumber handlers in 1887. The author notes that this was the first sharp conflict in the area between an employers' organization and a labor union and that its elements of excitement and disorder, involvement of the public, clashes with police and arrests, attempted mediation from the outside, and investigation by a government official set a pattern for future labor disputes.

A Symposium on Andrew Furuseth. New Bedford, Mass.: Darwin Press [1949?] 233 pp.

A compilation of statements and addresses in tribute to Andrew Furuseth, a selection of Furuseth's letters, speeches, and statements, and miscellaneous materials related to American seamen and Furuseth. Having special reference to Pacific Coast seamen's history are "The Furuseth Calendar" (pp. 25–29), excerpts from *The Sailors' Union of the Pacific* by Paul S. Taylor (pp. 92–144), and two articles by Paul Scharrenberg, "My Association with Furuseth" and "Furuseth" (pp. 194–203).

Taft, Philip. "The Unlicensed Seafaring Unions," *Industrial and Labor Relations Review,* vol. 3, Jan. 1950, pp. 187–212.

Sketches the history and development of the various units comprising the maritime unions on the Atlantic and Pacific coasts and Great Lakes; stresses IWW and Communist influence at various times in these unions.

Taylor, Paul S. "Organization and Policies of the Sailors' Union of the Pacific," *Monthly Labor Review,* vol. 16, April 1923, pp. 11–20.

The article is an excerpt from Taylor's book on the Sailors Union which at the time was in press.

———. *The Sailors' Union of the Pacific.* New York: Ronald Press, 1923. 188 pp.

Tells of the part the SUP played in improving the conditions of Pacific Coast seafarers through economic and legislative action from its inception as the Coast Seamen's Union in 1885 to shortly after the national seamen's strike in 1921. Introductory material describes attempts at organization before 1885. Concluding chapters explain the organizational and policy structure of the union.

U.S. Works Progress Administration. *History of the Sailors Union of the Pacific.* Berkeley, 1936. 51 pp.

The history is broadly divided into three periods: the beginnings of the union to the loss of the 1921 strike; 1921 to the start of the 1934 west coast maritime strike; and the period immediately following. The first period closely parallels Paul S. Taylor's work of the same name, the author acknowledging the source. In the twenties the union fell victim to factional strife because of alleged IWW and Communist influence. The events of the mid-thirties are shown to have revived the SUP. It actively participated in the maritime strike of 1934 and later in the formation of the Maritime Federation of the Pacific.

West, George P. "Andrew Furuseth and the Radicals," *Survey,* vol. 47, Nov. 5, 1921, pp. 207–9.

Sketches Furuseth's labor philosophy and shows how he applied it when the SUP membership rejected an agreement on the steam schooners, calling on them to work with nonunion longshoremen.

———. "Andrew Furuseth Stands Pat," *Survey,* vol. 51, Oct. 15, 1923, pp. 86–90.

Pictures Andrew Furuseth standing alone fighting a united front of the shipowners and the IWW. Furuseth is quoted at length on his opposition to the IWW, industrial unionism, and concerted action with the longshoremen.

Wollett, Donald H., and Robert J. Lampman. "The Law of Union Factionalism—the Case of the Sailors," *Stanford Law Review,* vol. 4, Feb. 1952, pp. 177–214.

Covers the trial in July 1949 of John Mahoney, Seattle SUP member, for slander of the union's officials. The trial committee was composed of members selected at SUP headquarters in San Francisco.

———

American Federation of Labor. *Andrew Furuseth, 1854–1938.* [Washington, D.C., 1938] [16] pp.

Associated, Richfield, Standard, and Union Oil Companies; General Petroleum Corporation; Hilcone Steamship Company. *Read the Facts about the Tanker Strike.* San Francisco, 1935. [6] pp.

Auerbach, Jerold S. "Progressives at Sea: The La Follette Act of 1915," *Labor History,* vol. 2, Fall 1961, pp. 344–60.

Bloch, Louis. "The Seamen's Right to Strike," *American Labor Legislation Review,* vol. 32, June 1942, pp. 73–81.

California. Bureau of Labor Statistics. *Fifth Biennial Report, 1891–1892.* Sacramento, 1893. "Investigation: Coast Seamen," pp. 166–89.

———. ———. *Investigation, June 29 to July 10, 1887 by the Commissioner of the Bureau into the Condition of Men Working on the Waterfront and on Board of Pacific Coast Vessels.* Sacramento, 1887. 107 pp.

Coast Seamen's Union of the Pacific Coast. *Constitution and History.* [San Francisco] A. W. Publishing Co., 1885. 48 pp.

Cross, Ira B. "The First Seamen's Unions," *Coast Seamen's Journal,* vol. 21, July 8, 1908, pp. 1, 2, 7, 10.

———. "The Sailor in '49," *Coast Seamen's Journal,* vol. 20, June 19, 1907, pp. 2, 14.

Dickson, Samuel. *Tales of San Francisco.* Stanford: Stanford University Press, 1957. Book 2, chap. 14, "Shanghai Kelly," pp. 386–95.

Dillon, Richard H. *Embarcadero.* New York: Coward-McCann, 1959. Chap. 13, "Shanghai Days in San Francisco," pp. 291–313.

Drury, Horace B. "The Labor Policy of the Shipping Board," *Journal of Political Economy,* vol. 29, Jan. 1921, pp. 1–28.

Fanning, Pete. *Great Crimes of the West.* San Francisco: By the author [1929?] "Cruelty on the High Seas," pp. 124–34.

Forsyth, Ralph Kendall. "The Wage Scale Agreements of the Maritime Unions," *Annals of the American Academy of Political and Social Science,* vol. 36, Sept. 1910, pp. 95–111.

Harrison, Gregory A. *Oral Argument and Supplementary Data before the United States Maritime Commission in the Matter of Minimum Manning Scales, Minimum Wage Scales and Reasonable Working Conditions.* [San Francisco? 1937?] 32 pp. Supplementary statement. 53 pp.

Healey, James. *Foc's'le and Glory-Hole.* A study of the merchant seaman and his occupation. New York: Merchant Marine Publishers Association, 1936. Chap. 13, "Seamen and Organized Labor," pp. 148–63.

Hohman, Elmo Paul. *Seamen Ashore.* A study of the United Seamen's Service and of merchant seamen in port. New Haven: Yale University Press, 1952. 426 pp.

Hudson, Roy B. "The Fight of the Seamen for Militant Unionism," *Communist,* vol. 15, March 1936, pp. 220–29.

Ingram, John. "The National Union of Marine Cooks and Stewards, C.I.O.: A Case Study in Bureaucracy and Democracy in American

Trade Unions." Unpublished M.A. thesis. University of California, Berkeley, 1951. 294 pp.

Inland Boatmen's Union of the Pacific: Its Birth and Growth. [San Francisco, 1937?] 36 pp.

International Juridical Association. *Report on the Status and Working Conditions of Seamen in the American Merchant Marine.* New York: Waldorf Press [1936?] 36 pp.

International Longshoremen's and Warehousemen's Union and National Union of Marine Cooks and Stewards. *The Waterfront Is the Union Front; Nailing the Shipowners' Lies.* San Francisco, 1948. [12] pp.

International Seamen's Union of America. *The American Seaman in His Relation to the Merchant and Naval Services.* A summary of the historical and economic aspects of the subject; also a recapitulation of the features contained in H.R. 11193 and S. 6155. San Francisco, 1910. 34 pp.

———. *Handy-Billy Book of New Century Pamphlets for Seamen.* Chicago: Hollister Bros., 1901. 40 pp.

———. *A Memorial to the U.S. Senate and House: Unskilled Sailors, Greatest Danger to Lives of Passengers.* San Francisco [1910?] 13 pp.

———. Pacific District Committee. *The Seamen's Union.* San Francisco, 1923. 8 pp.

Johnson, Alvin S. "Andrew Furuseth," *New Republic,* vol. 9, Nov. 11, 1916, pp. 40–42.

Joint Strike Committee and Tanker Negotiating Committee. *Memorandum of Terms of Employment of Licensed and Unlicensed Personnel on Oil Tankers, Dated April 5, 1935, as Amended April 6, 19 and 24, 1935.* Committee recommendations. [San Francisco, 1935?] Various pagings.

Kennedy, Phillip B. "The Seamen's Act," *Annals of the American Academy of Political and Social Science,* vol. 63, Jan. 1916, pp. 232–43.

Krigsman, Henry A. "A History of the Masters, Mates and Pilots of America—an Organization of Merchant Marine Officers." Unpublished M.A. thesis. Purdue University, 1954. 78 pp.

Lampman, Robert J. "Collective Bargaining of West Coast Sailors, 1885–1947: A Case Study in Unionism." Unpublished Ph.D. dissertation. University of Wisconsin, 1950. 324 pp.

Lang, Frederick J. "The Government Offensive Against the Merchant Seamen," *Fourth International,* vol. 3, Oct. 1942, pp. 303–9.

———. *Maritime: A Historical Sketch and a Workers' Program.* New York: Pioneer Publishers, 1945. 171 pp.

Macarthur, Walter. *American Seamen's Law: Supplement.* San Francisco, 1936. 16 pp.

———, comp. *Handbook—Navigation Laws of the United States.* Sections and acts applicable to shipment and discharge of seamen; qualifications of licensed officers, manning scales. . . . 3d ed. San Francisco: James H. Barry, 1918. 146 pp.

———, comp. *The Seaman's Contract, 1790–1918.* A complete reprint of the laws relating to American seamen, enacted, amended and repealed by the Congress of the United States. San Francisco: James H. Barry, 1919. 234 pp.

MacMullen, Jerry. "Windjammer Days in San Diego," *California Historical Society Quarterly,* vol. 22, Dec. 1943, pp. 349–54.

Marine Cooks and Stewards. *Delegates Handbook.* Rev. ed. San Francisco, 1949. 41 pp.

———. *The Ship Committee's Job.* San Francisco, 1939. 16 pp.

Marine Engineers Beneficial Association, No. 35, San Francisco. *Constitution and By-Laws.* [San Francisco] Baird and Henderson [1885] 53 pp.

Maritime Federation of the Pacific. *Maritime Workers Demand a New Deal.* A program for an American merchant marine and a summary of the anti-labor policies followed by the Bureau of Marine Inspection and Navigation. Compiled in collaboration with C.I.O. Maritime Committee, National Maritime Union, and W. L. Standard, Admiralty Lawyer. San Francisco [1939] 38 pp.

Marshall, Thomas C. *Into the Streets and Lanes: The Beginnings and Growth of the Social Work of the Episcopal Church in Diocese of Los Angeles, 1897–1947.* Claremont, Calif.: Saunders Press, 1948. Chap 6, "The Seamen's Church Institute," pp. 79–92.

Master Mariners' Mutual Aid Society of San Francisco. *Rules and Regulations.* San Francisco: Jos. Winterburn & Co., 1875. 11 pp.

The National Seamen. *Proposed Constitution for One National Industrial Union of All Seamen.* Submitted by a committee of the Pacific Coast Marine Firemen, Oilers, Watertenders and Wipers Association; Sailors Union of the Pacific; Marine Cooks and Stewards Association of the Pacific Coast; Inland Boatmen's Union of the Pacific; and National Maritime Union of America. San Francisco, 1937. 52 pp.

National Union of Marine Cooks and Stewards. *Story of the National Union of Marine Cooks and Stewards, Told in the words of an Old Timer who Sailed the Pacific in Topmasters and Still Sails.* San Francisco [1946?] 19 pp.

Pacific Coast Marine Fireman's Union. *Constitution and By-Laws.* San Francisco: S.F. Printing Co., 1886. 9 pp.

Pacific Coast Marine Firemen, Oilers, Watertenders and Wipers Association. *Agents Conference, May 1, 1945.* San Francisco, 1945. 112 pp.

Sailors Union of the Pacific. *Harry Lundeberg, 1901–1957.* San Francisco, 1957. 12 pp.

———. *Statement re Historical Background of Sailors' Right to Work Cargo in Steam Schooners.* [San Francisco, 1950] 10 + [40] pp.

———. *To the Membership: CIO? Independent? AFL? Steady as She Goes.* San Francisco, 1937. [10] pp.

[San Francisco Seamen's Institute] *Seamen's Church Institute of San Francisco.* [San Francisco: John Henry Nash, 1917?] [15] pp.

Schrader, Ralph A. "Organized Labor and Panama Ships." Unpublished M.A. thesis. University of California, Berkeley, 1955. 181 + 80 pp.

Seafarers' Federation of the Pacific. *Minutes of Meeting to Discuss Question of Seafarers' Federation.* [San Francisco, 1938] 14 pp.

Seamen's Protective Union of San Francisco. *Constitution and By-Laws.* San Francisco: Crane & Raveley, 1878. 22 pp.

Steamshipmen's Protective Association of San Francisco. *History, Constitution and By-Laws.* San Francisco: Cooperative Labor Press, 1886. 24 pp.

Taft, Philip. *The Structure and Government of Labor Unions.* Cambridge: Harvard University Press, 1954. Chap. 5, "The Unlicensed Seafaring Unions," pp. 181–212.

Taylor, Paul S. "Chapters from the Early History of the Seamen of the Pacific Coast." Unpublished M.A. thesis. University of California, Berkeley, 1920. 67 pp.

———. "Eight Years of the Seamen's Act," *American Labor Legislation Review,* vol. 15, Mar. 1925, pp. 52–63.

Thor, Howard A. "A History of the Marine Engineers' Beneficial Association." Unpublished M.A. thesis. University of California, Berkeley, 1954. 255 pp.

U.S. Bureau of Labor Statistics. *The Earnings and Employment of Seamen on United States Flag Ships.* Bull. no. 1238. Washington, 1958. 90 pp.

———. *International Seamen's Union of America: A Study of Its History and Problems,* by Arthur E. Albrecht. Bull. no. 342. Washington, 1923. 119 pp.

————. *Workmen's Compensation and the Protection of Seamen*. Bull. no. 869. Washington, 1946. 93 pp.

U.S. Congress. House. Committee on Merchant Marine and Fisheries. *Hearings.* 76th Cong., 1st sess., on H.R. 4051 (hiring of seamen). Washington, 1939. Testimony: Bruce Hannon, MFP, pp. 13–48; Roy A. Pyle, ACA, pp. 48–57; Jack O'Donnell, MCS, pp. 57–62; Harry Bridges, ILWU, pp. 62–87; W. L. Welsh, MFOWW, pp. 87–89; Samuel Kagel, MEBA, pp. 89–94; Harry Lundeberg, SUP, SIU, pp. 94–104; Walter D. Fisher, MFP, pp. 206–29.

————. Joint Committee on Labor-Management Relations. *Hearings on the Operation of the Labor-Management Relations Act, 1947.* 80th Cong., 2d sess. Part 1. Washington, 1948. Testimony of Vincent J. Malone, president of MFOWW, pp. 177–236.

————. Senate. *Employment of Chinese on Vessels Flying the American Flag....* 57th Cong., 1st sess., S. Doc. 254. Washington, 1902. 17 pp.

————. ————. Committee on Labor and Public Welfare. *Communist Domination of Certain Unions*. Report of the Subcommittee on Labor and Labor-Management Relations. 82d Cong., 1st sess., S. Doc. 89. Washington, 1951. "Report of Executive Board Committee appointed by President Murray to investigate charges against the National Union of Marine Cooks and Stewards," pp. 31–41; "American Communications Association," pp. 43–57.

————. ————. ————. *To Legalize Maritime Hiring Halls*. Hearings on S. 1044 before the Subcommittee on Labor and Labor Management Relations. 82d Cong., 1st sess. Washington, 1951. Testimony of James R. Gormley, MFOWW, pp. 81–91.

U.S. Laws, Statutes.... *Act of Congress Creating the Office of Shipping Commissioner*. San Francisco: Women's Cooperative Print, 1873. 20 pp.

U.S. Maritime Commission. "In the Matter of Minimum Manning Scales, Minimum Wage Scales and Reasonable Working Conditions." Stenographer's minutes. Washington, 1937. 248 pp.

U.S. War Shipping Administration. *Comparative Analysis of Union Agreements of General Agents of the War Shipping Administration, Covering Unlicensed Personnel on Dry Cargo Vessels as of March 1, 1944.* 431 pp. As of October 1, 1945. 53 pp.

Weintraub, Hyman. *Andrew Furuseth, Emancipator of the Seamen*. Berkeley: University of California Press, 1959. 267 pp.

White, Donald S. *Seafaring Men and Automation: Some Educational Approaches*. In cooperation with the Marine Cooks and Stewards Union, AFL-CIO. San Francisco [1961] 27 pp.

TRANSPORTATION

MOTOR TRUCK

Beck, Dave. *Forward with America.* The program and policies of the Western Conference of Teamsters as our country prepares for a great era of peacetime production. An address delivered at the Tenth Western Conference of Teamsters, Seattle, April 1, 1946. Washington, D.C.: International Brotherhood of Teamsters, 1946. [29] pp.

Dave Beck, vice-president of the International Brotherhood of Teamsters and chairman of the Western Conference, defines the Teamsters' philosophy of labor relations and interprets the objectives of the Western Conference in the light of that philosophy.

Cross, Ira B. *Collective Bargaining and Trade Agreements in the Brewery, Metal, Teaming and Building Trades of San Francisco, California.* University of California Publications in Economics, vol. 4, no. 4. Berkeley: University of California Press, 1918. "The Teaming Trades," pp. 300–30.

States that neither the unions nor the employers in the draying industry were as well organized as other groups covered in this study to carry on effective collective bargaining, and that agreements, with a few exceptions, involved only individual union and employer groups. Each teaming trade is dealt with separately, its organizational history briefly told, and its wage rates, hours, and working conditions before and after organization reviewed.

Gillingham, John B. *The Teamsters Union on the West Coast.* Berkeley: Institute of Industrial Relations, University of California, 1956. 90 pp.

Discusses the rapid growth of the Teamsters Union on the Pacific Coast, the diversity of its jurisdiction, and the special problems of structure and internal administration arising from this diversity. Emphasized is the union's multi-employer bargaining pattern, its relations with other unions, often marked by sharp jurisdictional conflict, and its general trade-union philosophy. Includes a number of statistical tables.

Leiter, Robert D. *The Teamsters Union: A Study of Its Economic Impact.* New York: Bookman Associates, 1957. 304 pp.

A number of references to the California Teamsters' history and problems, both brief and extended, are included in a study of the Teamsters Union as a national organization.

Page, Thomas Walker. "The San Francisco Labor Movement in 1901," *Political Science Quarterly,* vol. 17, Dec. 1902, pp. 664–88.

States that the teamsters' strike of 1901 is worthy of careful study because "the principles at issue were of fundamental importance to our industrial system," and because as an aftermath of the strike a political movement developed which gave the unions virtual control of the city government. The strike itself is described and an attempt is made to evaluate the significance of its outcome.

Robinson, Robert M. "San Francisco Teamsters at the Turn of the Century," *California Historical Society Quarterly,* vol. 35, March 1956, pp. 59–69; Sept. 1956, pp. 145–53.

Traces the development of trade-union organization among San Francisco teamsters from 1853 to 1902. The early San Francisco teamsters are shown to have been, in the main, self-employed, and their organization was more in the nature of a guild than a trade union. Toward the end of the century, when large-scale firms became typical in the teaming trades, the working teamsters had their own organization. In 1901 this local, affiliated nationally with the Team Drivers' International and locally with the City Front Federation, went through its first real test of strength in a long and arduous strike against the Draymen's and the Employers and Manufacturers Associations. The result is indicated to have been indefinite.

Rosenberg, Ed R. "The San Francisco Strikes of 1901," *American Federationist,* vol. 9, Jan. 1902, pp. 15–18.

An account, by the secretary of the San Francisco Labor Council, of the Employers Association's campaign against organized labor in San Francisco and the strikes it provoked on the part of workers in their self-defense, culminating in the hard-fought strike of the teamsters and their affiliates in the City Front Federation in 1901.

Bernstein, Irving. "The Politics of the West Coast Teamsters and Truckers," *Proceedings,* Tenth Annual Meeting, Industrial Relations Research Association, New York, Sept. 5–7, 1957. Publication no. 20, pp. 12–31.

California. Legislature. Joint Legislative Fact-Finding Committee on Agricultural and Industrial Labor. *Special Report, Covering Investigation of Alleged Abuses by Swampers and Lumpers in the Handling of Produce at the Main Los Angeles Produce Markets.* Sacramento, 1945. 40 pp.

Chatom, Paul, Jr. "Industrial Relations in the Brewery, Metal and Teaming Trades of San Francisco." Unpublished M.A. thesis. University of California, Berkeley, 1915. 123 pp.

[Conboy, William J.] Teamster Life in San Francisco before World War I. As told in answers to questions by Corinne L. Gilb for the Institute of Industrial Relations Oral History Project, University of California, Berkeley. Spring 1957. 16 pp. Typewritten.

"Dave Beck, Labor Faker at 25 G's a Year," *March of Labor,* vol. 2, Nov. 1950, pp. 6–7, 27.

Draymen and Teamsters Union of San Francisco. *Constitution and By-Laws*. San Francisco: Women's Co-operative Printing Office, 1879. 36 pp.

Hackmen's Protective Benevolent Association, San Francisco. *Constitution, By-Laws and Rules*. San Francisco: Alta California Printing House, 1875. 17 pp.

Harrington, Michael. *The Retail Clerks*. New York: Wiley, 1962. "The Teamsters," pp. 73–78.

Miller, Joe. "Dave Beck Comes Out of the West," *Reporter,* vol. 9, Dec. 9, 1953, pp. 20–23.

Neuberger, Richard L. "Labor's Overlords—Bridges and Beck," *American Magazine,* vol. 125, March 1938, pp. 16–17, 166–70.

Robinson, Robert McClure. "A History of the Teamsters' Union in the San Francisco Bay Area, 1850–1950." Unpublished Ph.D. dissertation. University of California, Berkeley, 1951. 497 pp.

Robson, R. Thayne. "The [West Coast] Trucking Industry," *Monthly Labor Review,* vol. 82, May 1959, pp. 547–51.

San Francisco Labor Council. *Strike Fund, April 23, 1901 to November 30, 1901*. San Francisco [1901?] 22 pp.

"Teamsters' Dave Beck," *Fortune,* vol. 38, Dec., 1948, pp. 191–98.

[Thompson, Roy B.] The Trucking Industry, 1930–1950. An interview by Corinne L. Gilb for the Institute of Industrial Relations Oral History Project, University of California, Berkeley. June–Aug. 1958. "Labor Relations in California," pp. 307–85. Typewritten.

Todd, Elinore Adele. "History of the Milk Wagon Drivers' Union of San Francisco County, 1900–1933." Unpublished M.A. thesis. University of California, Berkeley, 1953. 294 pp.

U.S. Congress. Senate. Committee on Education and Labor. *Violations of Free Speech and Rights of Labor*. Hearings, 76th Cong., 3d sess. Washington, 1940. Part 53. "Teamster Activity in Los Angeles," pp. 19397–430.

Yorke, Rev. Peter C. Series of letters on teamsters' strike, in San Francisco *Examiner,* Sept. 25–28, 30, Oct. 1, 1901.

RAILROAD

The "City Guard," a History of Company "B", First Regiment Infantry, N.G.C., During the Sacramento Campaign, July 3 to 26, 1894, by Lieutenant George Filmer, Corporal A. McCulloch, Privates W. J. Hayes and Wm. D. O'Brien. San Francisco: Filmer-Rollins Electrotype Co., 1895. 263 pp.

The Pullman strike as viewed by a San Francisco National Guard unit dispatched to Sacramento along with other California National Guard units to take possession of the railroad yards and start the trains running. Since some of the units were unwilling or reluctant to take military action against the strikers, the mission was at first unsuccessful, but with the later arrival of a regular army unit the strike was broken and railroad operations were resumed.

Leach, Frank A. *Recollections of a Newspaperman.* San Francisco: Samuel Levinson, 1917. Chap. 13, "Newspaper Life in Oakland," pp. 256–86.

Part of the chapter, pp. 264–73, discusses the Pullman railroad strike of 1894.

McGowan, Joseph A. *History of the Sacramento Valley.* New York: Lewis Historical Publishing Co., 1961. "Industrial Armies and the Pullman Strike," vol. 2, pp. 96–105.

Describes the experiences of Sacramento and other valley centers with the industrial "Armies" in 1894 and 1897, and reviews the dramatic course of the Pullman railroad strike of 1894 in the Sacramento Valley and especially in Sacramento.

Stimson, Grace Heilman. *Rise of the Labor Movement in Los Angeles.* Berkeley: University of California Press, 1955. Chap. 13, "The Pullman Strike," pp. 161–71.

Describes the structural characteristics of railroad trade-union organization in the Los Angeles area at the time of the Pullman strike, its relationship to the general trade-union movement in Los Angeles, and the course and outcome of the strike locally.

Bacon, T. R. "The Railroad Strike in California," *Yale Review,* vol. 3, Nov. 1894, pp. 241–50.

California. Bureau of Labor Statistics. *Seventh Biennial Report, 1895–1896.* Sacramento, 1896. "Railroad Strike, San Francisco Printing Pressmen's and Painters' Strikes," pp. 149–60.

———. ———. *Fifteenth Biennial Report, 1911–1912.* Sacramento, 1912. "Steam Railroads—Number of Employees and Wages," pp. 596–601.

[California. Industrial Welfare Commission] Before the Industrial Welfare Commission, State of California. In the matter of proposed Order No. 9 NS. Public Hearings, May 28, 1943. San Francisco: Stenotype Reporting Co., 1943. 210 pp.

————. Before the Wage Board Appointed by the Industrial Welfare Commission for the Transportation Industries, State of California—May 8, 1943. In the matter involving Order No. 9 NS. Los Angeles, 1943. 47 pp. Typewritten

————. Executive Session of the Wage Board Appointed by the California Industrial Welfare Commission for the Transportation Industries, State of California—May 9, 1943. In the matter involving proposed Order No. 9 NS. Los Angeles, 1943. 199 pp. Typewritten.

————. Interstate Railway Carriers Motion before the Industrial Welfare Commission of the State of California, to eliminate such carriers from the scope of proposed Order No. 9 NS . . . in the matter of proposed Order No. 9 NS relating to the wages, hours and working conditions of women and minors employed in the transportation industry. [San Francisco?] 1943. Various pagings.

California Committee for Railroad Safety. *The People's Case for Railroad Safety: No on #3*. Richmond, Calif. [1948?] 35 pp.

Carrasco, H. C. Address at testimonial banquet, San Francisco, February 21, 1939. 8 pp.

Estes, George. *Railway Employees United*. Portland, Ore.: by the author, 1931. 79 pp.

Friedman, Morris. *The Pinkerton Labor Spy*. New York: Wilshire Book Co., 1907. "Destruction of the United Brotherhood of Railway Employees," pp. 184–89.

"History of Railway Shopmen's Memorable Strike," *East Bay Labor Journal*, Supplement, vol. 1, May 24, 1924, pp. 11, 37.

Railway Brotherhoods. California State Legislative Board. *Report on the 52nd Session of the California Legislature, 1937*. [San Francisco, 1937] 26 pp.

U.S. Presidential Emergency Board [Railway] Testimony of Hale Holden, chairman of the Southern Pacific Company, in 1938 national railway wage reduction controversy. Washington, 1938. Doc. no. 23193, pp. 1–12.

LOCAL TRANSPORTATION

Lilienthal, Lillie Bernheimer. *In Memoriam: Jesse Warren Lilienthal*. San Francisco: John Henry Nash, 1921. Chap. 8, "The United Railroads," pp. 155–207.

Cites the many things Jesse W. Lilienthal did for his employees as president of the United Railroads in San Francisco. The claim is made that these employees were contented and that the more obvious this contentment was, the more insistent labor leaders were to organize the men. Appended material includes a reprint of an address made by Lilienthal before the American Railway Association dealing with welfare work, particularly as it applied to his employees, and an account of the employment conditions of United Railroads employees in 1917.

Plehn, Carl C. "The Adjustment of Street-Carmen's Wages in San Francisco," *Journal of Political Economy,* vol. 12, Dec. 1903, pp. 1–17.

The outstanding issue in the 1903 dispute between the United Railroads and the streetcarmen was the rate of pay. Arbitration was resorted to, and because the writer considers the method of appraisement important for students of economics, he reviews the arguments advanced by both sides and the reasoning of the arbitrator in reaching a decision.

Quick, H. C. *The Only Official Souvenir History of the Street Railway Employees Strike of San Francisco, April 19 to 26, 1902.* San Francisco: Walter N. Brunt Press, 1902. 106 pp.

Reviews the difficulties the carmen encountered in trying to organize for bargaining with the United Railroads. In spite of these difficulties, they did succeed in organizing, and after a week's strike, with the sympathy of the public and the cooperation of the Union Labor Party administration, they won all major demands.

Schmidt, Emerson P. *Industrial Relations in Urban Transportation.* Minneapolis: University of Minnesota Press, 1937. "Strikes in San Francisco," pp. 178–83.

A record of attempts by San Francisco's street railway employees from 1901 to 1917 to negotiate with the employers of the privately owned street railway lines. Describes the organization of a union in 1901, partially successful strikes in 1902 and 1906, and unsuccessful strikes in 1907 and 1917, noting the widespread use by the employers of strikebreakers and the violence their use provoked.

Young, John P. *San Francisco: A History of the Pacific Coast Metropolis.* San Francisco: S. J. Clarke Publishing Co., 1912. Vol. 2, chap. 65, "Graft Prosecutions and Other Troubles after the Fire," pp. 873–96.

Includes accounts of the carmen's strikes in 1902, 1906, and 1907 for higher wages and shorter hours, and a comment on the violent nature of the 1907 strike because of the widespread use of strikebreakers.

Board of Arbitration. Report in the Wage Controversy between San Francisco–Oakland Terminal Railways and Carmen's Union, Division No. 192, Amalgamated Association of Street and Electric Railway Employees of America. [San Francisco] 1918. 17 pp. Typewritten.

Ford, Tirey L. Argument . . . in the Matter of the Arbitration of Certain

Differences between the Amalgamated Association of Street Railway Employees of America, Division No. 205 and United Railroads of San Francisco. San Francisco [1903?] 64 pp.

Heller Committee for Research in Social Economics. *Spending Ways of a Semi-Skilled Group.* Cost of Living Studies IV. A study of the incomes and expenditures of ninety-eight streetcar men's families in the San Francisco East Bay Region. University of California Publications in Economics, vol. 5, no. 5. Berkeley: University of California Press, 1931. Pp. 295–366.

In the Supreme Court of the State of California. Los Angeles Metropolitan Transit Authority, Plaintiff and Respondent, v. The Brotherhood of Railroad Trainmen, et al., Defendants and Appellants. [Sacramento? 1960?] Decision and Dissenting Opinion. 33 pp.

[Key System Transit Company] Argument and Brief in the Matter of the Arbitration Proceedings between Amalgamated Association of Street and Electric Railway Employees of America, Division No. 192 and Key System Transit Company, Oakland, California, 1925. San Francisco: Pernau-Walsh, 1925. 50 + 113 pp.

The Labor Bureau. *Report on Financial Condition of the Municipal Railway of San Francisco.* Prepared for Carmen's Division No. 518, Amalgamated Association of Street and Electric Railway Employees of America. San Francisco, 1923. 33 pp.

Omnibus R.R. Company, San Francisco. *Rules and Regulations for Conductors.* San Francisco: A. L. Bancroft Co., 1873. 8 pp.

Powers, Laura Bride. "The Peace Strike in San Francisco," *Overland,* vol. 39, June 1902, pp. 980–82.

"A Strike Called by Outsiders to Compel Recognition of a Union...," *Law and Labor,* vol. 5, Dec. 1923, pp. 335–38.

Taylor, Beatrice V. "Labor Relations on the Street Railways of San Francisco." Unpublished M.A. thesis. University of California, Berkeley, 1928. 110 pp.

"Wage Chronology No. 39: Pacific Greyhound Lines, 1945–53," *Monthly Labor Review,* vol. 77, Dec. 1954, pp. 1340–54.

BUILDING AND CONSTRUCTION

Bertram, Gordon W., and Sherman J. Maisel. *Industrial Relations in the Construction Industry: The Northern California Experience.* Berkeley: Institute of Industrial Relations, University of California, 1955. 70 pp.

Describes the organization and structure of the construction industry as they relate to collective bargaining and reviews the industry's past labor relations. The following periods are reviewed: 1869–1896, when unregulated competition prevailed; 1896–1921, a period of union dominance; 1921–1935, when the open shop was dominant; and the period following 1936, when collective bargaining was resumed. The writers note that the industry now accepts the unions as stabilizing influences because they assure uniform wage rates in the bargaining area, stabilize wage rates and other costs for an agreed period of time, and supply a skilled and disciplined work force.

Brown, Jack. "San Francisco Rank and File Movement," *Labor Herald,* vol. 1, April 1922, pp. 21–23.

Tells of a movement which resulted from a strike and lockout of building trades workers in San Francisco in 1921. Claiming that officials of the building trades unions had failed to take effective action against the lockout, the rank and file of these unions organized an auxiliary unit, the General Conference of the Building Trades, and succeeded in calling a general strike of all building trades in the San Francisco Bay Area. The strike ended in failure after the Building Trades and Central Labor Councils withdrew their support, and the workers were forced to return to work under open-shop conditions.

California. Bureau of Labor Statistics. *Second Biennial Report, 1885–1886.* Sacramento, 1887. Chap. 9, "Investigations," pp. 325–442.

The major investigation is "An inquiry as to the condition of the laborers employed by the contract on the seawall at San Francisco," and in part deals with the non-enforcement of the eight-hour law.

Cross, Ira B. *Collective Bargaining and Trade Agreements in the Brewery, Metal, Teaming and Building Trades of San Francisco, California.* University of California Publications in Economics, vol. 4, no. 4. Berkeley: University of California Press, 1918. "The Building Trades," pp. 331–42.

Maintains that the Building Trades Council, in contrast to other trade-union groups in the San Francisco area, as a matter of policy did not follow collective bargaining procedures based on trade agreements. It is pointed out that the building trades unions nevertheless had secured benefits for their members equal to or better than those of the other groups. The author examines the reasons for the obvious effectiveness of the Building Trades Council despite its rejection of collective bargaining procedures.

Haber, William. *Industrial Relations in the Building Industry.* Cambridge: Harvard University Press, 1930. Chap. 14, "The American Plan in San Francisco," pp. 400–41.

Reviews the history, tactics, and leadership of the San Francisco Building Trades Council as representative of the city's organized labor, and appraises the causes of its complete defeat in 1921 by open-shop forces. Examines the nature, principles, and functions of the San Francisco Industrial Association and the American Plan, which replaced the power of the Building Trades Council.

Perlman, Selig, and Philip Taft. *History of Labor in the United States, 1896–1932.* Vol. 4, *Labor Movements.* New York: Macmillan, 1935. Chap. 7, "The Labor Barony on the Pacific Coast," pp. 71–81.

Chiefly a review of the formation in 1896 of the San Francisco Building Trades Council and its growth into a powerful organization that for twenty-five years dictated conditions in the building industry; the methods that accounted for its powerful position; and its relationship to the San Francisco Labor Council and the Union Labor Party.

Ryan, Frederick L. *Industrial Relations in the San Francisco Building Trades.* Norman, Okla.: University of Oklahoma Press, 1936. 241 pp.

The study is divided into four periods: 1849–1869, when the master workman and journeyman relationship was general in construction and when the rules of that relationship were derived from the customs of the crafts; 1869–1896, a period of increasing division of labor, replacement of the master workman by the contractor, division of the crafts, and efforts of the craftsmen to organize permanent trade-union organizations; 1896–1921, the period during which the thoroughly organized crafts and the autocratically controlled Building Trades Council, through the practice of "business unionism," generally dominated industrial relations; 1921–1935, when "business unionism" and narrow craft interests no longer sufficed, the building trades workers were defeated by the employers, and the open shop became general in the building industry.

U.S. Congress. Senate. Commission on Industrial Relations. *Final Report and Testimony.* 64th Cong., 1st sess., S. Doc. 415. Washington, 1916. "Labor Conditions in Construction Camps," vol. 6, pp. 5087–168.

Testimony: John G. Tyler, Utah Construction Co., pp. 5106–14; Ruben Ready, labor agent, pp. 5127–39; A. L. Wilde, secretary-treasurer, Steam Shovelmen's Union, San Francisco, pp. 5139–46.

Bertram, Gordon William. "Industrial Relations in the Northern California Construction Industry." Unpublished Ph.D. dissertation. University of California, Berkeley, 1957. 487 pp.

Building Trades Council of San Francisco. *Arguments for Increase in Wage for Fifteen Crafts.* Submitted in arbitration proceedings, 1921. San Francisco: James H. Barry, 1921. 95 pp.

"Building Trades—San Francisco: Bonus Contract of the Industrial Association of San Francisco," *Monthly Labor Review,* vol. 16, Jan. 1923, pp. 107–9.

California. Division of Labor Statistics and Research. "California Construction Employment," *Bulletins,* Aug. 1948–June 1950, pp. CE1–23.

———. Governor's Conference on Employment. *Proceedings.* Sacramento, 1949. Construction Section, Public and Private. Various pagings.

Cross, Ira B. "The San Francisco Building Trades," *in* John R. Commons, ed., *Trade Unionism and Labor Problems*. 2d series. Boston: Gin and Co., 1921. Chap. 31, pp. 477–88.

"Enforcement of 'American Plan' in Building Industry by the Industrial Association . . . ," *Law and Labor,* vol. 7, May 1925, pp. 111–15.

The Labor Bureau. "Supplementary Report on Wages, Cost of Living and General Business Conditions." Prepared for Pile Driving and Bridge Contractors Association and Pile Drivers, Bridge, Dock and Wharf Builders Union No. 34. San Francisco, 1925. 7 pp. Typewritten.

Los Angeles Building and Construction Trades Council. Testimonial dinner honoring C. J. Haggerty, Los Angeles, December 10, 1952. [Los Angeles? 1953?] 64 pp.

Los Angeles Chamber of Commerce. Construction Industries Committee. *Apprenticeship: A Profitable Investment for Everyone*. Los Angeles, 1947. 22 pp.

Murray, Sam. "The Passing of a Building Trades Boss," *Industrial Pioneer,* vol. 2, April 1925, pp. 26–28.

Oricello, Joseph C. "The Work of Apprenticeship Committees: An Evaluation of the Operation of Selected San Francisco Building Trades Committees." Unpublished Ed.D. dissertation. University of California, Berkeley, 1954. 354 pp.

Pierson, Frank C. "Building Trades Bargaining Plan in Southern California," *Monthly Labor Review,* vol. 70, Jan. 1950, pp. 14–18.

Pile Drivers, Bridge, Wharf and Dock Builders, Local 34. *How to Organize the Job*. San Francisco [1943?] 55 pp.

San Francisco Union No. 22 of the Brotherhood of Carpenters and Joiners of America. *Constitution and By-laws*. San Francisco: Barry, Baird and Co., 1882. 24 pp.

U.S. Congress. Senate. Commission on Industrial Relations. *Final Report and Testimony*. 64th Cong., 1st sess., S. Doc. 415. Washington, 1916. "The Painters' Strike in San Francisco," vol. 6, pp. 5475–84.

AIRCRAFT

Allen, Arthur P., and Betty V. H. Schneider. *Industrial Relations in the California Aircraft Industry*. Berkeley: Institute of Industrial Relations, University of California, 1956. 59 pp.

An analysis of the development of trade-union organization and collective bargaining in the Southern California airframe industry. The emphasis is on the relations between the six chief airframe producers and the two major unions in the industry, the United Automobile Workers and the International Association of Machinists. Includes a review of some of the jurisdictional problems of the two unions.

Olmstead, Edwin. *Your Union and How It Operates.* North Hollywood, Calif.: Aeronautical Industrial District Lodge 727 [1945?] 27 pp.

Includes a statement of achievements in improved wage rates and working conditions, and a program for the future.

―――――

Feise, Richard. "Aircraft: Stabilization of Wages, the West Coast," *in* Institute of Labor Studies, *Year Book of American Labor.* New York: Philosophical Library, 1945. Vol. 1, chap. 14, pp. 261–66.

Golden, Clinton S., and Virginia D. Parker, eds. *Causes of Industrial Peace under Collective Bargaining.* New York: Harper, 1955. Part 2, Condensations of Thirteen Case Studies. "Lockheed Aircraft Corporation and the Machinists (AFL)," by Clark Kerr and George Halverson, pp. 157–82.

Gray, Robert D. *Systematic Wage Administration in the Southern California Aircraft Industry.* Monograph no. 7. New York: Industrial Relations Counselors, 1943. 90 pp.

"Half a Million Workers," *Fortune,* vol. 23, March 1941, pp. 96–98, 163–66.

Hamlisch, Robert T. "Wage Chronology No. 24: North American Aviation, 1941–51," *Monthly Labor Review,* vol. 74, June 1952, pp. 683–87.

Mayo, Elton, and George F. Lombard. *Teamwork and Labor Turnover in the Aircraft Industry of Southern California.* Business Research Study no. 32. Boston: Graduate School of Business Administration, Harvard University, 1944. 40 pp.

"Postwar Adjustment of Aircraft Workers in Southern California," *Monthly Labor Review,* vol. 63, Nov. 1946, pp. 706–11.

United Auto Workers (CIO), Local 683. *Dear Brother: A Letter to You from a North American Aircraft Worker.* Los Angeles [1941?] 10 pp.

U.S. Bureau of Labor Statistics. *Southern California Aircraft Workers in Wartime.* Work and Wage Experience Studies, Report no. 6. Washington, 1947. 17 pp.

―――. *Wage Rates in California Airframe Industry, 1941,* by Louis M. Solomon and N. Arnold Tolles. Bull. no. 704. Washington, 1942. 26 pp.

―――. *Wage Stabilization in the California Airframe Industry, 1943.* Bull. no. 746. Washington, 1943. 16 pp.

U.S. Federal Security Agency. Social Security Administration. *Nineteen Employee-Benefit Plans in the Airframe Industry,* by Abe Friedson and Joseph Zisman. Washington, 1951. 63 pp.

U.S. National Youth Administration. *An Occupational Study of the Aircraft Manufacturing Industry in California,* by Edward G. Stoy and Francis W. Strong. N.p., 1939. 69 pp.

"Wage Chronology No. 24: North American Aviation, Supplement No. 2, 1953–57," *Monthly Labor Review,* vol. 80, April 1957, pp. 460–65.

"Wage Chronology No. 24: North American Aviation, Supplement No. 3, 1957–61," *Monthly Labor Review,* vol. 84, June 1961, pp. 629–34.

Welty, Malcolm W., comp. *Labor Contract Clauses in the Automotive and Aviation Parts Manufacturing Industry.* Detroit: Automotive and Aviation Parts Manufacturers, 1945. 488 pp.

MINING

Brissenden, Paul F. "Labor Turnover among Employees of a California Copper Mining and Smelting Company," *Monthly Labor Review,* vol. 8, May 1919, pp. 63–84.

Intended to show the relative stability of mine and smelter workers.

Browne, J. Ross. *Mining Adventures: California and Nevada, 1863–1865.* Balboa Island, Calif.: Paisano Press, 1961. Chap. 1, "To Bodie Bluff," pp. 3–13; chaps. 4–5, "The Hacienda," "Town on the Hill," pp. 171–78.

An account of days spent in the mining country and among the miners.

Goss, Helen Rocca. *The Life and Death of a Quicksilver Mine.* Los Angeles: Historical Society of Southern California, 1958. 150 pp.

Reminiscences of life at the Great Western Mine in Lake County, California, by members of the family of Andrew Rocca, superintendent of the mine from 1876 to 1900. The recollections cover aspects of life at the mine settlement, the operations at the mine, its predominantly Chinese work force, the division of labor, hours, and wage rates. Of special interest is a chapter describing the workaday life of the Chinese.

Morefield, Richard Henry. "Mexicans in the California Mines, 1848–53," *California Historical Society Quarterly,* vol. 35, March 1956, pp. 37–46.

Reviews the fierce competition for profitable claims in the gold fields and how it affected the thousands of Mexicans, many of them experienced miners, who had been among the first to stake out claims. The many methods used, including extreme violence, to deprive them of their claims are described. Tells how they were welcomed back as the first wage workers after placer mining was exhausted and industrialists took over the mining of gold.

Paul, Rodman W. *California Gold: The Beginning of Mining in the Far West.* Cambridge: Harvard University Press, 1947. Chap. 17, "From Sunday Carnival to Labor War, 1857–1873," pp. 311–33.

> "One could almost say that within the short span of twenty-five years California mining had passed through a cycle that commenced with what the economists call 'home crafts' and ended with what the socialists term 'proletarian industry.'" Discusses the transition from the mining of small private claims to large-scale industrial mining and gives an account of the organization of trade unions among the miners and the rise of disputes with the mine operators, resulting in strikes which in one instance involved the intervention of the state militia.

U.S. Congress. House. *Mining Statistics West of the Rocky Mountains.* 42d Cong., 1st sess., Ex. Doc. no. 10. Washington, 1871. Chap. 1, "California," pp. 8–92.

> Contains references to employment and wages in various mines.

U.S. Work Projects Administration. *Employment and Income from Gold Placering by Hand Methods, 1935–1937.* Philadelphia, 1940. 142 pp.

> During the depression of the 1930's many unemployed workers were led by glowing accounts of gold finds to seek an income from hand placer mining. This report lists the negative findings of a study made to determine if it was possible to realize a livelihood from that source. The study is national in scope but it was found that California accounted for 70 per cent of this type of mining.

Burrows, A. "In a Modern Gold Mining Camp," *Overland,* vol. 9, April 1887, pp. 337–40.

California. Bureau of Labor Statistics. "The Gold Mines and Laboring Conditions on the 'Mother Lode,' California, 1912." San Francisco, 1912. 75 pp. Typewritten.

———. ———. *Tenth Biennial Report, 1901–1902.* Sacramento, 1902. "Wages, Hours of Labor per Diem … of Miners in the State of California," pp. 16–24.

Conway, Alan, ed. *The Welsh in America: Letters from the Immigrants.* Minneapolis: University of Minnesota Press, 1961. "On the Mining Frontiers," pp. 231–82.

Dufault, David V. "The Chinese in the Mining Camps of California, 1848–1870," *Historical Society of Southern California Quarterly,* vol. 41, June 1959, pp. 155–70.

Foote, M. "A California Mining Camp," *Scribner's Monthly,* vol. 15, Feb. 1878, pp. 480–93.

Friedman, Morris. *The Pinkerton Labor Spy.* New York: Wilshire Book Co., 1907. "Frank E. Cochran," pp. 178–83.

Harries, Norman Hayden. "Cornish and Welsh Mining Settlements in California." Unpublished M.A. thesis. University of California, Berkeley, 1956. 164 pp.

Morefield, Richard Henry. "The Mexican Adaptation in American California, 1846–1875." Unpublished M.A. thesis. University of California, Berkeley, 1955. Chap. 1, "Hewers of Wood and Drawers of Water: Mexicans in the Mines of California, 1848–1853," pp. 3–31.

Paul, Rodman W. *California Gold: The Beginning of Mining in the Far West.* Cambridge: Harvard University Press, 1947. Chap. 8, "Basic Conditions for a Transitional Era," pp. 116–23.

"The Quicksilver Mine of New Almaden," *Hutchings California Magazine,* vol. 1, Sept. 1856, pp. 97–105.

U.S. Congress. Senate. Committee on Labor and Public Welfare. *Communist Domination of Certain Unions.* Report of the Subcommittee on Labor and Labor-Management Relations. 82d Cong., 1st sess. S. Doc. 89. Washington, 1951. "International Union of Mine, Mill and Smelter Workers," pp. 97–109.

U.S. Works Progress Administration. *Small-Scale Placer Mines as a Source of Gold, Employment, and Livelihood in 1935.* Philadelphia, 1937. Sec. 2, "California," pp. 10–22.

LUMBER

Hudson, James Jackson. "The California National Guard, 1903–1940." Unpublished Ph.D. dissertation, University of California, Berkeley, 1952. Pp. 120–30.

Refers to the National Guard's part in the breaking of the lumber strike at McCloud.

———. "The McCloud River Affair of 1909: A Study in the Use of State Troops," *California Historical Society Quarterly,* vol. 35, March 1956, pp. 29–35.

"In the spring of 1909 the California National Guard was called upon to quell a riot of several hundred Italian lumbermen in the Siskiyou County town of McCloud." In explanation of this statement the account adds that as a result of a strike against the McCloud River Lumber Company over labor conditions, "Some 700 Italian workmen not only refused to work but also threatened to prevent nonstrikers from doing so...." Further details describe the participation of the National Guard in the dispute and its eventual outcome.

Olson, Culbert L. *State Papers and Public Addresses, January 2, 1939–January 4, 1943*. Sacramento, 1942. Part 3, "California's Labor Problems," Radio address delivered over Columbia Broadcasting System, March 19, 1939. Pp. 183–86.

Has reference to CIO–AFL jurisdictional disputes at the lumber mills in Westwood, Lassen County, and at the Central Valley Project jobs in Shasta County.

Strong, Anna Louise. *My Native Land*. New York: Viking, 1940. Chap. 9, "The Westwood War," pp. 124–34.

Tells how the workers of the Red River Lumber Company organized a CIO local of lumberworkers and struck against a wage cut and how, in retaliation, the company vigilantes drove the strikers out of the company-owned town. When some days later they returned, they found an AFL union installed in the headquarters of a defunct company union. At the time of writing, in 1939, the question of representation had not yet been resolved.

California. Bureau of Labor Statistics. *Sixteenth Biennial Report, 1913–1914*. Sacramento, 1914. "The Lumber Industry in California: A Survey of Labor, Living and Other Conditions," pp. 51–150. Illustrated.

Haueter, Lowell. "Westwood, California: The Life and Death of a Lumber Town." Unpublished M.A. thesis. University of California, Berkeley, 1956. 179 pp.

[Hill, Fentress] *The Redwood Strike*. Testimony of Fentress Hill before U.S. House Committee on Education and Labor, March 3, 1947 and before U.S. Senate Committee on Labor and Public Welfare, March 4, 1947. N.p. [1947?] 15 pp.

Industrial Workers of the World. *The Lumber Industry and Its Workers*. Chicago, n.d. Chaps. 4–5, "Private Monopoly of Natural Resources," "How Rich Grafters Got Possession of the Timber Lands of the Country," pp. 21–40.

Jackson, Dan Denty. "The International Woodworkers of America." Unpublished M.A. thesis. University of California, Berkeley, 1953. 139 pp.

Jensen, Vernon H. *Lumber and Labor*. New York: Farrar and Rinehart, 1945. "The West," pp. 99–113.

Kleinsorge, Paul L. "The Lumber Industry," *Monthly Labor Review*, vol. 82, May 1959, pp. 558–63.

"Labor Situation in Western Logging Camps and Sawmills," *Monthly Labor Review*, vol. 55, Dec. 1942, pp. 1125–33.

Schleef, Margaret Louise. "Rival Unionism in the Lumber Industry." Unpublished M.A. thesis. University of California, Berkeley, 1950. 154 pp.

U.S. Bureau of Labor Statistics. *Industrial Relations in the West Coast Lumber Industry,* by Cloice R. Howd. Bull. no. 349. Washington, 1924. 120 pp.

———. "Labor Relations in the California Lumber Industry." San Francisco, 1945. 47 pp. Typewritten.

———. *Wages and Hours of Labor in the Lumber Industry in the United States, 1928.* Bull. no. 497. Washington, 1929. 77 pp.

———. *Wages in the Basic Lumber Industry, 1944.* Bull. no. 854. Washington, 1945. 47 pp.

"Wages in West Coast Sawmills, February 1952," *Monthly Labor Review,* vol. 76, March 1956, pp. 272–75.

Wattenburger, Ralph Thomas. "The Redwood Lumbering Industry on the Northern California Coast, 1850–1900." Unpublished M.A. thesis. University of California, Berkeley, 1931. "The Lumberjack," pp. 14–18; "Labor," pp. 53–59.

OIL

Brissenden, Paul F. "Labor Policies and Labor Turnover in the California Oil Refining Industry," *Monthly Labor Review,* vol. 8, April 1919, pp. 23–52.

A case study of labor turnover in two oil refineries. One of the aims of the study was to determine the degree of instability of unskilled labor as compared to skilled labor.

Marsh, E. P. "Wage Adjustments in California Oil Fields," *Monthly Labor Review,* vol. 11, Oct. 1920, pp. 9–23.

"This article will be a chronicle of what happened in one industry in utilizing the organized strength of both groups . . . in bringing about an added measure of contentment to both workers and employers without strikes or lockouts . . . ." An appendix contains the President's Mediation Commission's suggested wage schedules and working conditions for pipeline, field, and refinery workers.

O'Connor, Harvey. *History of the Oil Workers International Union (CIO).* Denver: OWIU-CIO, 1950. 442 pp.

California's oil workers are given a prominent place in the history of the OWIU as the California locals had been of vital importance in the building of the union. A general history (pp. 1–98) covers pioneering efforts at organization before the turn of the century, limited successes during and immediately after the first world war, almost total extinction between 1922 and 1933, the union's revival in 1933, and its continuous growth since. The general history is followed by individual histories of the locals, including those of California (pp. 101–397).

Dunn, Robert W. *Company Unions: Employers' "Industrial Democracy."* New York: Vanguard Press, 1927. "Shell Oil Company of California," pp. 65–68.

Held, Walter J. "Why I Like to Work for My Company." San Francisco: Standard Oil Co. of California, 1937. 9 pp.

The Labor Bureau. "Data on Wages, Cost of Living and the Financial Condition of the Shell Oil Company of California." Prepared for the representatives of employees of Shell Oil Company of California at wage conference held at Santa Barbara, August 27, 1923. Los Angeles, 1923. 38 pp. Typewritten.

"Pacific Coast Tankers' Strike," *Monthly Labor Review,* vol. 41, Aug. 1935, pp. 380–82.

Standard Oil Company (California). *"Standard Oil Spirit," a Discussion of the Relationship between the Personnel and Management of the Standard Oil Company (California).* San Francisco, 1923. 62 pp.

Swindell, G. M. "The Labor Situation in the California Oil Fields," *Mining and Oil Bulletin,* vol. 4, Dec. 1917, pp. 5–7.

U.S. Congress. Joint Committee on Labor-Management Relations. *Hearings on the Operation of the Labor-Management Relations Act of 1947.* 80th Cong. 2d sess. Part 1. Washington, 1948. Testimony of T. S. Petersen, Standard Oil Company of California, pp. 450–501.

U.S. National Labor Relations Board. In the matter of Standard Oil Company of California and Oil Workers International Union, Local 299. Case no. R-265. Decided March 3, 1938. Washington, 1938. 7 pp.

U.S. Work Projects Administration. *Technology, Employment, and Output per Man in Petroleum and Natural-Gas Production,* by O. E. Kiessling and others. Philadelphia, 1939. 346 pp.

White, Gerald T. *Formative Years in the Far West: A History of Standard Oil Company of California and Predecessors Through 1919.* New York: Appleton-Century-Crofts, 1962. Chap. 20, "The Human Element," pp. 520–40.

Zitnik, Louis James. "The Trend of Collective Bargaining in Petroleum Production, Refining, and Pipe Line Transportation Department in California." Unpublished M.A. thesis. University of California, Berkeley, 1947. 177 pp.

SHIPYARD

Archibald, Katherine. *Wartime Shipyard: A Study in Social Disunity*. Berkeley: University of California Press, 1947. 237 pp.

During World War II, the author, whose normal place was in the academic world, went to work at Moore Dry Dock in Oakland, California. For two years she observed, discussed, questioned, and listened, and then wrote the story of the tens of thousands of workers gathered there from all corners of the country. The author portrays the extreme prejudice against the women in the shipyard, the "Okies," and the racial and national minorities, all, however, united in hatred of the Negro. As the yard is seen as a society, factors of importance to the society—status patterns, unions, class consciousness, and shipyard nationalism—are analyzed.

"Adjustment of Shipbuilding Disputes on the Pacific Coast," *Monthly Labor Review,* vol. 6, March 1918, pp. 67–76.

Bing, Alexander M. *Wartime Strikes and Their Adjustments*. New York: Dutton, 1921. Chap. 3, "Shipbuilding," pp. 20–32.

Douglas, P. H., and F. E. Wolfe. "Labor Administration in the Shipbuilding Industry during Wartime," *Journal of Political Economy,* vol. 27, Jan. 1919, pp. 145–87; May 1919, pp. 362–96.

Finnie, Richard, comp. and ed. *Marinship*. The history of a wartime shipyard told by some of the people who helped build the ships. San Francisco: Taylor and Taylor, 1947. "Recruitment," "Hiring Hall," pp. 39–55; "Placement," pp. 58–61; "Contractual Labor Relations," pp. 88–93; "Yard Labor Relations," "Women in the Crafts," pp. 211–30.

Hedley, George. *Twelve Weeks in a Shipyard*. Oakland, Calif.: Pacific Coast Labor School, 1942. 12 pp.

International Brotherhood of Boilermakers, Iron Shipbuilders and Helpers, Local No. 513. *Richmond: "Arsenal of Democracy."* Berkeley: Tam Gibbs Co. [1947?] 103 pp.

Journeymen Ship and Steamboat Joiners' Association of the Port of San Francisco. *Constitution, By-Laws and Rules of Order*. San Francisco: Cubery and Co., 1884. 14 pp.

Journeymen Shipwrights' Association of the Port of San Francisco. *Constitution and By-Laws*. San Francisco: Women's Co-operative Printing Office, 1883. 15 pp.

Journeymen Shipwrights' Association of San Francisco. *An Address to Shipowners*. San Francisco, 1899. 19 pp.

Markley, Arthur. "What the Workers Think," *Sunset,* vol. 40, May 1918, pp. 13, 90, 92.

Maslin, Marshall, ed. *Western Shipbuilders in World War II*. Oakland, Calif.: Shipbuilding Review Publishing Association, 1945. "Shipyard and Marine Shop Laborers' Union, Local 886," pp. 15–17; "The Shipyard Worker . . . ," pp. 75–77; "Housing for Human Beings—the Story of How Shipyard Workers Were Sheltered," pp. 91–96.

Pacific Coast Zone Shipbuilding Stabilization Conference, San Francisco, July 12–Aug. 26, 1943. *Minutes of Labor's Working Committee*. [San Francisco, 1943] Various pagings.

Richmond Shipbuilding Corporation. *Full Ahead: Richmond Shipyard Number Two*. Richmond, Calif., 1942. 132 pp. [Manual for shipyard workers]

"Wage Chronology No. 21: Pacific Coast Shipbuilding, 1941–51," *Monthly Labor Review,* vol. 74, March 1952, pp. 300–5; Supplement no. 1: vol. 76, May 1953, pp. 514–15; Supplement no. 2: vol. 77, March 1954, pp. 290–91; Supplement no. 3: vol. 82, April 1959, pp. 411–15.

Woehlke, Walter V. "The Shipyard Hold-Up," *Sunset,* vol. 40, March 1918, pp. 11–13, 71–72.

———. "The Wooden Span," *Sunset,* vol. 40, June 1918, pp. 36–38, 60, 62–63.

METAL

Cross, Ira B. *Collective Bargaining and Trade Agreements in the Brewery, Metal, Teaming and Building Trades of San Francisco, California*. University of California Publications in Economics, vol. 4, no. 4. Berkeley: University of California Press, 1918. "The Metal Trades," pp. 274–99.

Provides brief sketches of each union in the Iron Trades Council, giving its organizational background, nature of its membership, its jurisdiction, and the wages, hours, and shop conditions it enjoyed. The organizational features of the two employers' organizations, the California Metal Trades Association and the California Foundrymen's Association, as well as their collective bargaining relations with the Iron Trades Council, are described.

"The San Francisco Iron Strike: First Paper," *Overland,* vol. 6, July 1885, pp. 39–47.

An ironworker discusses the issue that caused the ironworkers to strike in February 1885. This was an attempt by the employers to institute a 15 per cent wage cut, which was defeated by the ironworkers' strike action. The author analyzes the employers' purported reasons for the cut and seeks to justify the ironworkers' action against it.

Scott, Irving M. "Iron Molders Union No. 164 of San Francisco," *Overland,* vol. 17, March 1891, pp. 292–304.

A strike of molders in 1890 serves as the occasion for a critical appraisal of the Molders Union. The author quotes sections of the union's constitution and reviews the union's conduct in previous strikes to demonstrate that its tenets are contrary not only to the interests of the San Francisco employers but also to those of Pacific Coast industries generally, to the well-being of society, and to the welfare of the state.

Vassault, F. I. "The Iron Molders' Strike," *Overland,* vol. 16, Aug. 1890, pp. 113–21.

Sees a degree of hostility and bitterness between the workers and employers in the molders' strike, unknown in past California labor-employer conflicts.

Amalgamated Sheet Metal Workers International Alliance, Local Union No. 104, San Francisco. *Souvenir Pictorial History of Local Union 104,* by James A. Feeny. San Francisco, 1910. 121 pp.

Columbia Steel Company, Pittsburg Works. *Report of Industrial Management and Industrial Relations Lecture Conference for Supervisory Group.* Pittsburg, Calif., 1937. Unpaged.

Iron Molders Union No. 164 of San Francisco. *By-Laws.* San Francisco: C. W. Nevin and Co., 1883. 12 pp.

Iron Workers League No. 20, San Francisco. *Constitution and By-Laws.* San Francisco: Joseph Winterburn and Co., 1868. 15 pp.

Machinists Union of California. *Constitution and By-Laws.* San Francisco: Bruce's Printing House, 1885. 38 pp.

Mechanics Institute. *Proceedings of the Reception Tendered to the Workmen of the Union Iron Works by the Mechanics Institute of San Francisco, December 22, 1893.* San Francisco: James H. Barry [1893?] 29 pp.

National Planning Association. *Causes of Industrial Peace under Collective Bargaining: Lockheed Aircraft Corporation and International Association of Machinists.* Case Study no. 6, by Clark Kerr and George E. Halverson. Washington, 1949. 87 pp.

Representative Council of the Iron Trade of San Francisco. *Constitution, Rules of Order and Order of Business.* San Francisco: Frank Eastman and Co., 1885. 14 pp.

PRINTING

Franklin Printing Trades Association. *Organized Felony: The Picket and the Wrecking Crew, Weapons of San Francisco's Labor Monopoly.* [San Francisco, 1914?] 20 pp.

Contends that the San Francisco printing pressmen's strike, in progress since June 1913, reflects the control of San Francisco by a labor monopoly, and seeks to prove its contention by reviewing what it considers to be the impossible demands of the striking union.

Hunt, Rockwell D. *California's Stately Hall of Fame*. Publications of the California History Foundation, no. 2. Stockton: College of the Pacific, 1950. "Harrison Gray Otis, Publisher of the Los Angeles Times," pp. 489–94.

A sympathetic sketch.

McMurtrie, Douglas Crawford. *The Pacific Typographical Society and the California Gold Rush of 1849*. A forgotten chapter in the history of typographical unionism in America. Chicago: Ludlow Typograph Co., 1928. 20 pp.

A reprint of an article from the *Alta California* of October 28, 1853, which affords evidence of trade-union organization among printers dating back almost to the beginning of newspaper publishing in California. The article relates to a conflict between the *Alta California* and other newspapers and the Pacific Typographical Society over wage rates, which eventually resulted in the dismissal by the *Alta California* of all union men and their replacement by printers brought from the East. (*Note:* The introduction to the reprinted article states that it had first appeared in the *Alta California* on October 28, 1851. This date may be a typographical error, as the correct date is October 28, 1853.)

Otis, Harrison Gray. "A Long, Winning Fight Against the 'Closed Shop,' " *World's Work*, vol. 15, Dec. 1907, pp. 9675–79.

The publisher of the Los Angeles *Times* tells of the strike of 1890 which initiated the conflict between the paper and the Typographical Union and of the union's use of the boycott and other means of attack in its opposition to the policy of the *Times*. He maintains that the paper is the real friend of labor and that the public has supported its policy.

Stimson, Grace Heilman. *Rise of the Labor Movement in Los Angeles*. Berkeley: University of California Press, 1955.

Chap. 3, sec. 1, "The Printers Lead the Way," pp. 32–42.

Tells of the organization of Typographical Union Local 174 of Los Angeles in 1875, possibly the first bona fide union organized in that city. The union faced many difficulties in its first years of existence, gaining only very modest improvements for its members and experiencing its first skirmishes with Harrison Gray Otis, proprietor of the Los Angeles *Times*.

Chap. 9, "The 'Big Strike,' " pp. 104–22.

An account of the continued conflict from 1890 to 1895 between the Typographical Union and the *Times*. The conflict, begun as a skirmish in 1883, had now developed into full-scale strikes and boycotts against the newspaper, with growing support for the printers from local, state, and national central labor bodies as they came to realize that the bitter resistance of the *Times* sprang from opposition to trade unionism itself and from a belief in the open shop. The entrance of the newly organized Merchants Association on the side of the *Times* in 1893 added to that realization.

[Brown, Seth] Seth Brown and the I.T.U. in Los Angeles, 1911–1950. An interview by Corinne L. Gilb for the Institute of Industrial Relations Oral History Project, University of California, Berkeley. 1957. 150 pp. Typewritten.

Eureka Typographical Union. *List of Officers.* Together with a list of active members, in the Federal Army, on the Honorary Roll and those expelled. San Francisco, 1863. 3 pp.

French, Will J. "Organized Printers of the Western Metropolis," *in* International Typographical Union, *57th Convention, Official Souvenir.* San Francisco, 1911. Unpaged.

The Labor Bureau. Brief for the Union in Arbitration Proceedings between San Francisco Stereotypers' and Electrotypers' Union No. 29 and San Francisco Newspaper Publishers' Association, May 25, 1922. San Francisco, 1922. 105 pp. Typewritten.

———. Prima Facie Argument on Wages in Arbitration Proceedings between Pressmen's and Assistants' Union No. 24 and Bookbinders' and Bindery Women's Union Nos. 31–125, and Printers' Board of Trade, Franklin Printing Trades Association, Employing Bookbinders' Association, March 17, 1922. San Francisco, 1922. 47 pp. Typewritten.

Opinion and Decision. In the Matter of the Arbitration Proceedings between San Francisco Typographical Union No. 21 and San Francisco Printers' Board of Trade and Franklin Printing Trades Association, August 15, 1924. San Francisco, 1924. 28 pp.

Peixotto, Jessica B. *How Workers Spend a Living Wage.* Cost of Living Studies II. A study of the incomes and expenditures of eighty-two typographers' families in San Francisco. Heller Committee for Research in Social Economics. University of California Publications in Economics, vol. 5, no. 3. Berkeley: University of California Press, 1929. Pp. 161–245.

San Francisco Lithographers Pension Trust. *San Francisco Lithographers Pension Plan.* San Francisco, 1950. 35 pp.

San Francisco Typographical Union No. 21. *Constitution, By-Laws, Rules of Order and Scale of Prices.* San Francisco: Frank Eastman and Co., 1885. 41 pp.

———. *The Printers' Appeal.* San Francisco, 1880. 4 pp.

San Jose Typographical Union No. 231. Union's Closing Argument in Arbitration Proceedings between San Jose Typographical Union No. 231 and Santa Clara County Graphic Arts Association. [San Jose?] 1925. 24 pp. Typewritten.

Selvin, David Frank. "History of the San Francisco Typographical Union." Unpublished M.A. thesis. University of California, Berkeley, 1935. 98 pp.

U.S. Work Projects Administration. *History of Journalism in San Francisco.* 7 vols. San Francisco, 1939–40. Vol. 2, chap. 3, "The Front Office... ; First Labor Relations; Printers Wage Scale Fight," pp. 53–58.

"Wage Chronology No. 29: San Francisco Printing, 1939–51," *Monthly Labor Review,* vol. 75, Sept. 1952, pp. 289–98.

Weiss, David. "An Example of Arbitration in the San Francisco Newspaper Publishing Industry," *Monthly Labor Review,* vol. 17, Aug. 1923, pp. 13–21.

AUTOMOBILE

Berger, Bennett M. *Working Class Suburb: A Study of Auto Workers in Suburbia.* Berkeley: University of California Press, 1960. 143 pp.

Investigates some of the social and economic consequences for the employees of a Ford Motor Company assembly plant after it was moved, in 1955, from Richmond, California, to Milpitas, a suburban area north of San Jose, California. The investigation aimed generally to determine whether the working-class families involved were adopting middle-class behavior, beliefs, and aspirations—the so-called suburbanization process. The author maintains that an examination of the considerable information gathered from answers to a detailed questionnaire and personal interviews showed that these working-class families were unaffected by the suburbanization process and generally retained their class consciousness as workers.

Gordon, Margaret S., and Ann H. McCorry. "Plant Relocation and Job Security: A Case Study," *Industrial and Labor Relations Review,* vol. 11, Oct. 1957, pp. 13–36.

In 1954 the management of a San Francisco Bay area automobile plant shifted production of automobiles and trucks to its plant in the Los Angeles area. Those of the workers who had the necessary seniority were offered employment at the new location. The study, in the main, aims to determine the factors affecting job security which influenced the workers to accept or reject the offer. Age, race, and skill are found to be among the determining factors.

Stern, James Lawrence. "The Role of the Local Union: A Case Study of Local 844, UAW-CIO." Unpublished Ph.D. dissertation. University of California, Berkeley, 1954. 378 pp.

The local studied is that of the Dodge plant in San Leandro, California.

WAREHOUSING

Heide, Paul. *Welcome to Warehouse Local 6, I.L.W.U.-C.I.O.* Illustrated by Giacomo Patri. [San Francisco] Local 6 [1944?] [15] pp.

The vice-president of the local welcomes new members and discusses union matters with them. He tells them what they can expect from the union and what the union expects from them as he discusses the dispatching system, the union's position against discrimination, its democratic structure, the various committees and their functions, and other essential union matters.

Warehouse Union, Local 6. *Behind the Waterfront: History of Warehousemen's Union, I.L.W.U., Local 6.* Designed and illustrated by Giacomo Patri. San Francisco [1943?] 32 pp.

Traces the growth of the far-flung local of the Warehousemen's Union from a membership of 15 in 1934 to 18,000 in 1943, and from a single unit to six units, subsidiaries of units, and nine branches in northern California. Reference is made to some of the major disputes with the warehouse employers and to some of the jurisdictional disputes the local had to resolve. Stresses the importance of committees and shop stewards in its organizational structure.

Clinton, J. Hart. *Negotiating a Warehousing Labor Contract.* San Francisco: Distributors Association of Northern California, 1949. 13 pp.

APPAREL

Palmer, Emily. *A Survey of the Garment Trades in San Francisco.* University of California, Bureau of Research in Education, Study no. 3. Berkeley, 1921. 87 pp.

The survey was prompted by a shortage of operators in San Francisco garment factories in 1919. Its purpose was to gather information on the nature of the work, the composition of the work force, working conditions, and wage scales—information which was to be used to determine the advisability of establishing training schools for operators. Included is a brief history of the making of ready-to-wear garments in San Francisco as an occupation for girls.

Pesotta, Rose. *Bread upon the Waters.* Edited by John Nicholas Beffel. New York: Dodd, Mead, 1944. Chaps. 2–8, pp. 19–90; chaps. 30–33, pp. 332–92.

A national organizer for the International Ladies' Garment Workers Union describes her efforts in 1933 and 1934 to organize the garment workers in Los Angeles and San Francisco. In later chapters she tells of the changed conditions in the Los Angeles garment industry which brought her back there for another round of organization in 1940 and 1941.

California. State Reconstruction and Reemployment Commission. *Apparel Manufacturing in California.* Sacramento, 1945. 77 pp.

Head, Frances Catherine. "Trade Unionism in the Clothing Industries of San Francisco." Unpublished M.A. thesis. University of California, Berkeley, 1935.

ILGWU Locals 266–482–496–84S. *Here Are the Union Garment Workers in Los Angeles; They Are on the March.* Report to the members, 1947–1950. Los Angeles, 1950. 16 pp.

Journeymen Tailors Protective Union of San Francisco. *Constitution and By-Laws.* San Francisco: E. C. Hughes, 1877. 24 pp.

Keane, Barbara Ingham. "The Clothing Industry in California." Unpublished M.A. thesis. University of California, Berkeley, 1943. Chap. 3, "Workers in the California Clothing Industry," pp. 27–53.

[Matyas, Jennie] Jennie Matyas and the I.L.G.W.U. An interview by Corrinne Gilb for the Institute of Industrial Relations Oral History Project, University of California, Berkeley. Berkeley, 1957. 409 pp. Typewritten.

Pesotta, Rose. "Sub-Cellar Garment Shops in San Francisco's Chinatown," *Justice* (ILGWU), April 1934, p. 7.

AMUSEMENT

Bledsoe, William. "Revolution Came to Hollywood," *American Mercury,* vol. 49, Feb. 1940, pp. 152–60.

Comments on Communist influence in Hollywood unions, especially those of the talent groups, and on the effect of the Soviet-Nazi pact on that influence.

California. Bureau of Labor Statistics. *Twenty-second Biennial Report, 1925–1926.* Sacramento, 1926. "Fluctuations in Employment and Wage Rates in Motion Picture Industry," pp. 131–54.

A study of employment conditions in the motion picture industry in California devoted mainly to manual workers, office employees, and the extras. Shows the earnings of the extras, and discloses the exceptional degree of irregularity of employment among them, the abuses they are subjected to in obtaining employment, and some of the steps taken to eliminate these abuses.

Dawson, Anthony P. "Hollywood's Labor Troubles," *Industrial and Labor Relations Review,* vol. 1, July 1948, pp. 638–47.

Examines the seedier side of employment and wages in the movie industry, the significance of jurisdiction to those people who are affected by it, and some steps that could be taken to lessen jurisdictional conflict and ensure more employment security.

Dunne, Father George H. *Hollywood Labor Dispute: A Study in Immorality.* Los Angeles: Conference Publishing Co. [1950?] 44 pp.

Contends that the strike of the Conference of Studio Unions (CSU) in 1946 was in fact a lockout and was the final move in a joint conspiracy of the motion picture producers and the top officials of the International Alliance of Theatrical Stage Employees (IATSE) to destroy the CSU. To throw light on the purposes of this conspiracy, the author reviews the history of the IATSE from 1934 to 1941, when it was controlled by a Chicago crime syndicate with the alleged cooperation of many of the motion picture producers for mutual gain. As many of the key officials of that period were still in controlling positions in 1946, it is implied that not much had changed and that the alleged cooperation between producers and IA leaders was still in effect.

Johnson, Malcolm. *Crime on the Labor Front.* New York: McGraw-Hill, 1950. Chap. 2, "Hollywood Shakedown," pp. 14–33.

A Pulitzer Prize winning journalist, known for his exposé of the infiltration of crime syndicates into some major unions, writes about the "take" in the movie industry by the Capone gang in the 1930's through their control of the IATSE. According to this account, the "take," starting with token sums but eventually running into millions, began with the partnership of Willie Bioff, a minor criminal, and George E. Browne, business agent of IATSE Local 2, and in time broadened out to include the Capone gang and the unwilling and sometimes even willing co-operation of top executives in the movie industry. The final apprehension and prose-cution of the criminal gang revealed possible state and national political influence, but the subject, it is indicated, was never developed by the prosecution.

Lovell, Hugh, and Tasile Carter. *Collective Bargaining in the Motion Picture Industry.* Berkeley: Institute of Industrial Relations, University of California, 1955. 54 pp.

Reviews the economic and technological development of the motion picture in-dustry, noting the industry's special characteristics that have influenced the nature of collective bargaining practices; examines the collective bargaining experiences of the various groups engaged in the production of motion pictures, including those affiliated with the International Alliance of Theatrical Stage Employees, and the Screen Actors and Screen Writers Guilds; concludes with comments on some possible future problems the development of television may pose for the motion picture unions.

"More Trouble in Paradise," *Fortune,* Nov. 1946, pp. 154–59, 215–25.

Describes the involved structure of unionism in the Hollywood movie industry, with its numerous craft organizations and resulting jurisdictional disputes. The rival unions are discussed and some of their recent history is reviewed.

Reagan, Ronald. "Report to Members," *Screen Actor,* vol. 2, March 1960, pp. 2–13. [Strike issue]

The president of the Screen Actors Guild reports to striking members on late developments in negotiations with the producers and reviews the issues and events that forced the Guild to call the strike, the first since its organization in 1933.

Ross, Murray. *Stars and Strikes: Unionization of Hollywood.* New York: Columbia University Press, 1941. 233 pp.

Traces the beginnings and growth of trade unions and the development of em-ployer-employee relations in the motion picture industry in the years between the first and second world wars. Although the organizational activities, problems, and experiences of all the groups engaged in movie-making are discussed, those of the extras are given special consideration. Also discussed are the vain efforts of Actors

Equity to gain jurisdiction of the screen actors, the opposition of the actors and writers to the Academy of Motion Picture Arts and Sciences, considered by them a company union, and the eventual recognition by the producers of the Screen Actors and Writers Guilds. Emphasized throughout is the special composition of the studio labor force which makes for jurisdictional conflict.

Screen Actors Guild. *Memorandum re 1945 Hollywood Strike.* Hollywood, 1945. 19 pp.

The Guild contends that the thirty years of jurisdictional "wars," "truces," and "armistices" in the motion picture industry are due to the fundamental difference between the craft nature of the American Federation of Labor and the semi-industrial character of the IATSE. It maintains that the strike of Painters Local 1421 is a reflection of this fundamental difference, and as the SAG's efforts to mediate the dispute have failed, it is justified in assuming a neutral position.

———. *The Story of the Screen Actors Guild.* Hollywood, 1960. 24 pp.

Seeks to acquaint new members with key features of the Guild. Tells of its organization in 1933 and of its growth from six to fifteen thousand members. Describes its organizational and financial structure, jurisdiction, contractual relations, affiliations, approach to political questions, and services to members.

American Federation of Radio Artists. *AFRA Speaks for Itself.* Radio address, Hollywood, Calif., 1945. 6 pp.

Conference of Studio Unions. *The Government of the United States Gives You the Facts.* From the Report on Challenges Issued by the National Labor Relations Board, 21st Regional Office, June 12, 1945. Los Angeles, 1945. 11 pp.

Council of Hollywood Guilds and Unions. *The Truth about Hollywood.* Hollywood, Calif. [1944?] 32 pp.

Film Technicians of the Motion Picture Industry. *Flashes from Hollywood.* Hollywood, Calif., 1947. [18] pp.

" 'Freedom of Press' Held Not a Shield for Unlawful Picketing . . . ," *Law and Labor,* vol. 13, May 1931, pp. 107–10.

Green, Anna. "Musicians' Union of San Francisco." Unpublished M.A. thesis. University of California, Berkeley, 1929. 159 pp.

Harding, Alfred. "The Motion Pictures Need a Strong Actors' Union," *American Federationist,* vol. 36, March 1929, pp. 282–89.

International Alliance of Theatrical Stage Employees. *Decision by Executive Council Committee of the AFL on Hollywood Jurisdictional Controversy.* Hollywood, Calif.: Harmon Press, 1945. 15 pp.

The Labor Bureau. "Report on the Theatrical Industry." Prepared for the San Francisco Musicians, Local No. 6, American Federation of Musicians. San Francisco, 1922. 67 pp. Typewritten.

"Limelight on 'Roy,'" *Fortune,* vol. 47, May 1953, pp. 76–78.

Musicians Mutual Protective Union of San Francisco. *Constitution and By-Laws.* San Francisco: William M. Hinton and Co., 1886. 12 pp.

"Picketing of Patrons of Motion Picture Theaters...," *Law and Labor,* vol. 12, Sept. 1930, pp. 204–5.

"Picketing Under Cover of Selling Newspapers in Front of the Theatre...," *Law and Labor,* vol. 13, Sept. 1931, pp. 204–7.

Reagan, Ronald. "The Screen Actors," *American Federationist,* vol. 54, May 1947, pp. 12–13, 37.

Ross, Murray. "Labor Relations in Hollywood," *Annals of the American Academy of Political and Social Science,* vol. 254, Nov. 1947, pp. 58–64.

Screen Publicists Guild. *The Story of the Screen Publicists Guild.* [Los Angeles? 1939?] 32 pp.

U.S. Congress. House. Committee on Education and Labor. *Jurisdictional Disputes in the Motion-Picture Industry.* Hearings before a Special Subcommittee. 80th Cong., 1st sess. Washington, 1948. 3 vols. 2445 pp.

U.S. Department of Labor. Wage and Hour Division. *An Exemptions Survey of the Motion Picture Industry,* by Edred M. Cocking. [Washington] 1941. 107 pp.

Walsh, Richard F. "For Your Entertainment; The I.A.T.S.E.: How It Was Born, How It Grew, What It Does," *American Federationist,* vol. 58, May 1951, pp. 23–26.

FOOD PROCESSING

California. Bureau of Labor Statistics. *Fifteenth Biennial Report, 1911–1912.* Sacramento, 1912. "The Alaska Salmon Canneries," pp. 56–61.

Treats of post-season claims of cannery workers based in California. Among the claims dealt with are deficiencies in wage payments and the levying of false and exorbitant charges by cannery operators and labor contractors.

———. Industrial Welfare Commission. *The Regulation of the Fruit and Vegetable Canning Industry of California.* Sacramento, 1917. 176 pp.

Reports on working conditions and earnings for 1915, and includes a preliminary report on the possibility of seating women cannery workers.

Cross, Ira B. *Collective Bargaining and Trade Agreements in the Brewery, Metal, Teaming and Building Trades of San Francisco, California.* University of California Publications in Economics, vol. 4, no. 4, Berkeley: University of California Press, 1918. "The Brewery Trades," pp. 251–73.

Outlines the pattern of collective bargaining in the brewery trades, considering it in many respects the most perfect in the district. The history and structure of the unions and of the employer associations are described and the major terms of early and later agreements analyzed. Wage schedules provided by some of the agreements are included.

Emmet, Boris. *The California and Hawaiian Sugar Refining Corporation of San Francisco, California.* Stanford University Press, 1928. "Industrial Relations Department," pp. 55–99; "Labor Stabilization," pp. 220–31.

States that the Industrial Relations Department was organized to satisfy the prime interests the management believes the workingman to have: a good annual income, security of employment, insurance against loss of earnings due to sickness or disability, good and cheap housing, and interesting community life. How the Industrial Relations Department goes about satisfying these interests is described in some detail. The section on "Labor Stabilization" analyzes the plant's labor turnover for the years 1923–1927.

United Brewery Workmen's Union of the Pacific Coast. *Statement: A Concise History of the Present Difficulties and the Causes Thereof; An Address to All Trade-Unionists and the General Public.* San Francisco: James H. Barry, 1891. 39 pp.

Contrasts the favorable conditions of the organized brewers on the Pacific Coast with the less favorable conditions of the brewers in the East, maintaining that these differences are the basis of the conflict with the national union. Contends that the conflict is with the leaders of the national union and not with the membership, and calls on the members and trade unionists generally to repudiate attempts of the national union to organize dual locals on the Pacific Coast.

Western Council of Cannery and Food Process Workers Unions. *The Sebastopol Story, 1954–1956.* Western Conference of Teamsters [1956?] [10] pp.

Tells of a two-year battle to organize a union among two thousand cannery workers in the apple orchard country of Sebastopol, California. The use of economic pressures and the blacklist by the employers and their disregard for an NLRB decision forced the workers to take strike action. Despite the use of open force by the employers, the strike ended in the successful organization of the cannery workers.

Anthony, Donald. "Labor Conditions in the Canning Industry in the Santa Clara Valley of California." Unpublished Ph.D. dissertation. Stanford University, 1928. 102 pp.

California. Bureau of Labor Statistics. *Fifth Biennial Report, 1891–1892.* Sacramento, 1893. "Breweries," pp. 101–66.

———. ———. *Special Report: Labor Conditions in the Canning Industry.* Sacramento, 1913. 34 pp.

———. Industrial Welfare Commission. *Report on Wage Board in the Fruit and Vegetable Canning Industry,* by Katherine Philips Edson. San Francisco, 1916. 16 pp.

California CIO Council. *Economic Material on the California Cannery Industry.* [Los Angeles?] 1946. Various pagings.

D'Avee, William. "Monterey and the Canned Sardine," *What's Doing* (Monterey, Calif.), vol. 1, Sept. 1946, pp. 16, 38–39, 41. [Sardine Number]

Howell, Marjorie. "California Cannery Unions." Unpublished M.A. thesis. Stanford University, 1946. 69 pp.

Schlüter, Hermann. *The Brewing Industry and the Brewery Workers' Movement in America.* Cincinnati, Ohio: International Union of United Brewery Workmen of America, 1910. "Struggle and Strife on the Pacific Coast," pp. 173–77.

Smith, Kenneth Hugh. "Industrial Relations in the California Fruit and Vegetable Canning Industry." Unpublished M.A. thesis. University of California, Berkeley, 1946. 248 pp.

Thomas, Mike. "Cannery Row—Boom to Bust in One Generation: The Short Life Cycle of Monterey's Sardine Industry," *Monterey Peninsula Herald,* April 15–22, 1959.

U.S. Bureau of Labor Statistics. *Labor Unionism in American Agriculture,* by Stuart Jamieson. Bull. no. 836. Washington, 1945. "The Canning Industry," pp. 149–55.

U.S. National Youth Administration. *An Occupational Study of the Fruit and Vegetable Canning Industry in California,* by Edward G. Stoy and Francis W. Strong. n.p., 1938. 41 pp.

U.S. Women's Bureau. *Earnings and Hours in Pacific Coast Fish Canneries.* Bull. no. 186. Washington, 1941. 30 pp.

FISHING

Crutchfield, James A. "Collective Bargaining in the Pacific Coast Fisheries: The Economic Issues," *Industrial and Labor Relations Review,* vol. 8, July 1955, pp. 541–56.

A study of collective bargaining problems posed by the system of compensation in the fishing industry.

Randall, Roger L. "Labor Agreements in the West Coast Fishing Industry: Restriction of Trade or Basis of Industrial Stability?" *Industrial and Labor Relations Review,* vol. 3, July 1950, pp. 514–41.

> A discussion of the relationship between the fishermen and the cannery operators and wholesale fish dealers. As the legal status of the fishermen and their right to bargain collectively had been questioned, the discussion aims to determine whether the relationship is that of independent vendor to buyer or that of employee to employer.

Bamford, Edwin F. *Social Aspects of the Fishing Industry at Los Angeles Harbor.* Sociological Monograph no. 18. Los Angeles: Southern California Sociological Society, 1921. 15 pp.

California. State Board of Control. *California and the Oriental: Japanese, Chinese and Hindus.* Report to Governor William D. Stephens. Sacramento, 1920. "Fishing Industry," pp. 101–10.

California CIO Council. *The California Fisheries.* San Francisco: International Fishermen and Allied Workers of America, 1947. 200+ pp.

Dondo, Anna. "A Fisherman's Wage," *Overland,* vol. 82, June 1924, pp. 271, 282.

CULINARY

Josephson, Matthew. *Union House, Union Bar: The History of the Hotel and Restaurant Employees and Bartenders International Union, AFL-CIO.* New York: Random House, 1956. 369 pp.

> Underscores the importance of the California locals and their leading member, Hugo Ernst, in the development of the international union. The early organizational and strike activities of the then independently organized San Francisco cooks and waiters are described on pages 46–49, and the later, broadened activities of the California locals, as part of the international union, are discussed in chap. 5, "The 'Western Movement,' " pp. 108–128, and on pages 264–71.

California. Industrial Welfare Commission. *Women in Public Housekeeping Occupations.* San Francisco, 1942. Unpaged.

Eaves, Edward Paul. "A History of the Cooks' and Waiters' Unions of San Francisco." Unpublished M.A. thesis. University of California, Berkeley, 1930. 101 pp.

Joint Board of Culinary Workers. *The Truth about the Hotel Strike.* San Francisco [1937] 8 pp.

Kennedy, Van Dusen. *Arbitration in the San Francisco Hotel and Restaurant Industries*. Philadelphia: University of Pennsylvania Press, 1952. 113 pp.

U.S. Women's Bureau. *Employment in Hotels and Restaurants*. Bull. no. 123. Washington, 1936. 105 pp.

White Cooks, Waiters and Employees Protective and Benevolent Union of the Pacific Coast. *Constitution, By-Laws and Rules of Order*. San Francisco: C. W. Nevin and Co., 1886. 39 pp.

WHITE COLLAR GROUPS

STORE EMPLOYEES

California State Council of Retail Clerks. *Thousands of People Like You: Meet a Union Member*. Illustrated by Giacomo Patri. San Francisco [1944?] 19 pp.

> Appeals to retail clerks yet unorganized to join the Retail Clerks Union. Text and illustrations relate how the union was organized and tell of the gains in wages and working conditions the union made possible.

Crook, Wilfrid H. *Communism and the General Strike*. Hamden, Conn.: Shoestring Press, 1960. " 'Repeat Performance,' Oakland, 1946," pp. 188–95.

> Examines the causes and the outcome of the strike and makes special mention of the course followed by Teamsters Union officials.

Department Store Strike Committee. *Here's Our Story*. Department Store Employees Union, Local 1100, Janitors No. 87, Elevator Operators No. 117, Joint Board of Culinary Workers. San Francisco [1941?] [6] pp.

> A message to the public from the striking employees of The Emporium, Sears Roebuck & Co., and J. C. Penney Co., explaining what conditions store employees have worked under, how wages and some of the conditions have improved through trade-union organization, and why they had to strike to gain a further increase in wages and full recognition for their union.

Kirstein, George G. *Stores and Unions: A Study of the Growth of Unionism in Dry Goods and Department Stores*. New York: Fairchild Publications, 1950. Chap. 8, "The History of the AFL's Retail Union, 1937–1950," pp. 93–103.

> Reviews the issues in the San Francisco retail strike of 1938 which lasted 55 days and involved over 7000 clerks, and seeks to determine the causes of the strike's virtual failure by examining the strategies employed by both the union and the employers. Included also is a summary of the Oakland general strike of 1946 which was touched off by a minor strike of retail clerks.

Selvin, David F. *Local 373, The Union That Knows How*. Vallejo, Calif.: Retail Clerks Union, Local 373, AFL [1951?] 10 pp.

> Deals with its jurisdiction, and the wage rates, hours, and working conditions of its members.

Dickinson, Shoi Balaban. "The Significance of Interaction between Status Levels: A Case Study of a Major Department Store." Unpublished Ph.D. dissertation. University of California, Berkeley, 1955. 265 pp.

Douma, Frank Hartzell. "The Oakland General Strike." Unpublished M.A. thesis. University of California, Berkeley, 1951. 172 pp.

Dunlap, Marjorie Elise. "Personnel Policies and Practices in Five San Francisco Department Stores." Unpublished M.A. thesis. University of California, Berkeley, 1936. 165 pp.

Harrington, Michael. *The Retail Clerks.* New York: Wiley, 1962. "Local 770, Los Angeles," pp. 46–53.

Jay, Richard E. "A Case Study in Retail Unionism: The Retail Clerks in the San Francisco–East Bay Area (Alameda County)." Unpublished Ph.D. dissertation. University of California, Berkeley, 1953. 524 pp.

[Jinkerson, Claude] Grocery Clerks, Local 648 in San Francisco: An Interview with Claude Jinkerson, Maurice Hartshorn and Other Union Officials. Conducted by David Selvin and Corinne L. Gilb for the Institute of Industrial Relations Oral History Project, University of California, Berkeley. San Francisco, 1957. 179 pp. Typewritten.

Lehman, Lloyd. "The Oakland General Strike," *Political Affairs,* vol. 26, Feb. 1947, pp. 173–81.

Retail Department Store Employees Union, San Francisco Local 1100. *It's Our City Too.* San Francisco [1938?] [8] pp.

Selvin, David F. *Union Profile: The Fifty Years of Grocery Clerks Union, Local 648.* San Francisco: Local 648, 1960. 137 pp.

"Supervisor Bargaining by Rank-and-File Unions," *Stanford Law Review,* vol. 5, July 1954, pp. 674–92.

OFFICE WORKERS

Community Chest of San Francisco. *Classification and Pay Plan.* San Francisco, 1947. 106 pp.

Hoos, Ida Russ Akoff. "Automation in the Office: A Sociological Survey of Occupational and Organization Changes." Unpublished Ph.D. dissertation. University of California, Berkeley, 1959. 387 pp.

Kanninen, Toivo P. "Salaries of Office Workers: Los Angeles, California, March 1950," *Monthly Labor Review,* vol. 71, Oct. 1950, pp. 470–73.

Pacific Gas and Electric Co. *Clerical Wage Survey, May, 1946.* San Francisco, 1946. 19 pp.

San Francisco Employers Council. *Office Workers: Salaries and Personnel Practices, San Francisco Bay Area, Midyear, 1947.* San Francisco, 1947. 32 pp.

United Employers, Inc. *Office Workers' Salaries and Personnel Practices, San Francisco Bay Area, Mid-Year 1948.* Oakland, 1948. 34 pp.

U.S. Bureau of Labor Statistics. *Office Workers: Salaries, Hours of Work, Supplementary Benefits, San Francisco–Oakland, February, 1948.* [San Francisco?] 1948. 33+ pp.

U.S. Women's Bureau. *Office Work in Los Angeles, 1940.* Bull. no. 188-2. Washington, 1942. 64 pp.

Wallstrom, Faith. "Unionization of Clerical Workers: Conditions and Prospects." Unpublished M.A. thesis. University of California, Berkeley, 1961. Chap 4, "Organizing Office Workers" [Local 29, OEIU, Oakland] pp. 62–92.

GOVERNMENT EMPLOYEES

Bay District Joint Council of Building Service Employees, AFL. *A Statement on Behalf of San Francisco's "Miscellaneous" Employees to the Board of Supervisors of the City and County of San Francisco.* San Francisco, 1954. 24 pp.

California. Civil Service Commission and State Board of Control. *Report to the Senate and the Assembly Relative to Names, Titles and Salaries of State Officers and Employees.* Sacramento, 1921. 157 pp.

———. Commission on Pensions of State Employees. *Report.* Sacramento, 1929. 62 pp.

———. State Personnel Board. *Final Report of Findings of the State of California Employment and Wage Survey.* Sacramento, 1938. 117 pp.

———. ———. *Pay Scales in the California Civil Service.* [Sacramento?] 1936. 80 pp.

Carrasco, H. C. "Shall Public Employees Organize in Bona Fide Unions?" Address at a meeting of employees of the State Hospital, Stockton, Calif., July 22, 1939. San Francisco, 1939. 5 pp.

"Civil Service in California," *Transactions of the Commonwealth Club of California,* vol. 16, Dec. 1921, pp. 299–346.

Contra Costa County Employees Union, Local 302, AFL-CIO. *Proposed Adjustments in Salaries and Working Conditions.* N.p., 1956. 24 pp.

Crouch, Winston W., and Dean E. McHenry. *California Government: Politics and Administration.* Berkeley: University of California Press,

1949. Chap. 14, "Personnel and Civil Service," pp. 266–79; chap. 19, "Labor, Employment and Welfare," pp. 346–63.

East Bay Municipal Employees Union, Local 390, AFL-CIO. *Statement to the Personnel Board, City Manager and City Council of the City of Berkeley concerning Wages and Related Benefits.* [Berkeley] 1960. 15 pp.

Fietz, Louise Adelaide. "Personnel Relations of the City and County of San Francisco with Its Unionized Employees." Unpublished M.A. thesis. University of California, Berkeley, 1947. 154 pp.

Gallagher, Donald. *The Legal Aspects of Collective Bargaining for California Public Employees.* Prepared for the California State Employees Association. San Francisco, 1959. 82 + 7 pp.

Irwin, Charlotte Martin. "Unions of White-Collar WPA Workers in the Bay Region, November 1935 to May 1937." Unpublished M.A. thesis. University of California, Berkeley, 1938. 191 pp.

Los Angeles County Fire Department Fire Fighters Association No. 1014. *What Is a Professional Fireman Worth? Answer: Professional Wages for Professional Work.* Los Angeles, 1956. 108 pp.

San Francisco. Board of Supervisors. *Annual Salary Ordinance, 1958–1959, and Salary Standardization Ordinances.* San Francisco, 1959. 159 pp.

San Francisco City and County Employees Union, Local 400. *Unions for City Employees?* San Francisco, 1951. 8 pp.

San Francisco City and County Employees Union, Local 503, United Public Workers of America, CIO. *The Case for a Substantial Pay Increase.* Statement submitted to the Civil Service Commission of San Francisco on the salary and wage survey, December 1946. San Francisco: CIO Council, 1947. 10 pp.

Town Hall, Los Angeles. Municipal and County Government Section. *Wage Setting Methods in the Local Government Jurisdictions of the Los Angeles Area.* Report by Henry Reining, Chairman. June 1950. 22 pp.

U.S. Bureau of Labor Statistics. *Earnings and Wage Practices in Municipal Governments of 15 Cities, 1944.* Bull. no. 848. Washington, 1945. 21 pp.

Yin, Chia-Chen. "The Evaluation of Personnel in the California State Civil Service: A Study of the Reports of Performance in the California State Service." Unpublished M.A. thesis. University of California, Berkeley, 1950. 129 pp.

PROFESSIONAL WORKERS

de Ford, Miriam Allen. *They Were San Franciscans.* Caldwell, Ida.: Caxton Printers, 1947. Chap. 4, "Kate Kennedy," pp. 144–52.

Tells of Kate Kennedy's successful fight to gain tenure for teachers and equal pay for women teachers.

U.S. Work Projects Administration, Southern California. *So the Public May Know.* [Los Angeles? 1939?] 33 pp.

An illustrated directory of the activities of the Professional and Service Projects Divisions of the Work Projects Administration in Southern California.

Anderson, Oscar E. *Teachers' Salaries in California for 1946–1947.* San Francisco: California Teachers Association, 1947. 19 pp.

Ballf, Harry Ambrose. "The Employment of Teachers in California." Unpublished Ph.D. dissertation. University of California, Berkeley, 1959. 132 pp.

California. Senate. Special Committee on Governmental Administration. *Study on Employee and Teacher Benefit Programs.* Partial Report— Senate Res. No. 40, 1957. Sacramento, 1959. 119 pp.

———. University. Bureau of Public Administration. *A Study of the Salaries, Education and Experience of Library Employees in the State of California as of May 1, 1930.* Berkeley, 1931. [35] pp.

Edson, Katherine Philips. "Student Nurses and the Eight Hour Law in California," *Survey,* vol. 31, Jan. 24, 1914, pp. 499–500.

French, John H. "The Structure and Cost of Salary Schedules in Unified School Districts in Southern California." Unpublished Ed.D. dissertation. University of California, Los Angeles, 1952. 256 pp.

Kubik, Robert Mitchell. "Teacher Transfer in Selected Large Elementary School Systems in California." Unpublished Ed.D. dissertation. University of California, Berkeley, 1957. 313 pp.

"Mr. Hearst as an Employer," by one of his employees, *Overland,* vol. 50, Dec. 1907, pp. 557–60.

Noble, Emily Harris. *Status and Professional Preparation of Recreation Center Executives and Workers in California, 1929.* University of California Publications in Education, vol. 6. Berkeley: University of California Press, 1931. Pp. 217–83.

Stone, James C. "Supply and Demand: Certificated Personnel in California Public Schools, 1953," *California Schools,* vol. 24, July 1953, pp. 281–312.

U.S. Work Projects Administration. *History of San Francisco Journalism.* 7 vols. San Francisco, 1940. Vol. 3, *History of the San Francisco–Oakland Newspaper Guild,* by Russell Quinn. 116 pp.

White, Mary L. "The Training School for Nurses in San Francisco," *Overland,* vol. 60, Feb. 1887, pp. 123–28.

SPECIAL GROUPS

CHILD LABOR

California. Assembly. Interim Committee on Finance and Insurance. *Report on Youth Employment*. Assembly Interim Committee Reports, 1955–1957. Vol. 15, no. 15. Sacramento, 1957. 86 pp.

Includes material on the "Berkeley Workreation Camp Program," pp. 19–24, 44–58.

————. Bureau of Labor Statistics. *Thirteenth Biennial Report, 1907–1908*. Sacramento, 1908. "Child Labor," pp. 187–98.

Reports on the operation of the child labor law and some of the difficulties encountered in enforcing it; reviews the distribution of minors in selected industries.

————. ————. *Fourteenth Biennial Report, 1909–1910*. Sacramento, 1910. "Child Labor," pp. 18–32.

A general discussion of child labor and child labor laws in California.

————. ————. *Fifteenth Biennial Report, 1911–1912*. Sacramento, 1912. "Child Labor," pp. 21–28.

Speaks of the recent progress made by the Bureau toward elimination of child labor in California.

————. Department of Employment. Employment Service. *Youth Employment Programs in California*. Sacramento [1959?] 482 pp.

Contains statements by 120 communities outlining their youth employment activities.

"Digest of Child Labor Laws and Regulations Applicable in California," *California Law Review*, vol. 13, 1920, pp. 404–19.

Includes both California and federal laws and regulations.

Eaves, Lucile. *A History of California Labor Legislation*. Berkeley: The University Press [1910] Chap. 10, "Laws Regulating the Labor of Children," pp. 287–310.

Deals with state legislation adopted between 1858 and 1907 regulating the labor of minors engaged as apprentices or otherwise employed. Discusses the difficulties experienced in enforcing the statutes, particularly those dealing with the minimum age at which minors may be employed and maximum hours they may be worked.

French, Will J. "Are California Children Protected from Child Labor?" *Alameda County Public Health News,* vol. 7, Nov. 1929, pp. 3–7.

French was director of the California Department of Industrial Relations in 1929.

Juvenile Protective Association. *Child Labor on the Stage in San Francisco, California.* San Francisco, 1924. 30 pp.

Discusses the results of an investigation made by the Juvenile Protective Association and the California Bureau of Labor Statistics of the conditions under which children in San Francisco were employed in vaudeville performances. The investigation revealed that commercial dancing teachers and theatrical interests were employing minors in performances in violation of the child labor law; that children were being engaged in performances that were unchildlike in character and were often vulgar and objectionable; that they received little or no compensation for their work; that legal restraints were inadequate; and that the restraints that did exist were not being enforced. A number of corrective steps are recommended.

Sidel, James E. *Pick for Your Supper: A Study of Child Labor among Migrants on the Pacific Coast.* Publication no. 378. New York: National Child Labor Committee, 1939. 67 pp.

Cites facts and figures on child labor in the agricultural fields of Washington, Oregon, and California. The information on the extent of employment of children in the fields and its effect on their health and education was gained from specially conducted field studies. Recommendations are offered to eliminate some practices and to reform others.

———

Belanger, Laurence L. "Career Guidance for Girls," *Bulletin of the State Department of Education,* vol. 29, March 1960, pp. 1–119.

California. Bureau of Labor Statistics. *Thirteenth Biennial Report, 1907–1908.* Sacramento, 1908. "Child Labor Law," "Decisions of Supreme Court Affecting Child Labor Laws," pp. 327–39.

———. Department of Industrial Relations. *Wartime Relaxations of Laws Governing Employment of Women and Minors.* Sacramento, 1944. 31 pp.

———. Division of Labor Law Enforcement. *Digest of California Child Labor Laws, 1961.* Sacramento, 1961. 10 pp.

———. Division of Labor Statistics and Law Enforcement. *Report on Industrial Accidents to Minors Under Sixteen Years of Age During One Year, from July 1, 1926 to June 30, 1927,* by Louis Bloch. [Sacramento?] 1927.

———. University. Division of Vocational Education. Research and Service Center. *An Analysis of Department Store Occupations for Juniors.* Part Time Series no. 13, Bull. no. 2 (in cooperation with the State Board of Education). Berkeley, 1920. 48 pp.

California Newspaper-Boy Foundation, Inc. *Officers, History, Articles of Incorporation, List of Members.* [San Francisco? 1947?] 11 pp.

California Women's Committee of Councils of National and State Defense. *Child Labor and Education.* Children's Year Bull. no. 2. Sacramento: California State Printing Office, 1918. 6 pp.

Carrasco, H. C. Address before the Conference on Child Labor, University of California, Berkeley, July 13, 1939. 15 pp.

———. Address before the 52d Annual Convention of the California Newspaper Publishers Association, Coronado, Calif., January 20, 1940. 6 pp.

———. *The Day of Rest, Child Labor and Labor Contractors' Laws as Applied to Agriculture.* Address before the California State Chamber of Commerce, Los Angeles, December 5, 1940. San Francisco, 1940. 16 pp.

Central Casting Corporation. *Rules and Regulations Governing the Employment of Minors in the Production of Motion Pictures.* Hollywood, 1936. 11 pp.

Duffy, Margaret Hessell. "A Study of the State and Federal Laws Governing the Employment of Minors in California." Unpublished M.A. thesis. University of California, Berkeley, 1942. 57 pp.

Duke, Emma. "California the Golden," *American Child,* vol. 2, Nov. 1920, pp. 233–56. Illustrated.

Hogan, Elodie. "Children of the Streets," *Californian Illustrated,* vol. 4, Sept. 1893, pp. 517–26.

McCauley, Sister Mary Thomas Aquinas. "The Development of the Child-Labor Laws of California." Unpublished M.A. thesis. University of California, Berkeley, 1957. 91 pp.

Olson, Alden G. "History and Development of Child-Labor Legislation in California." Unpublished Ed.D. dissertation. Stanford University, 1945. 145 pp.

Schlesinger, (Mrs.) Bert. "What California Did in 1919 for Child Protection," *American Child,* vol. 1, Aug. 1919, pp. 145–48.

Sharp, Theresa Louise. "The Administration of the Child Labor Laws of California." Unpublished M.A. thesis. University of California, Berkeley, 1934. 134 pp.

Spooner, Fred K., and J. W. Halleen. "Young Workers in War Time: Supervised Student Labor on Farms—The Stockton Plan," *Child,* vol. 8, July 1943, pp. 3–7.

Stone, Marion Faas. "Industrial Accidents to Employed Minors in California in 1932," *Monthly Labor Review,* vol. 39, Nov. 1934, pp. 1078–94.

Thomas, Ruth Esther. "The Relation of Child Labor to Juvenile Delinquency: A Study of the Work Records of 203 Boys at the Preston School of Industry." Unpublished M.A. thesis. University of California, Berkeley, 1935. 93 pp.

United Employers, Inc. *Employment of Women and Minors: Analysis of California and Federal Labor Regulations*. Oakland, 1945. 22 pp.

U.S. Bureau of Labor Standards. *State—Child Labor Standards*. Bull. no. 158 (revised). Washington, 1960. "California," pp. 17–21.

U.S. Children's Bureau. *Vocational Guidance and Junior Placement: Twelve Cities in the U.S.* Publication no. 149 (Employment Service Publication "A"). Washington, 1925. "Oakland: History of the Vocational Guidance Movement," pp. 413–33.

U.S. Federal Writers' Project. "Labor in California Cotton Fields." [Oakland? 1938?] "Child Labor," pp. 72–78. Typewritten.

Weiss, Benjamin S. "Employment of Children in the Motion Picture Industry," *Journal of Applied Sociology,* vol. 6, Dec. 1921, pp. 11–18.

WOMEN IN INDUSTRY

California. Bureau of Labor Statistics. *Third Biennial Report, 1887–1888*. Sacramento, 1888. "Working Women," pp. 14–108.

Includes a review of wages and working conditions.

Eaves, Lucile. *A History of California Labor Legislation*. Berkeley: The University Press [1910] Chap. 11, "Laws for the Protection of the Women Workers of California," pp. 311–17.

Discusses the difficulties experienced in attempts to obtain needed state legislation regulating the labor of women workers, showing that improvements in working conditions for women have been gained only through the efforts of the trade unions.

Hundley, Norris C., Jr. "Katherine Philips Edson and the Fight for the California Minimum Wage, 1912–1923," *Pacific Historical Review,* vol. 29, Aug. 1960, pp. 271–85.

Tells of Katherine Edson's successful fight for the passage of a state minimum wage law and later for its enforcement, as part of her lifelong interest in the protection of working women and children. Her task, it is observed, was doubly difficult because organized labor was divided on the issue, with San Francisco labor leaders assailing the law and Los Angeles labor leaders supporting it. Employer organizations unanimously opposed it.

Mathews, Lillian Ruth. *Women in Trade Unions in San Francisco*. University of California Publications in Economics, vol. 3, no. 1. Berkeley: University of California Press, 1913. 100 pp.

Examines the history of trade-union organization, wage rates, hours of work, and working conditions of fifteen union groups, composed entirely of women or in which women form an important part. Wage schedules are listed for some of the larger groups, such as the laundry, bindery, garment, and cracker workers, and are contrasted with schedules of other major cities in the United States. An appendix contains publicity material used by the Anti-Jap Laundry League.

California. Bureau of Labor Statistics. *Ninth Biennial Report, 1899–1900.* Sacramento, 1900. "Female Labor in the State of California," pp. 35–46.

———. ———. *California Supreme Court Decision Upholding the Constitutionality of the Eight Hour Law for Women.* Sacramento, 1912. 7 pp.

———. Division of Labor Statistics and Research. *Women Workers in California Manufacturing Industries, 1955.* [San Francisco?] 1956. 17 pp.

———. Industrial Welfare Commission. *Second Biennial Report, 1915–1916.* Sacramento, 1916. "Employment of Women and Minors in the Garment Trades of California," by Bertha von der Nienburg, pp. 77–168.

———. ———. *Minimum Wages for Women in the Laundry Industry in the State of California,* by Paul A. Sinsheimer. Minority report. San Francisco, 1923. 15 pp.

———. ———. *Seating of Women and Minors in the Fruit and Vegetable Canning Industry of California,* by Harold Mestre. Bull. no. 2a. Sacramento, 1919. 14 pp.

———. ———. *Summary of Industrial Welfare Commission Orders, Governing Wages, Hours, and Working Conditions of Women and Minors.* Sacramento, 1953. 26 pp.

———. ———. *What California Has Done to Protect Its Women Workers.* Preliminary report. Sacramento, 1921. 14 pp.

———. ———. *What California Has Done to Protect the Women Workers.* Sacramento, 1929. 35 pp.

California State Federation of Labor and California State Industrial Union Council. *Opening Statement and Brief before the Manufacturing Wage Board in the Matter of Amending the Manufacturing Wage Order Covering Wages, Hours and Working Conditions for Women and Minors in Manufacturing Industries.* San Francisco, 1942. 85 pp.

Carrasco, H. C. *Relaxation of the Enforcement of the Eight Hour Law for Women in National Defense Industries.* Address before Town Hall, Los Angeles, February 17, 1942. 9 pp.

H.A.D. "Employment of Women in San Francisco," *Overland,* vol. 4, Oct. 1884, pp. 387–91.

Obenauer, Marie L. "Working Hours, Earnings and Duration of Employment of Women Workers in Selected Industries of Maryland and California," *Bulletin of the Bureau of Labor,* vol. 23, Sept. 1911, pp. 347–465.

Peixotto, Jessica B. "Women of California as Trade Unionists." Publications of the Association of Collegiate Alumnae, Series 3, no. 18. Dec. 1908. Pp. 40–49.

Ploeger, Louise Margaret. "Trade Unionism among the Women of San Francisco, 1920." Unpublished M.A. thesis. University of California, Berkeley, 1920. 131 pp.

Smith, Alice Prescott. "The Battalion of Life: Our Woman's Land Army and Its Work in the West," *Sunset,* vol. 41, Nov. 1918, pp. 30–33.

U.S. Commissioner of Labor. *Working Women in Large Cities.* Fourth Annual Report. Washington, 1889. 631 pp.

U.S. Women's Bureau. *Part Time Jobs for Women: A Study in Ten Cities.* Bull. no. 238. Washington, 1951. 82 pp.

———. *A Survey of Laundries and Their Women Workers in 23 Cities.* Bull. no. 78. Washington, 1930. 166 pp.

———. *Women Workers in Ten Production Areas and Their Postwar Employment Plans.* Bull. no. 209. Washington, 1946. 56 pp.

———. *Women's Emergency Farm Service on the Pacific Coast in 1943,* by Frances W. Valentine. Bull. no. 204. Washington, 1945. 36 pp.

"Women in Industry: Employment and Living Conditions of Women in California," *Monthly Labor Review,* vol. 6, Jan. 1918, pp. 114–20.

Wood, Ada May. "Employment Opportunities for Women in California." Unpublished Ed.D. dissertation. Stanford University, 1952. 174 pp.

CONVICT LABOR

California. Bureau of Labor Statistics. *First Biennial Report, 1883–1884.* Sacramento, 1884. Chap. 7, "Convict Labor," pp. 144–65.

Summarizes the testimony given before the Labor Commissioner on the negative effect of the competition of convict labor on free labor and recommends modification of the convict contract system.

———. ———. *Second Biennial Report, 1885–1886.* Sacramento, 1887. Chap. 5, "Convict Labor," pp. 118–52.

Includes a report by the Bureau on a protest from the Federated Trades Council of San Francisco on the "Effects of Competition of Convict Labor with Freemen."

California Taxpayers Association, *Report on Prison Labor in California,* by John M. Peirce. Association Report no. 92. Los Angeles, 1930. 41 pp.

Reviews past and present utilization of prison labor in California and discusses some of the problems encountered in its use. Legislation is suggested to effect improvements in the future use of prison labor.

Devlin, Robert T. "Prison Labor," *Overland,* vol. 7, May 1886, pp. 504–8.

Describes the three methods employed in the use of prison labor in California and how these methods have operated at different times.

Eaves, Lucile. *A History of California Labor Legislation.* Berkeley: The University Press [1910] Chap. 15, "Laws for the Regulation of Convict Labor," pp. 351–68.

Deals with the decades of conflict over the state's use of its convict labor, under the lease and contract systems, to produce commodities for the open market in competition with free labor and private industry, and the legislative measures which eventually resolved the conflict.

Meek, B. B. "Prison Labor on California State Highways: Success of Prison Road Camps Analyzed," *Tax Digest,* vol. 9, Feb. 1931, pp. 49–52.

Includes some comment on the charge that prison labor has deprived free labor of employment.

State Prison System of California; Immigration. San Francisco, 1857. 8 pp.

Contends that although California needs immigrants, especially skilled laborers, immigration is discouraged by the prospect of competition with contract convict labor.

U.S. Prison Industries Reorganization Administration. *The Prison Labor Problem in California: A Survey.* Washington, 1937. 84 pp.

Examines the California prison labor system and finds it inadequate. As prison production can be sold only to the state, the study surveys the state's need for various commodities and makes suggestions toward increasing production while at the same time avoiding competition with other agencies. Among the recommendations are an increase in prison camp assignments and engagement in general forestry work.

Blow, Ben. *California Highways.* San Francisco: H. S. Crocker Co., 1920. Chap. 6, "Convict Labor," pp. 41–47.

California. Bureau of Labor Statistics. *Ninth Biennial Report, 1899–1900.* Sacramento, 1900. "State Prisons, County Jails, Reformatory Institutions and Convict Labor," pp. 8–13.

——. Department of Corrections. Correctional Industries Commission. *How Prisoners Can Become Community Assets.* Sacramento, 1953. 10 pp.

———. Division of Highways. *Manual of Instructions Governing Highway Construction Using Prison Labor.* [Sacramento?] 1946. 127 pp.

Chernin, Milton. "Convict Road Work in California." Unpublished Ph.D. dissertation. University of California, Berkeley, 1938. 284 pp.

Eddy, Elford. "Hope for the Convict," *Sunset,* vol. 52, June 1924, pp. 20–21, 60.

Peirce, John M. "California's Prison Labor Problems Reviewed," *Tax Digest,* vol. 9, Jan. 1931, pp. 20–21.

U.S. Library of Congress. *List of References on Prison Labor.* Washington, 1915. 74 pp.

Wallace, Mrs. Ernest. "Industries in a Women's Prison," *Tax Digest,* vol. 9, April 1931, pp. 21–22.

LABOR MARKET

SUPPLY OF LABOR

Brissenden, Paul F. "Labor Turnover in the San Francisco Bay Region," *Monthly Labor Review,* vol. 8, Feb. 1919, pp. 45–62.

"A summary analysis of the results of a statistical study of the payroll and 'hiring and firing' records of twelve California companies for the year ending June 1, 1918."

Gordon, Margaret S. "Immigration and Its Effect on Labor Force Characteristics," *Monthly Labor Review,* vol. 82, May 1959, pp. 492–501.

Seeks to determine the nature of the relationship between the growth of the population and the growth of the work force in California, Oregon, and Washington. The period studied is 1930–1958. The three states are examined both as a region and individually. Statistical tables and graphs accompany the text.

———. "The Older Worker and Hiring Practices," *Monthly Labor Review,* vol. 82, Nov. 1959, pp. 1198–1205.

Examines the factors influencing hiring practices with respect to the older worker, as reflected in a wide-area survey by the U. S. Bureau of Employment Security and a study of the San Francisco area by the Institute of Industrial Relations of the University of California, Berkeley. The San Francisco study indicated that hiring practices were affected by such general factors as occupation, industry, and size of firm, and by such specific factors as training programs, seniority systems, insurance costs, and pension plans. Statistical tables classify some of the findings.

McEntire, Davis. *The Labor Force in California: A Study of Characteristics and Trends in Labor Force Employment and Occupations in California, 1900–1950.* Berkeley: University of California Press, 1952. 101 pp.

Analyzes the changes in the size and composition of the California work force as indicators of economic and social change. Special attention is given to the influence of age and sex in changes in the employment pattern. The study, throughout, notes relationships or the lack of them between the California and the national labor forces. Statistical tables are used extensively.

Palmer, Gladys L., and Carol P. Brainerd. *Labor Mobility in Six Cities: A Report on the Survey of Patterns and Factors in Labor Mobility, 1940–1950.* New York: Social Science Research Council, 1954. 177 pp.

Los Angeles and San Francisco were among the cities surveyed.

Buchanan, John Park. "Occupational Survey of Ventura County." Unpublished Ed.D. dissertation. Stanford University, 1948. 175 pp.

California. Department of Education. "Californians at Work: Facts and Figures on the California Labor Force for School Guidance Workers," *Bulletin,* vol. 24, Jan. 1955. 53 pp.

———. Department of Industrial Relations. *Middle-Aged and Older Workers in California.* Special Bull. no. 2. San Francisco, 1930. 98 pp.

———. Division of Labor Statistics and Research. *Estimated Number of Wage and Salary Workers in Non-Agricultural Establishments by Industry, California, 1939–1955.* [San Francisco?] 1956. 27 pp.

———. ———. *Estimated Number of Wage and Salary Workers in Non-Agricultural Establishments, by Industry: Los Angeles–Long Beach Metropolitan Area, 1949–1952.* [San Francisco?] 1956. 8 pp.

———. Economic Development Agency. *California Statistical Abstract, 1962.* Sacramento, 1963. Sec. H, "Labor Force, Employment and Earnings," pp. 61–93.

California State Chamber of Commerce. *Employment in California: Preliminary Report, 1929–1934.* [San Francisco? 1935?] 12 pp.

———. *Labor Supply for National Defense in California.* [San Francisco?] 1941. 23 pp.

California State CIO Council. *Report and Recommendations on the War Manpower Problem in California.* Submitted to the Win-the-War Convention of the Council, Oct. 9–11, 1942. Hollywood, 1942. 35 pp.

Crouch, Winston W., and Dean E. McHenry. *California Government, Politics and Administration.* Berkeley: University of California Press, 1949. Chap. 19, "Labor, Employment and Health," pp. 346–63.

Eliot, Charles W., and Cecil L. Dunn. *Jobs and Security after Victory.* Los Angeles: Haynes Foundation, 1944. 44 pp.

Gershenson, M. I. "Wartime and Postwar Employment Trends in California," *Monthly Labor Review,* vol. 64, April 1947, pp. 576–88.

Kidner, Frank L. *California Business Cycles.* Berkeley: University of California Press, 1946. "Changes in the Pattern of Employment," pp. 14–26.

Malm, F. Theodore. "Hiring Procedures and Selection Standards in the San Francisco Bay Area," *Industrial and Labor Relations Review,* vol. 8, Jan. 1955, pp. 231–52.

Nichols, Ward Matthews, and William Morris Williams. "Employment by Occupation and Industry for San Francisco." Unpublished Ed.D. dissertation. Stanford University, 1950. 386 pp.

Pacific Coast Board of Intergovernmental Relations. *People, Jobs and Income on the Pacific Coast, 1949–1960.* San Francisco [1950?] "Employment Trends in California, with Estimates of Maximum Increases to 1960," pp. 71–95.

Parker, Harold Kermit. "Population, Employment and Post High School Education in the Monterey Peninsula." Unpublished Ed.D. dissertation. Stanford University, 1952. 248 pp.

Paul, Glen Watson, and William Schultz. "An Occupational Survey of Greater Modesto." Unpublished Ed.D. dissertation. Stanford University, 1950. 221 pp.

Pearman, Lester M. "Prospective Labor Supply on the West Coast," *Monthly Labor Review,* vol. 64, April 1947, pp. 563–75.

Thompson, Warren S. *Growth and Changes in California's Population.* Los Angeles: Haynes Foundation, 1955. Chaps. 10–16, "The Labor Force," "Occupation and Industrial Composition," "Economic Status," "Migrants to California, 1935–1940 and 1949–1950," pp. 107–254.

U.S. Bureau of Labor Statistics. *Impact of War on the San Diego Area: Employment and Occupational Outlook.* Industrial Area Study no. 20. [San Francisco?] 1944. 52 pp.

U.S. Veterans Administration. *Occupations and Industries in the Pacific States: California, Oregon, Washington.* V.A. Pamphlet 7-7.9. Washington, 1955. 64 pp.

U.S. Work Projects Administration. *Monterey Peninsula.* Berkeley, 1941. Part 1, "Monterey: The People; the Industries," pp. 64–71.

U.S. Works Progress Administration. *California: A Guide to the Golden State.* New York: Hastings House, 1939. Part 1, "Workingmen," pp. 95–108.

WAGES AND HOURS

California. Bureau of Labor Statistics. *First Biennial Report, 1883–1884.* Sacramento, 1884.

Chap. 2, "The Labor Question," pp. 9–15, reviews the labor supply, the level of wages, and trends in the length of the workday. Chap. 6, "Employers and Employees," pp. 129–43, includes a wage and cost-of-living survey.

———. ———. *Third Biennial Report, 1887–1888.* Sacramento, 1888. "Unions and Labor Organizations," pp. 109–92.

Discusses wages, hours, strikes, and Chinese unions.

———. ———. *Sixteenth Biennial Report, 1913–1914.* Sacramento, 1914. "The Portland Cement Industry in California," pp. 151–81. Illustrated.

Includes a survey of wages and labor conditions.

Eaves, Lucile. *A History of California Labor Legislation.* Berkeley: The University Press [1910] Chap. 7, "The Length of the Work Day in California," pp. 197–228.

A review of California labor's contest for a shorter workday, beginning with the passage in the state legislature of a ten-hour bill in 1853 and continuing into the long struggle for the eight-hour day on both public and private work. Discusses the factors that influenced activity for a shorter workday; opposition to the eight-hour day; attempted and successful state and national eight-hour legislation; and court tests involving such legislation.

Hittell, John S. *The Commerce and Industries of the Pacific Coast of North America.* San Francisco: A. L. Bancroft & Co., 1882. Chap. 5, "The Labor Supply," pp. 99–120.

Lists the daily, weekly, and monthly wages being paid for various kinds of labor on the Pacific Coast and compares them with wage rates paid in other centers; describes the major labor associations on the Pacific Coast and briefly touches on Chinese labor competition.

Kenaday, Alexander M. *The Record of the Eight Hour Bill in the California Legislature, Session 1865–66.* San Francisco, 1867. 16 pp.

The president of the Trades Union reports for the special committee appointed by the union to further the passage of an eight-hour law, which was then agitating California as well as other parts of the country. The report shows that the committee succeeded in getting the bill passed in the Assembly in its original form, but could not muster enough support in the Senate to prevent a crippling amendment.

Lester, Richard A., and Edward A. Robie. *Wages under National and Regional Collective Bargaining: Experience in Seven Industries.* Industrial Relations Section, Department of Economics and Social Institutions, Princeton University. Princeton: Princeton University Press, 1946. Chap. 8, "Uniform Time Rates in West Coast Pulp and Paper," pp. 79–88.

Undertaken to throw light on a basic problem in collective bargaining—wage uniformity versus wage diversity—the survey points to the west coast pulp and paper industry as having achieved a high degree of wage uniformity. It examines the special factors and the industry's bargaining pattern which make wage uniformity desirable and possible and cites conditions that may make it difficult to maintain such uniformity.

Stafford, W. V. "Labor Conditions in California," *California's Magazine,* vol. 1, July 1915, pp. 57–62.

A description, in compact form, by a former California State Labor Commissioner of the state's work force, showing its composition, distribution in agriculture and in industrial enterprises, and prevailing hours and wages. Includes a separate listing of unionized crafts and their wage schedules.

Winn, A. M. Address delivered before the Mechanics' State Council, the Eight-Hour Associations, and United Mechanics, San Francisco, June 3, 1870. 15 pp.

The president of the Mechanics' State Council replies to the reasoning of those opposing the eight-hour day. He seeks in particular to convince employers that they stand to gain from the shorter workday, pointing to recent mechanization that has lessened the need for long hours of labor.

Young, John P. *San Francisco: A History of the Pacific Coast Metropolis.* San Francisco: S. J. Clarke Publishing Co., 1912. Vol. 1, chap. 29, "Labor Conditions and the Cost and Mode of Living," pp. 243–53.

Discusses wage rates for various types of labor during the first few years after the discovery of gold and contrasts them with the cost of living during the same period.

———

Belloc, Nedra Bartlett. *Wages in California: War and Postwar Changes.* Berkeley: University of California Press, 1948. 97 pp.

California. Bureau of Labor Statistics. *Seventh Biennial Report, 1895–1896.* Sacramento, 1896. "The Eight Hour Day," pp. 92–101.

———. Civil Service Commission. Special Committee. *Report on Cost of Living Survey.* Sacramento, 1923. 84 pp.

———. Department of Industrial Relations. *Estimated Employment, Total Wages, and Average Earnings and Hours Worked, 1940–1947.* San Francisco, 1948. 40 pp.

———. Division of Labor Statistics and Law Enforcement. *The Cost of Living in California, 1914–1922 and 1939–1941,* by Frances Moore. Sacramento, 1941. 34 pp.

———. ———. *Union Scales of Wages and Hours of Labor, 1929 and 1930.* Together with a Directory of California Reporting Trade Unions. Special Bull. no. 4. Sacramento, 1931. 72 pp.

———. Division of Labor Statistics and Research. *Earnings and Hours, by Industry, California, 1955.* [San Francisco?] 1956. 31 pp.

———. ———. *Earnings and Hours, Selected Industries, California, 1949–1950.* [San Francisco?] 1951. 49 pp.

———. ———. *Wages and Hours in Children's Institutions, California, 1958.* San Francisco, 1959. 39 pp.

———. ———. *Wages and Hours in Institutions for Aged Persons, California, 1958.* San Francisco, 1959. 42 pp.

———. ———. *Wages and Hours in Nursing and Convalescent Homes, California, 1958.* San Francisco, 1959. 45 pp.

——. ——. *Wages and Hours in Private Hospitals, California, 1958.* San Francisco, 1959. 68 pp.

——. ——. *Wages and Hours in Private Mental Institutions, California, 1958.* San Francisco, 1959. 46 pp.

Community Chest of San Francisco. *Salary Guide.* San Francisco, April 1955. 39 pp.

Kanninen, Toivo P. "Occupational Wages in Philadelphia and San Francisco," *Monthly Labor Review,* vol. 71, Dec. 1950, pp. 684–87.

Liggett, Hazel M. *The Relation of Wages to the Cost of Living in Los Angeles, 1915–1920.* Sociological Monograph no. 19. Los Angeles: Southern California Sociological Society, 1921. 10 pp.

Los Angeles County. *Wage and Salary Survey in Los Angeles County, March 1950.* Los Angeles, 1950. 15 pp.

Luck, Mary Gorringe. *Wartime and Postwar Earnings, San Francisco, 1944–1946.* Berkeley: University of California Press, 1948. 129 pp.

MacFarlane, Ruth. *Wage Rate Differentials: Comparative Data for Los Angeles and Other Urban Areas.* Los Angeles: Haynes Foundation, 1946. 164 pp.

Pacific Coast Labor Bureau. *Statement in Support of Reduction in Hours of Work per Week.* Prepared for the International Longshoremen's and Warehousemen's Union. Submitted before the California Industrial Welfare Commission. [Los Angeles?] May 27, 1941. 21 pp.

Shapiro, Solomon. "Income on the West Coast," *Monthly Labor Review,* vol. 64, April 1947, pp. 599–609.

U.S. Bureau of Labor Statistics. *Net Spendable Real Earnings in Four West Coast Cities, 1940–June 1958,* by Max D. Kossoris. San Francisco Regional Report no. 5. San Francisco, 1958. 20 pp.

——. *Wage and Salary Relationships in Los Angeles and San Francisco Metropolitan Areas, January 1952.* San Francisco, 1953. 18 pp.

Winn, A. M. *Valedictory Address, as President of the Mechanics State Council of California, January 11, 1871.* San Francisco: Cooperative Printing Co., 1871. 6 pp.

EMPLOYMENT AND UNEMPLOYMENT

Atherton, Gertrude. *California: An Intimate History.* New York: Boni & Liveright, 1927. Chap. 21, " 'The Chinese Must Go,' " pp. 290–307.

A novelist writes about the San Francisco labor scene in the 1870's, stressing such dramatic episodes as Denis Kearney's leadership of San Francisco's unemployed, the anti-Chinese and other disturbances involving the unemployed, and the activities of William T. Coleman's Pick-Handle Brigade.

Cahn, Frances, and Valeska Bary. *Welfare Activities of Federal, State, and Local Governments in California, 1850–1934.* Berkeley: University of California Press, 1936. Chap. 5, "The Unemployed," pp. 198–247.

A review of various types of aid to California unemployed workers administered by government and sometimes by private agencies during periods of economic recession or depression: in the 1870's and 1890's, the depressions between 1900 and 1920, 1921–22, and 1929. Concludes with a summary of the methods and procedures followed by governmental agencies in gathering data on unemployment.

California. Bureau of Labor Statistics. *Fourteenth Biennial Report, 1909–1910.* Sacramento, 1910. "Employment Agencies," pp. 36–42.

Discusses some of the problems found in the regulation and control of employment agencies, and recommends some changes in their regulation and control.

———. Division of Labor Law Enforcement. *Private Employment Agencies in California, 1950.* Sacramento, 1951. 14 pp.

A report of placements made and fees charged by private employment agencies in 1950, with comparative statistical data for 1940 and 1949.

———. State Relief Administration. Division of Special Surveys and Studies. *Transients in California.* San Francisco, 1936. 293 pp. and appendix.

States that the study was undertaken to discover the extent of the problem, to determine how the communities were meeting it, and to find desirable and practical solutions. The study is regional in nature and includes thirteen major California cities.

Cheit, Earl F. "Unemployment Disability Insurance in California," *Monthly Labor Review,* vol. 82, May 1959, pp. 564–71.

Tells how the program of benefits for nonoccupational disability was instituted, describes its provisions, compares the program with insurance plans of other states, and discusses some of the problems involved in its administration. Statistical tables accompany the text.

Cross, William T., and Dorothy E. Cross. *Newcomers and Nomads in California.* Stanford University Press, 1937. 149 pp.

Deals with the problem of indigent relief for the migratory population of California in the early years of the depression of the 1930's, and the intensification of the problem with the influx of thousands of "dust bowl" migrants between 1933 and 1936, when local emergency relief measures proved inadequate and the participation of federal agencies became necessary.

George, Henry. *Why Work Is Scarce, Wages Low, and Labor Restless.* San Francisco: Weekly Star Print, 1878. 14 pp.

Contends that it is not Chinese immigration nor the exhaustion of the placers that is responsible for unemployment and low wages. George maintains that the true reasons are the monopolization of the land and its resultant high cost. To correct these conditions he suggests a number of remedies, the chief one being a tax on the value of land.

Gordon, Margaret S. *Employment Expansion and Population Growth: The California Experience, 1900–1950.* Berkeley: University of California Press, 1954. 192 pp.

The purpose of the study, the introduction indicates, is to examine historical trends and fluctuations in the growth of population and employment in California as aids in determining any possible future trends. Among the questions considered, with the aid of numerous charts, graphs, and tables, are the following: What has been the nature of the relationship between population growth and the rate of expansion of employment in individual industries or groups of industries? Is there evidence that, with increasing industrialization, employment is becoming less stable in the state? Why has the rate of population growth and of net in-migration shown marked fluctuations?

Huntington, Emily H. *Doors to Jobs: A Study of the Organization of the Labor Market in California.* Berkeley: University of California Press, 1942. 454 pp.

A detailed examination of the many agencies and organizations, both public and private, which participate in placing unemployed workers in jobs. Among the major ones considered are the California State Employment Service, fee-charging employment agencies, and placement departments of trade unions and employers' organizations. A concluding chapter summarizes the composition of the California labor market.

————. *Unemployment Relief and the Unemployed in the San Francisco Bay Region, 1929–1934.* Berkeley: University of California Press, 1939. 106 pp.

The study is based on a sample of cases in San Francisco, Oakland, and Berkeley and refers to conditions in 1929, 1932, and 1934 when unemployment relief was mainly a county responsibility. The statistical method is used extensively.

Jordan, Lois (Mother). *The Work of the White Angel Jungle of San Francisco Waterfront.* San Francisco: Mother Lois Jordan Book Co., 1935. 54 pp.

The White Angel Jungle was a direct relief project organized and managed by Lois Jordan (generally referred to at the time as "Mother Jordan") during the early part of the depression of the 1930's. She tells how she conducted the project, obtained support for it, and defended herself at times against charges of fraudulent practices.

London, Charmian. *The Book of Jack London.* New York: Century, 1921. Vol. 1, chap. 11, "Tramping the Road," pp. 147–64.

Treats of London's stay with Kelly's "Army" in 1894 (California Division of Coxey's Army).

London, Jack. *The Road.* New York: Macmillan, 1907. "Two Thousand Stiffs," pp. 175–95.

Deals with Kelly's Army, the California division of Coxey's Army.

Los Angeles. Municipal Industrial Commission. *Fifth Annual Report of the Los Angeles Public Employment Bureau, Year Ending June 30, 1918.* Los Angeles, 1918. [18] pp.

Includes a discussion of a proposal to transfer the activities of the Bureau to the U. S. Employment Service.

McGowan, Joseph A. *History of the Sacramento Valley.* New York: Lewis Historical Publishing Co., 1961. Vol. 2, chap. 56, "The Depths of Depression," pp. 255–74.

Describes the economic conditions in the Sacramento Valley in the 1930's, telling of the depression's varying effect on different counties but particularly on the population centers and the valley's migrant workers. Also described are the measures taken by county and federal agencies to meet the needs of the unemployed. Includes a review of the agricultural and cannery strikes in the valley during that period.

McMurry, Donald L. *Coxey's Army: A Study of the Industrial Army Movement of 1894.* Boston: Little, Brown, 1929. Chaps. 7–9, "The Industrial Armies of the West: Fry's Army," "Kelly's Army—From San Francisco to Iowa," "Through Iowa and on to Washington," pp. 127–96.

The author considers the California armies of the unemployed under Lewis C. Fry and Charles T. Kelly to have been the most important of Coxey's "Industrial Armies." He describes their trek across the continent in detail, including the armies' difficulties with food and transport; their clashes with massed railroad detectives, local police forces, and state militias; and their mixed reception by the people of the towns and cities along the way.

Panunzio, Constantine M., Wade Church, and Louis Wasserman. *Self-Help Cooperatives in Los Angeles.* Berkeley: University of California Press, 1939. 148 pp.

A study undertaken to discover the extent to which the self-help organizations were meeting the needs of their members. Involving some 1030 families, it describes the kind of people that constituted the units, tells why they joined them and how each participated in their activities, and discusses the probable future of these organizations. An appendix contains related statistical material.

Stimson, Grace Heilman. *Rise of the Labor Movement in Los Angeles.* Berkeley: University of California Press, 1955. Chap. 12, "On to Washington," pp. 154–60.

Deals with the depression in Los Angeles in 1893 and 1894. The inadequate measures taken by county agencies to cope with unemployment encouraged the organization of local contingents of Coxey's Army under Lewis C. Fry and Arthur Vinette.

The author indicates that although Coxey's Army fell short of its purpose, locally the trials of the Vinette contingent stirred public responsibility for the unemployed and resulted in some positive action.

U.S. Congress. Senate. Commission on Industrial Relations. *Final Report and Testimony*. 64th Cong., 1st sess., S. Doc. 415. Washington, 1916. "Unemployment in California," vol. 5, pp. 5029–85.

Testimony: Jesse W. Lilienthal, president, United Railroads, pp. 5031–40; Paul Scharrenberg, editor, *Coast Seamen's Journal,* and secretary-treasurer, State Federation of Labor, pp. 5040–52; John P. McLaughlin, California Labor Commissioner, pp. 5052–66.

U.S. Works Progress Administration. Division of Social Research. *Survey of Cases Certified for Works Program Employment in 13 Cities*. Series 4, no. 2. Washington, 1937. 46 pp.

San Francisco is included among the cities surveyed.

Workers Alliance of California. *We Were Investigated*. Factual statement of the Workers Alliance of California before the State Senate Investigating Committee and an open letter to State Legislators. San Francisco, 1939. 32 pp.

Describes the structure, functions, and aims of the Workers Alliance as an organization representing the unemployed workers in their relations with California state and county work relief agencies.

Bedford, Arthur. "The Unemployed Problem," *Overland,* vol. 64, July 1914, pp. 92–99.

Bloch, Louis. "Employment Agencies in California," *American Labor Legislation Review,* vol. 19, Dec. 1929, pp. 363–66.

Browne, Carl, and William McDevitt. *When Coxey's "Army" Marcht on Washington, 1894.* San Francisco, May 1944. 29 pp.

Bruce, Robert V. *1877: Year of Violence.* Indianapolis: Bobbs-Merrill, 1959. Pp. 266–70. [San Francisco]

California. Bureau of Labor Statistics. *Seventh Biennial Report, 1895–1896.* Sacramento, 1896. "The Free Employment System," pp. 11–71.

———. ———. *Ninth Biennial Report, 1899–1900.* Sacramento, 1900. "Employment Agencies," pp. 73–83.

———. Commission of Immigration and Housing. *Report on Unemployment.* Supplement to First Annual Report. Sacramento, 1914. 73 pp.

———. ———. *Report on Relief of Destitute Unemployed, 1914–1915.* Sacramento, 1915. 24 pp.

———. Committee on Soldiers' Employment and Readjustment. *Report, January 1, 1919 to February 14, 1920.* Sacramento, 1920. 16 pp.

———. Department of Employment. *Objectives and Functions of the Public Employment Service in California.* Sacramento, 1960. 17 pp.

———. ———. *Proceedings of the Governor's Conference on Employment, December 5-6, 1949.* Sacramento, 1950. 346 pp.

———. ———. *Proceedings of the Los Angeles County Conference on Employment.* Held at the University of California, Los Angeles, April 28 and 29, 1950. Sacramento, 1950. 188 pp.

———. ———. *Questions and Answers about California's Employment Security System.* Sacramento [1955?] 68 pp.

———. ———. Employment Stabilization Commission. *Operating Statistics, 1938-1947.* Report 522, no. 1. Sacramento, 1947. 56 pp.

———. Department of Industrial Relations. *Report of the Division of State Employment Agencies for 1926-1927 and 1927-1928.* [Sacramento?] 1928. 77 pp.

———. ———. State Unemployment Committee. *A County or Municipal Program for Combating Unemployment in California.* San Francisco, Jan. 1931. 11 pp.

———. Division of Labor Statistics and Research. *Supplemental Unemployment Benefit Plans; Severance Pay Plans; Recent Wage Settlements.* Industrial Relations Report no. 10. [San Francisco?] 1956. 35 pp.

———. Governor's Commission on Reemployment. *Report.* Sacramento, 1939. 95 pp.

———. State Emergency Relief Administration. *Economic Trends in California, 1929-1934.* San Francisco, 1935. Chap. 1, "Depression and Its Effect on Employment of Labor," pp. 1-17; chap. 2, "Trends in Cost of Living in California, 1929-1934, Inclusive, and Changes in Average Weekly Earnings in Manufacturing Industries," pp. 18-27.

———. ———. *Sacramento Depression Settlement Survey, 1935.* [Sacramento] 1936. 49 pp.

———. ———. *Survey of Social Work Needs of the Chinese Population of San Francisco* [San Francisco? 1934?] "Industry Survey," pp. 33-39.

———. State Relief Administration. *California Transient Service: Progress and Methods of Approach, August 1933-April 1935.* Edited by H. A. R. Carlton and E. S. Robison. San Francisco: "Nomad" (Transient Publication Project), 1935. 134 pp. Illustrated.

———. ———. *Job Analysis, Los Angeles County.* Feb. 1940. 48+ pp.

———. ———. *Review of Activities, 1933–1935.* Sacramento, 1936. 332 pp.

———. ———. *Unemployment Relief in Labor Disputes.* Los Angeles, Oct. 1939. 40 pp.

———. State Unemployment Commission. *Abstract of Hearings on Unemployment, April and May 1932.* San Francisco, 1932. 244 pp.

———. ———. *Report and Recommendations.* Sacramento, 1933. 810 pp.

———. ———. Labor Camp Committee. *Report on the State Labor Camps.* Prepared by S. Rexford Black. San Francisco, 1932. 47 pp.

———. Unemployment Reserves Commission. *A Study of Seasonal Employment in California.* Sacramento, 1939. 185 pp.

California CIO Council. *California CIO Council's 10 Point Program to Halt Growing Unemployment.* Los Angeles, 1954. 24 pp.

California Labor and Employment Exchange. *Articles of Association and By-Laws.* San Francisco: Bancroft & Co., 1871. 7 pp.

———. *Facts for Emigrants to California.* A circular issued to workingmen. San Francisco: Fred'k MacCrellish & Co., 1869. 12 pp.

"Consumers' Cooperation in California, 1934–1935," *Monthly Labor Review,* vol. 42, May 1936, pp. 1216–25.

Duke, Thomas S. *Celebrated Criminal Cases of America.* San Francisco: James H. Barry, 1910. "Dennis Kearney Riots," pp. 61–62.

Eaves, Lucile. "Where San Francisco Was Sorest Stricken," *Charities and the Commons,* vol. 16, May 5, 1906, pp. 161–63.

Eliot, Charles W. *Demobilization and Jobs.* Los Angeles: Haynes Foundation, 1944. 12 pp.

Emerson, Edwin, Jr. "The Reconstruction of San Francisco," *Out West,* vol. 25, March 1907, pp. 191–208.

Holmes, Avis Cecilia. "The California State Employment Service." Unpublished M.A. thesis. University of California, Berkeley, 1938. 130 pp.

Hutchinson, Wallace I. *Public Opinion of the Civilian Conservation Corps in California.* San Francisco: U.S. Forest Service, California Region, 1934. 10 pp.

Kerr, Clark. "Productive Enterprises of the Unemployed, 1931–1938." Unpublished Ph.D. dissertation. University of California, Berkeley, 1939. 4 vols. 1268 pp.

Kerr, Clark, and Arthur Harris. *Self-Help Cooperatives in California.* 1939 Legislative Problems, no. 9. Berkeley: Bureau of Public Administration, University of California, 1939. 26 pp.

Kerr, Clark, and Paul S. Taylor. "Self-Help Cooperatives in California," *in* E. T. Grether, ed., *Essays in Social Economics.* Berkeley: University of California Press, 1935. Pp. 191–225.

Luck, Mary Gorringe, and Agnes B. Cummings. *Standards of Relief in California, 1940.* Berkeley: University of California Press, 1945. Chaps. 4–6, "Cash Relief for the Unemployed," "Work Relief for the Unemployed," "Federal Aid to Migratory Agricultural Workers," pp. 16–57.

May, Samuel C. *The Post War Unemployment Problem in California, 1945–1947.* Berkeley: Bureau of Public Administration, University of California, Aug. 1945. 14 pp.

May, Samuel C., and Alfred G. Norris. *Estimates of California Employment and Unemployment, 1946–1947.* Berkeley: Bureau of Public Administration, University of California, 1946. 49 pp.

Morgan, Edward N. "The Unemployed in San Francisco," *New Review,* vol. 2, April 1914, pp. 194–99.

Mosk, Sanford A. "Unemployment Relief in California under the State Emergency Relief Administration," in *Essays in Social Economics.* Berkeley: University of California Press, 1935. Pp. 247–75.

Neff, Philip, and Annette Weifenbach. *Business Cycles in Los Angeles.* Los Angeles: Haynes Foundation, 1949. 32 pp.

―――. *Business Cycles in Selected Industrial Areas.* Berkeley: University of California Press, 1949. 274 pp.

Parker, Florence E. "Cooperatives in the Pacific States," *Monthly Labor Review,* vol. 64, April 1947, pp. 688–95.

Parker, Zelma E. "History of the Destitute Migrant in California, 1840–1939." Unpublished M.A. thesis. University of California, Berkeley, 1940. 181 pp.

San Francisco. Mayor's Unemployment Committee. *Report: Winter of 1921–22.* San Francisco, 1922. 16 pp.

―――. Unemployment Relief Administration. *Report of Survey.* Supplement to Journal of Proceedings (Board of Supervisors), Sept. 11, 1933. San Francisco, 1933. 122 pp.

Segrest, Earl C., and Arthur J. Misner. *The Impact of Federal Grants-in-Aid on California.* Berkeley: Bureau of Public Administration, University of California, 1954. Chap. 8, "Grants for Employment Security," pp. 241–78.

"Self-Help Activities of Unemployed in Los Angeles," *Monthly Labor Review,* vol. 36, April 1933, pp. 717–40.

"Self-Help Among the Unemployed in California," *Monthly Labor Review,* vol. 41, Dec. 1935, pp. 1504–9.

"Self-Help Among Unemployed of San Francisco Bay District," *Monthly Labor Review,* vol. 36, May 1933, pp. 1002–14.

Singleton, Richard C. "Employment Trends in California, 1870 to 1970," *in* Warren S. Thomas, *Growth and Change in California's Population.* Los Angeles: Haynes Foundation, 1955. Chap. 19, pp. 295–329.

Splitter, Henry Winfred. "Concerning Vinette's Los Angeles Regiment of Coxey's Army," *Pacific Historical Review,* vol. 17, Feb. 1948, pp. 29–36.

Survey Associates. *San Francisco Relief Survey: The Organization and Methods of Relief Used After the Earthquake and Fire of April 18, 1906.* New York: Russell Sage Foundation, 1913. 483 pp.

"Unemployed Co-operative Relief Association of San Jose, Calif.," *Monthly Labor Review,* vol. 36, May 1933, pp. 1022–24.

"Unemployment," *Transactions of the Commonwealth Club of California,* vol. 9, Dec. 1914, pp. 671–714.

U.S. Bureau of the Census. *Unemployment Bulletin: California, Unemployment Returns by Classes.* Fifteenth Census of the United States, 1930. Washington, 1931. 37 pp.

U.S. Work Projects Administration. *Recent Migration into Oakland, Calif. and Environs.* [Oakland?] 1942. 6 pp.

———. *Recent Migration into San Francisco.* [Oakland?] 1942. 6 pp.

U.S. Works Progress Administration. *Northern California's Three Years of Achievement under the Works Progress Administration, 1935–1938.* San Francisco [1938?] 43 pp. Profusely illustrated.

———. *A Study of Contemporary Unemployment and of Basic Data for Planning a Self-Help Cooperative in Palo Alto, California, 1935–1936.* San Francisco, 1936. 37+ pp.

Whiteman, Luther, and Samuel L. Lewis. *Glory Roads: The Psychological State of California.* New York: Crowell, 1936. "From Bartering to Reciprocal Economy," pp. 158–74; "Superbartering in California," pp. 175–87; "Epic, or Politics for Use," pp. 203–18.

Williamson, Mary Helen. "Unemployment Relief Administration in Kern County, 1935–1940." Unpublished M.A. thesis. University of California, Berkeley, 1941. 250 pp.

Wood, Samuel Edgarton. "State Activities for the Control and Welfare of Immigrants in California with Special Emphasis upon Co-operation with Federal Agencies." Unpublished M.A. thesis. University of California, Berkeley, 1933. 236 pp.

Wright, Allen Henry. "Unemployed Men for Unemployed Land," *Overland,* vol. 61, May 1913, pp. 486–91.

LABOR LEGISLATION

Bloch, Louis. "Some Effects of the Operation of the California Minimum Wage Law," *Monthly Labor Review,* vol. 17, Aug. 1923, pp. 1–12.

Seeks to prove, in particular, that the minimum wage did not tend to become the maximum and that the law had benefited women wage earners of the state.

Crum, Bartley C. *Mr. Justice Edmonds and Some Recent Trends in the Law of Civil Liberties.* Foreword by Chester H. Rowell. San Francisco: Pernau-Walsh Printing Co. [1942?] 29 pp.

An assessment of the contribution of Justice Douglas L. Edmonds of the California Supreme Court toward a liberal interpretation of California law, particularly in its application to civil liberties and labor's civil rights. Briefly reviews, as illustrative of Justice Edmonds' liberal approach, such court cases as the Bridges, Los Angeles *Times,* Bulcke, and Wahlenmaier contempt cases, the series of labor cases known as the "Howard Automobile cases," and others involving strikes, picketing, the closed shop, and the boycott. Numerous footnotes provide bibliographical details for the cases mentioned.

Eaves, Lucile. *A History of California Labor Legislation.* Berkeley: The University Press [1910] Chap. 19, "Judicial Restraint of the Actions of Trade Unions," pp. 394–438.

Reviews state judicial intervention in labor disputes and the use of the injunction by California and federal courts, during the period 1899–1907, to limit or prohibit picketing and the use of the boycott. Analyzes a number of injunction cases and tells of the efforts by labor to obtain state anti-injunction legislation.

Gellhorn, Walter. *The States and Subversion.* Ithaca, N.Y.: Cornell University Press, 1952. Chap. 1, "California: Regulation and Investigation of Subversive Activities," pp. 1–53.

Includes references to legislative investigation of Communist Party activities among California labor groups.

Kalish, Samuel. *The American Way to Labor Peace.* Los Angeles: Mercury Printing Co. [1939?] [21] pp.

Deals with the drive by Southern California employers' organizations for antiunion legislation.

Kuhl, Max J. *Argument on the Anti-Injunction Bill (S.B. 1035) before Hon. Wm. D. Stephens, Governor of California, Monday, May 21, 1917.* San Francisco: Chamber of Commerce [1917?] 47 pp.

Analyzes the various sections of the bill with a view to eliciting a veto. Similar to a number sponsored by the American Federation of Labor in other states, the bill had been passed by the California legislature and was before the governor for action. In addition to representing the San Francisco Chamber of Commerce, Kuhl spoke for similar organizations in other parts of California.

Murphy, John Luttrell. *Argument by J. L. Murphy before the New City Hall Commission in Support of His Resolution for Day Labor on the New City Hall.* San Francisco: Law Printing and Publishing Co., 1880. 31 pp.

Chiefly a plea for employment of the less skilled labor directly instead of through contractors, so that such labor would realize some of the contractors' profit.

National Lawyers Guild, San Francisco Chapter. *Report of Committee on Minimum Wage Enforcement.* San Francisco, 1938. 54 pp.

According to the committee, its investigation shows not only that the Industrial Welfare Commission and the Labor Commission have failed to enforce the California minimum wage law adequately but also that its enforcement has at times been sabotaged from above. It points to evidence of influence by political and industrial groups in the selection of key enforcement personnel and of improper financing of investigations by industrial interests. A number of political and legislative recommendations are made to assure more effective enforcement of the law.

Olson, Culbert L. *State Papers and Public Addresses, January 2, 1939–January 4, 1943.* Sacramento, 1942. Part 2, "Messages to the Legislature, 1941."

In "Hot Cargo and Secondary Boycott," pp. 137–46, the governor returns Senate Bill No. 877, outlawing secondary boycotts, without his signature, basing his objections to it on provisions of the federal and California constitutions. In "Unemployment Insurance," pp. 147–57, he states his objections to Assembly Bill No. 560 and returns it unsigned.

Tobriner, Mathew O. "The Organizational Picket Line, Lawful Economic Pressure," *Stanford Law Review,* vol. 3, 1950–1951, pp. 423–39.

Inquires into the juridical reasoning behind the decisions of the California Supreme Court in upholding the right of peaceful picketing for the purpose of organizing a nonunion plant or obtaining a union-shop contract, particularly from the point of view of the "Lawful Purpose Doctrine" which was the basis of the court's decisions.

Aaron, Benjamin, and William Levin. "Labor Injunctions in Action: A Five-Year Survey in Los Angeles County," *California Law Review,* vol. 39, March 1951, pp. 42–66.

Ames, Alden P. "Who Is a Vagrant in California?" *California Law Review,* vol. 25, Sept. 1935, pp. 616–20. [Reply to A. W. Grossman, below]

Benner, Frederic Campbell. "A Study of the Principle Developed in California Labor Law." Unpublished J.D. dissertation. University of California, Berkeley, 1924. 53 pp.

California. Attorney General. *Opinion Relative to Eight Hour Law,* by U. S. Webb. Sacramento, 1914. 50 pp.

————. Bureau of Labor Statistics. *Labor Laws of California,* by J. D. Mac-Kenzie, comp. Sacramento, 1909. 76 pp.

————. ————. *Proposed Labor Laws.* Compiled and recommended by E. L. Fitzgerald, Commissioner. Sacramento, 1896. 29 pp.

————. ————. *Tenth Biennial Report, 1901–1902.* Sacramento, 1902. "As Regards Enforcement of Some of the Labor Laws of California," pp. 32–45.

————. Commission for Fair Employment Practices. *In a Nut Shell: The Proposed Fair Employment Practices Law, Assembly Bill No. 971.* San Francisco, 1955. 4 pp.

————. District Court of Appeals. First Appellate District, Division Two. *Opinions Defining Rights of Union Organization, April 7, 1939.* James T. McKay v. Retail Automobile Salesmen's Local Union No. 1067; E. H. Renzel Co. v. Warehousemen's Union, I.L.A. 38-44, Anthony Montes, The Central Labor Council of Santa Clara County . . . ; C. S. Smith, Metropolitan Market Co., Ltd. v. The Amalgamated Meat Cutters and Butcher Workmen, Local Union 284. . . San Francisco: Recorder Printing and Publishing Co. [1939?] 14 pp.

————. Law Revision Commission. *Recommendation and Study Relating to Arbitration.* Sacramento, 1960. 64 pp.

————. ————. *A Study of California Arbitration Law with Suggested Revisions,* by Sam Kagel. San Francisco, 1960. 72 + 16 pp.

————. University. Bureau of Public Administration. *State Labor Relations Acts,* by Arthur Harris. 1939 Legislative Problems, no. 2. Berkeley, 1939. "Consideration of State Labor Relations Legislation in California," pp. 26–29.

California CIO Council. *Digest of Bills Important to Labor, Pending before 57th Session of the California Legislature.* San Francisco, 1947. 38 pp.

California State Chamber of Commerce. *Digest of California Labor Laws.* [San Francisco?] 1948. 41 pp.

California State Federation of Labor. *What They Promise to Do for Labor.* San Francisco, 1912. 27 pp.

———. *What They Promise to Do for Labor*. Replies of candidates to questions. San Francisco, 1916. 20 pp.

———. *Workers' Rights on Trial in California*. A handbook for speakers. San Francisco [1957?] 53 pp.

"Compulsory Health Insurance Proposed by Social Insurance Commission of California," *Monthly Labor Review,* vol. 4, April 1917, pp. 497–507.

Crockett, Earl C. "The History of California Labor Legislation, 1910–1930." Unpublished Ph.D. dissertation. University of California, Berkeley, 1931. 329 pp.

Cross, Ira B. "Eaves, History of California Labor Legislation," *American Economic Review,* vol. 1, March 1911, pp. 106–9. [Book review]

Eaves, Lucile. "History of California Labor Legislation—a Communication," *American Economic Review,* vol. 1, Sept. 1911, pp. 587–89. [Reply to Ira B. Cross]

———. *A History of California Labor Legislation*. Berkeley: The University Press [1910] Chaps. 8–9, "Laws for the Protection of the Wages of Labor," "Laws Regulating the Relationship of Employer and Employee," pp. 229–86; chap. 14, "Employment Agencies," pp. 335–50; chap. 18, "The Union Label," pp. 385–93.

"Employers Liability," *Transactions of the Commonwealth Club of California,* vol. 6, June 1911, pp. 85–107.

Grossman, A. W. "Who Is a Vagrant in California?" *California Law Review,* vol. 23, July 1935, pp. 506–18. [See Alden Ames, above]

Hanna, Warren L., ed. *The Workmen's Compensation Laws of California*. Albany, Calif.: Hanna Legal Publications, 1961. 469 pp.

Hichborn, Franklin. *Story of the Session of the California Legislature of 1911*. San Francisco: James H. Barry, 1912. Chap. 18, "Labor and the Legislature," pp. 225–35; chaps. 20–21, "Women's Eight Hour Bill," "The Compulsory Arbitration Bill," pp. 246–65.

———. *Story of the Session of the California Legislature of 1915*. San Francisco: James H. Barry, 1916. Chap. 17, "Labor and the Legislature," pp. 189–203.

———. *Story of the Session of the California Legislature of 1921*. San Francisco: James H. Barry, 1922. Chap. 21, "Labor and the 1921 Session," pp. 296–303.

"The Industrial Accidents Bill," *Transactions of the Commonwealth Club of California,* vol. 8, April 1913, pp. 103–53.

McGrath, Edward Gorham. "California Labor Legislation Concerning Industrial Disputes, 1941–1947, with Special Reference to 'Hot Cargo' and Secondary Boycott." Unpublished M.A. thesis. University of California, Berkeley, 1948. 76 pp.

Mathewson, Walter G. "Collection of Unpaid Wages in California," *American Labor Legislation Review,* vol. 19, Dec. 1929, pp. 411–15.

Mel, Marian L. "Labor Laws of California, Oregon and Washington," *Monthly Labor Review,* vol. 64, April 1947, pp. 675–87.

Mellor, M. L. "Fair Employment Practices: Legislative Trends and Proposals," *California Law Review,* vol. 38, Aug. 1950, pp. 514–24.

Minar, David William. "Voting Behavior on Recent Labor Measures in California." Unpublished M.A. thesis. University of California, Berkeley, 1951. 199 pp.

Pierson, Frank C. "Effects of the Taft-Hartley Act on Labor Relations in Southern California," *Proceedings,* 23rd Annual Conference of the Pacific Coast Economic Association, Los Angeles, Dec. 29–30, 1948. Pp. 76–82.

Rabinowitz, Herbert. "A Criticism of Certain Cases of Law." Unpublished J.D. dissertation. University of California, Berkeley, 1922. Various pagings.

"Recent Minimum Wage Orders in California," *Monthly Labor Review,* vol. 11, Nov. 1920, pp. 108–12.

"Results of Minimum Wage Legislation in California Canning Industry," *Monthly Labor Review,* vol. 6, Feb. 1918, pp. 138–42.

Rubens, William Charles. "The Labor Initiative of 1938: The Development of a New Orientation of Restrictive Labor Legislation in California." Unpublished M.A. thesis. University of California, Berkeley, 1950 222 pp.

San Francisco Employers Council. *Legislative Bulletin,* March 7, 1939–June 24, 1939. San Francisco, 1939. Various pagings.

Strong, George Alvin. "A Study of the Development of the California Law of Picketing." Unpublished M.A. thesis. University of California, Berkeley, 1952. 155 pp.

"The Supreme Court of California on Picketing," *Law and Labor,* vol. 3, Nov. 1921, pp. 250–53.

Triska, Joseph F. *The Juvenile Laws of California, Including Federal Statutes.* Los Angeles: Research Publishing Co., 1940. Chap. 7, "Employment," pp. 112–38; Appendix A, "Labor," pp. 296–306; Appendix

B, "A Summary of Orders Issued by the California Industrial Welfare Commission Fixing Minimum Wages, Maximum Hours, and Standard Conditions of Labor for Minors in the Various Trades and Industries," pp. 309–28.

United Progressive News. *One Hundred Votes.* An analysis of the 1937 session of the California Legislature. Los Angeles, 1938. 124 pp.

U.S. Bureau of Labor Statistics. *Labor Laws and Their Administration in the Pacific States,* by Hugh S. Hanna. Bull. no. 211. Washington, 1917. 150 pp.

"Workmen's Compensation; Employers' Liability," *Transactions of the Commonwealth Club of California,* vol. 7, Nov. 1912, pp. 461–514.

Wright, Allen G. *Brief Analysis of California's New Employers' Liability Act, Eight Hour Law for Women and New Mechanics Lien Law.* Report to the members of the Merchants Association of San Francisco. San Francisco: Merchants Association, 1911. 16 pp.

Young, Jack. *The People Be Damned.* A record of the 53d session of the State Legislature of California. San Francisco: People's World, 1939. 48 pp.

LABOR IN POLITICS

Bean, Walton. *Boss Ruef's San Francisco: The Story of the Union Labor Party, Big Business, and the Graft Prosecution.* Berkeley: University of California Press, 1952. 345 pp.

Tells the story of corruption in the San Francisco Union Labor Party municipal administration, 1901–1906, its exposure, and its prosecution. The widespread use of the police in the City Front Federation strike in 1901, and the belief by labor that the machinery of the city government generally had been placed at the disposal of the Employers Association in that strike, led labor to seek protection in independent political action. This, it is believed, accounted for the election of successive Union Labor Party administrations, which under the guidance of political boss Abraham Ruef followed an ever growing practice of selling municipal privileges to the public utility corporations. The graft prosecutions began in 1906 and had as their main aim the imprisonment of the corrupters: the leading captains of industry. The author shows that though the prosecutions provided in pitiless detail a case study of boss government and municipal corruption, and of the difficulties of reform, they did not realize that primary aim.

Bryce, James. *The American Commonwealth.* New York: Macmillan, 1910. Vol. 2, chap. 90, "Kearneyism in California," pp. 426–48.

Maintaining that events in California can be properly viewed only if one understands that "California, more than any other part of the union, is a country by itself, and San Francisco a capital," the author attempts to give the Workingmen's Party of California its proper place in California history. He concludes that it was of little lasting significance, excepting its major role in shaping the new state constitution.

Carlson, Oliver. *A Mirror for Californians.* Indianapolis: Bobbs-Merrill, 1941. Chap. 10, "The Workingmen's Party," pp. 238–62.

Assigning to the Workingmen's Party of California a place among the four most important movements of social protest in the history of California, the author discusses the rapid rise and equally rapid decline of both the party and Denis Kearney, its chief leader. The conditions which encouraged the organization of the Workingmen's Party—mass unemployment in the late seventies, the Chinese question, and the power of the railroad monopoly—are discussed, as are the varying fortunes of the party and the high point in its career, the influence it exerted in shaping a new constitution for California.

Cross, Ira B. *A History of the Labor Movement in California.* Berkeley: University of California Press, 1935. Chap. 10, "The International Workingmen's Association," pp. 156–65.

Describes the formation of the International Workingmen's Association, patterned after Karl Marx's First International, by Burnette Haskell in 1882, its organizational and ideological features, and the part it played in building the labor movement in California.

Davis, Winfield J. *History of Political Conventions in California, 1849–1892*. Publications of the California State Library, no. 1. Sacramento, 1893. Chaps. 27–29, "1877: Workingmen's Movement and the Kearney Excitement," "1878: The Workingmen's Excitement Growing in Intensity ...," "1879: Adoption of the New Constitution ...," pp. 365–402.

A chronological account of the agitation among the unemployed of San Francisco which led to the organization of the Workingmen's Party of California, the division in the party and victory of the Kearney faction, the leading role of the Workingmen's Party in framing a new state constitution, and the party's eclipse after the adoption of the constitution. Included are some of the party's resolutions and the list of delegates to the constitutional convention.

George, Henry. "The Kearney Agitation in California," *Popular Science Monthly,* vol. 17, Aug. 1880, pp. 433–53.

Seeks to debunk some of the fictions that had become prevalent about Denis Kearney, the Workingmen's Party of California, and the new state constitution. George contends that there was nothing socialistic or communistic, imported or native, about the Workingmen's Party; that it only reflected, in part, the general discontent in the country. He further contends that Kearney was not a labor leader but a small-time politician whom, out of fear, the monied class had built up; and that the new constitution was a fraud as far as the interests of the workingmen were concerned.

Gray, Arthur A. *History of California from 1542*. New York: Heath, 1934. Chap. 27, "The Workingmen's Party," pp. 448–59.

Intended for high school reading.

Kauer, Ralph. "The Workingmen's Party of California," *Pacific Historical Review,* vol. 13, Sept. 1944, pp. 278–91.

Outlines the history of the party, stressing its less spectacular but more vital features, and assesses its contribution to the interests of California labor.

The Labor Agitators, or the Battle for Bread. San Francisco: G. S. Greene [1878?] 31 pp.

Includes sections on "History of Workingmen's Party of California," "Venality of the Press," "The Battle for Bread," "Incidents of Chinese Life," "Dennis Kearney," and "Speeches of the Leaders."

McGowan, Joseph A. *History of the Sacramento Valley*. New York: Lewis Historical Publishing Co., 1961. Vol. 1, chap. 26, "Economic Problems and Political Action," pp. 334–42.

Includes an account of the fortunes of the Workingmen's Party of California in the Sacramento Valley in 1878 and 1879.

Mowry, George E. *The California Progressives.* Berkeley: University of California Press, 1951. Chap. 2, "The Struggle for the Cities," pp. 23–56.

Briefly reviews the Union Labor Party municipal government graft prosecutions in San Francisco, 1905–1912, and describes the Los Angeles political and labor scene during the same period. The effect of the confessions of the McNamara brothers on the fortunes of the Socialist Party in Los Angeles is emphasized.

Quint, Howard H. "Gaylord Wilshire and Socialism's First Congressional Campaign," *Pacific Historical Review,* vol. 26, Nov. 1957, pp. 327–40.

Gaylord Wilshire had the distinction of being the first candidate to campaign for a congressional seat as a socialist. The post was that of congressman from the southern California counties in the election of 1890, with Wilshire running under the banner of the Nationalist Party.

Steffens, Lincoln. "The Mote and the Beam, A Fact Novel," *American Magazine,* vol. 65, Nov. 1907, pp. 26–40; Dec. 1907, pp. 140–51; Feb. 1908, pp. 390–402.

Tells the story of the Abe Ruef–Eugene Schmitz graft prosecutions in San Francisco.

———. "William J. Burns, Intriguer," *American Magazine,* vol. 65, April 1908, pp. 614–25.

Describes Burns's detective work in the Abe Ruef–Eugene Schmitz graft prosecutions in San Francisco.

Stimson, Grace Heilman. *Rise of the Labor Movement in Los Angeles.* Berkeley: University of California Press, 1955.

Chap. 2, "Labor Ventures into Politics," pp. 13–31.

Discusses the organization and erratic and ineffectual course of the Workingmen's Party in Los Angeles. Organized in 1877, when no trade-union movement of any importance yet existed, the Workingmen's Party was in effect a fusion of groups representing farmers and reform elements in addition to workers. The party's affiliation with Denis Kearney's Workingmen's Party of San Francisco did not help it, and after a few unfruitful years it was absorbed by the Greenback Party.

Chap. 16, "Labor and Socialism," pp. 218–36.

Tells of the collaboration at the turn of the century of Los Angeles trade unionists, first, with the Socialist Labor Party and, later, with Social Democracy and its successor, the Socialist Party, and the varying degrees of success or failure of this collaboration.

Thomas, Lately. *A Debonair Scoundrel: An Episode in the Moral History of San Francisco.* New York: Holt, Rinehart and Winston, 1962. 422 pp.

A retelling of the story of graft and its prosecution in the San Francisco municipal administration of the Union Labor Party mayor, Eugene Schmitz.

Young, John P. *San Francisco: A History of the Pacific Coast Metropolis.* San Francisco: S. J. Clarke Publishing Co., 1912. Vol. 2, chap. 51, "The Sand Lot Troubles and the New Constitution," pp. 529–48.

A critical examination of Denis Kearney's activity as a labor leader, the organization and activity of the Workingmen's Party of California, and the party's role in the formulation and passage of a new state constitution in 1878.

Bean, Walton E. "Boss Ruef, the Union Labor Party, and the Graft Prosecution in San Francisco, 1901–1911," *Pacific Historical Review,* vol. 17, Nov. 1948, pp. 443–55.

Blake, Evarts I. *San Francisco and Its Municipal Administration.* A brief biographical sketch of some of the most prominent men who will preside over her destiny for at least two years. San Francisco: Pacific Publishing Co., 1902. 223 pp.

Bohn, Frank. "The Socialist Party and the California Labor Party," *International Socialist Review,* vol. 11, June 1911, pp. 762–67.

Bonnet, Theodore. *The Regenerators: A Study of the Graft Prosecution of San Francisco.* San Francisco: Pacific Printing Co., 1911. 251 pp.

Bruce, John. *Gaudy Century: The Story of San Francisco's Hundred Years of Robust Journalism.* New York: Random House, 1948. Chap. 25, "The Chinese Must Go," pp. 161–70; chap. 39, "Fire, Earthquake and Ruef," pp. 259–73.

Cain, Glen George. "Political Action by Organized Labor in Alameda County, California, with Special Reference to the 1956 Election." Unpublished M.A. thesis. University of California, Berkeley, 1957. 194 pp.

California Labor League for Political Education. *Constitution and Rules of Order.* Adopted by the CLLPE Convention, Santa Barbara, Oct. 13, 1950. Reprinted May 1954. 23 pp.

———. *You and Politics.* San Francisco, 1952. 11 pp.

Cleland, Robert Glass. *California in Our Time.* New York: Knopf, 1941. Chap. 2, "Graft," pp. 9–25.

"Confessions of a Stenographer; Being an Analysis of the Graft in San Francisco and the Underlying Causes That Led to It," *Overland,* vol. 50, Aug. 1907, pp. 101–9. Illustrated.

Dosch, Arno. "Rudolph Spreckels—the Genius of the San Francisco Graft Prosecutions," *Overland,* vol. 50, Nov. 1907, pp. 477–81.

Hart, Jerome A. *In Our Second Century: From an Editor's Notebook.*

San Francisco: Pioneer Press, 1931. Chap. 5, "The Sand Lot and Kearneyism," pp. 52–63.

Hichborn, Franklin. *"The System" as Uncovered by the San Francisco Graft Prosecution*. San Francisco: James H. Barry, 1915. 464 + xl pp.

Hunt, Rockwell D. *California's Stately Hall of Fame*. Publications of the California History Foundation, no. 2. Stockton: College of the Pacific, 1950. "Dennis Kearney, Sand Lot Politician," pp. 351–56.

Ingels, Helen Havens. "History of the Workingmen's Party of California." Unpublished M.A. thesis. University of California, Berkeley, 1919. 124 pp.

Kahn, Charles Herzl. "In-Group and Out-Group Responses to Radical Party Leadership: A Study of the Workingmen's Party of California." Unpublished M.A. thesis. University of California, Berkeley, 1951. 67 pp.

Larsen, Charles E. "The Epic Movement in California Politics, 1933–1934," *Pacific Historical Review,* vol. 27, May 1958, pp. 127–49.

Lewis, Austin. "The Day After," *International Socialist Review,* vol. 12, Dec. 1911, pp. 357–59.

———. "The Economic Fact: A Reply to 'An Appeal to the People of the West,' " *Overland,* vol. 45, Feb. 1905, pp. 165–71. [See John Roberts and Thomas Wilson, below]

Moremen, Merrill Raymond. "The Independent Progressive Party in California, 1948." Unpublished M.A. thesis. Stanford University, 1950. 263 pp.

Posner, Russell M. "A. P. Giannini and the 1934 Campaign in California," *Historical Society of Southern California Quarterly,* vol. 39, June 1957, pp. 190–202.

Roberts, John. "A Plea to the People of the West," *Overland,* vol. 45, Jan. 1905, pp. 49–58. [See Austin Lewis, above, and Thomas Wilson, below]

Rowell, Edward Joseph. "The Union Labor Party of San Francisco, 1901–1911." Unpublished Ph.D. dissertation. University of California, Berkeley, 1938. 264 pp.

Ruef, Abraham. "The Road I Traveled: An Autobiographic Account of my Career from University to Prison, with an Intimate Recital of the Corrupt Alliance ... ," in San Francisco *Bulletin,* May 21–Sept. 5, 1912.

San Francisco. Mayor's Committee. *Report of the Causes of Municipal Corruption in San Francisco*. As disclosed by the investigation of the Oliver Grand Jury, and the prosecution of certain persons for bribery and other offenses against the State. A reprint by the *California Weekly*. San Francisco: Rincon Publishing Co., 1910. 54 pp.

Shaffer, Ralph Edward. "A History of the Socialist Party of California." Unpublished M.A. thesis. University of California, Berkeley, 1955. 201 pp.

Socialist Party. *Facts as to Socialism*. Principles and Candidates of the Socialist Party, Campaign of 1911. San Francisco, 1911. 64 pp.

Stedman, J. C., and R. A. Leonard. *The Workingmen's Party: An Epitome of its Rise and Progress*. San Francisco: Bacon & Co., 1878. 120 pp.

Steffens, Lincoln. *The Autobiography of Lincoln Steffens*. New York: Harcourt, Brace, 1931. Part 3, chaps. 28–29, "San Francisco: A Labor Government," "How Hard It Is to Keep Things Wrong," pp. 552–69.

———— *Upbuilders*. New York: Doubleday, Page, 1909. Chap. 4, "Rudolph Spreckels, a Business Reformer," pp. 244–84.

Swisher, Carl Brent. *Motivation and Political Technique in the California Constitutional Convention, 1878–79*. Claremont, Calif.: Pomona College, 1930. 132 pp.

Welton, Claude Hamilton. "A New Type of Political Boss," *California Review,* vol. 2, Dec.–Jan. 1904, pp. 5–8.

Wilkins, M. W. "The California Situation," *International Socialist Review,* vol. 3, Jan. 1903, pp. 416–19.

Wilson, Thomas B. "Economic Fallacies," *Overland,* vol. 45, May 1905, pp. 452–54. [A reply to both John Roberts' "A Plea to the People of the West" and Austin Lewis' "The Economic Fact"]

Woehlke, Walter V. "From Henry George to 'Gene Schmitz,' " *Sunset,* vol. 38, April 1917, pp. 7–10, 93.

Workingmen's Party of California. *Address and Platform, Constitution and Rules of Order of the Workingmen's Party of California*. Adopted June 1881. San Francisco: W. T. Baggett & Co., 1881. 23 pp.

————. Alameda County Executive Committee. *Dennis Kearney and His Relations to the Workingmen's Party of California*. A campaign document. San Francisco: Faulkner & Fish [1878?] 34 pp.

LABOR AND LABOR-RELATED PRESS

Cross, Ira B. "Labor Papers on the Pacific Coast," *Labor Clarion,* vol. 7, June 5, 1908, pp. 2, 3, 7.

A review of the early development of the labor press in San Francisco, Los Angeles, Oakland, and the cities of the Northwest. Of particular interest is a discussion of papers which had a very brief existence and have since been all but forgotten.

National Industrial Conference Board. *Employee Magazines in the United States.* New York, 1925. 89 pp.

An appendix includes a listing of some twenty-five employee magazines published by California business firms.

U.S. Work Projects Administration. *The American Labor Press: Annotated Directory.* Introduction by John R. Commons. Washington, D.C.: American Council on Public Affairs, 1940. 120 pp.

Includes California publications, current at time of publication, under the headings of AFL and CIO National, International, and Local Unions; Independent Trade Unions; Communist and Socialist Parties; Other "Left Wing" Organizations; and General Labor publications.

Note: The items shown as follows are in the collections of the libraries indicated below, and were examined:
Banc.—Bancroft Library
S.F. Pub. Lib.—San Francisco Public Library
U.C.B.—University of California, Berkeley
I.L.W.U.—International Longshoremen's and Warehousemen's Union Research Library
The items shown as follows were not examined. They are discussed in these publications:
Cross Hist.—Ira B. Cross, *A History of the Labor Movement in California*
Cross Lab. Clar.—Ira B. Cross, "Labor Papers on the Pacific Coast," *Labor Clarion,* June 5, 1908
Stimson—Grace Heilman Stimson, *Rise of the Labor Movement in Los Angeles*

SAN FRANCISCO

AFL Cannery Reporter. Weekly and monthly. 1945–1954. Official publication of the California Council of Cannery Unions. Superseded by *Northern California Teamster.* Sometimes published in Oakland. (U.C.B.)

Alliance News. Monthly. 1904. Orientation: Open-shop advocacy. Published by the Citizens' Alliance of San Francisco. (Banc.)

American Labor Citizen. Weekly. 1939–1945. Suspended publication, Oct. 30, 1942–Feb. 15, 1943. Ceased publication, July 2, 1945. First published as an official western publication of the AFL and later as the official publication of the Bay Cities Metal Trades Council. (U.C.B.)

American Plan Progress. Semimonthly. 1925–1926. Orientation: Employers' approach to labor relations. Published by the Industrial Association of San Francisco. (S.F. Pub. Lib.)

Anti-Communist Bulletin. Approximately weekly. Nov. 14, 1935–Sept. 20, 1938 (nos. 39–80). Orientation: Questions affecting labor as viewed by the employers. Published by the Industrial Association of San Francisco. Superseded by the *Anti-Subversive Bulletin*. (U.C.B.)

Anti-Subversive Bulletin. Approximately monthly. Sept. 20–Nov. 22, 1938 (nos. 81–83). Orientation: Questions affecting labor as viewed by the employers. Published by the Industrial Association of San Francisco. Ceased publication with this issue. (U.C.B.)

A.O.U.W. Bulletin. Monthly. 1898–1899. Publication of the Ancient Order of United Workmen. (Banc.)

The Blast. Weekly. Jan. 15, 1916–June 1, 1917. Orientation: Anarchist. Editor and publisher: Alexander Berkman. (U.C.B.)

Caucasian and Workingmen's Journal. Weekly. Aug. 1869. Orientation: Anti-Chinese. Existed only briefly. (Cross Lab. Clar.)

Cigar Maker's Appeal. Weekly. 1880. Published by the Cigar Makers Union. Campaigned against the sale of Chinese-made goods. (Cross Lab. Clar.)

Coast Seamen's Journal. Weekly and monthly. Nov. 2, 1887–June 1937. Editors: Paul Scharrenberg, Walter Macarthur, and others. First published by the Coast Seamen's Union of the Pacific Coast; became official organ of the Sailors Union of the Pacific in 1891; became official organ of the International Seamen's Union as well as of the SUP in 1917 or 1918 under the name of the *Seamen's Journal*. (U.C.B.)

Commonwealth. Monthly. 1888–1889. Published also as *Kaweah Commonwealth*. Editor: Burnette G. Haskell. Official publication of the Kaweah Cooperative Colony. Sometimes published in Berkeley. (Banc.)

Council News. Monthly. Feb. 1953–Jan. 1954. Published also as *Teamster Bay Area Warehouse News*. Official publication of Teamster Bay Area Warehouse Council. (U.C.B.)

Daily Plebian. Daily. July 24–Aug. 16, 1871. Served as official organ of the American Labor Union. (Banc.)

Daily Star. Daily and weekly. Founded by James H. Barry in Feb. 1884. Changed to weekly soon after. Suspended publication in 1921. " ... not, strictly speaking, a labor paper, it was nevertheless an ardent champion of the rights of the working class. ... " (Cross Hist.)

Eight-Hour Herald. Monthly. 1889–1890. Organ of the Eight-Hour League. Succeeded by *The Future* in May 1890. (Cross Lab. Clar.)

Enterprise and Cooperator. Weekly. 1872. A merger of the South San Francisco *Enterprise* and the *Cooperator*. Published only for several months. (Banc.)

Evening Journal. Daily and weekly. Founded in 1871 as successor to the *People's Journal*. " ... it was not, strictly speaking, a labor paper, although it was strongly pro-labor in its views." (Cross Hist.; Banc.)

The Fo'cs'le Head. Approximately twice weekly. May–Sept. 1934. Published by the Marine Workers Industrial Union. (U.C.B.)

Free Society. Monthly and quarterly. Jan.–Aug. 1898; May 1899–June 1900. Orientation: "The advocate of communal living and individual sovereignty." (Banc.)

The Future. Monthly. Founded in May 1890 as successor to the *Eight-Hour Herald*. (Cross Lab. Clar.)

The Great Strike. 1877. Published by Carl Browne, secretary to Denis Kearney, as the organ of the Order of Caucasians. Lasted only briefly. (Cross Lab. Clar.)

Hays Valley Advertiser. Weekly. 1878. (Banc.)

Industrial Magazine. Monthly. Jan. 1867. Suspended after three issues. (Banc.)

Industrial Reformer. Weekly. Founded in 1871 by the Industrial Reformers, an anti-Chinese association. Survived for a short time only. (Banc.)

Industrial Relations Exchange; Industrial Relations Review. Monthly. 1921–1924. Published by the Industrial Relations Association of California. (U.C.B.)

Journal of Trades and Workingmen. Weekly. April 1865. Editor and publisher: Alexander M. Kenaday. Discontinued after five issues. (Cross Lab. Clar.)

Labor Action. Weekly. Nov. 28, 1936–May 1, 1937. Editor: James P. Cannon. Organ of the Socialist Party of California and also of the Western States Federation of the Socialist Party. (U.C.B.)

Labor Clarion. Weekly. Feb. 28, 1902–April 30, 1948. Editors: Will J. French, James W. Mullen, and others. Official journal of the San Francisco Labor Council and for a time also of the California State Federation of Labor. (Banc.)

The Labor Herald. 1894. Orientation: Labor in politics. (Cross Lab. Clar.)

Labor Herald. Biweekly. June 7, 1937–March 23, 1953. Published by the California State Industrial Council, CIO. Sometimes published in Oakland. (U.C.B.)

Labor Unity; also *San Francisco Labor Unity*. Weekly. 1919–1925. Orientation: Radical; Communist. Succeeded the *Rank and File*. (U.C.B.)

The Liberator. Weekly. Dec. 12, 1908–June 4, 1910. Founded to further the Schmitz-Ruef graft prosecutions. (Banc.)

Maritime Worker. Biweekly. 1935–1938? Published by the Waterfront Section of the Communist Party. (Banc.)

The New Union. Weekly. 1894–1895. (Banc.)

The Open Letter. Founded by Carl Browne in Nov. 1877. Adopted as the official organ of the Workingmen's Party of California. (Cross Lab. Clar.)

Our Union. Founded in the fall of 1887 by the Cooks and Waiters Union. Only a few issues were published. (Cross Lab. Clar.)

Pacific Coast Boycotter. Weekly. Founded in 1886 to further a boycott by the local typographical union against the *Morning Call* and *Evening Bulletin*. (Banc.)

Pacific Coast Maritime Report. Semimonthly. Feb. 5, 1947–Jan. 24, 1949. Orientation: Maritime labor relations as viewed by the shipping industry. (U.C.B.)

Pacific Coast Railroader. 1892. (Cross Lab. Clar.)

Pacific Coast Trades and Labor Journal. Founded July 1890; published only briefly. (Cross Lab. Clar.)

Pacific Seaman. Weekly. Sept. 1934– Feb. 1936. Editor and publisher: Carl Lynch. Claimed endorsement of the Pacific Coast District unions of the International Seamen's Union. Became the *American Seaman* in Nov. 1935 under independent status. (U.C.B.)

Pacific Union Printer. Founded in 1888 as the official organ of the Allied Printing Trades Council and printing trades unions in the San Francisco Bay region. Suspended publication in 1899. (Cross Lab. Clar.)

The People. Established in 1888; only a few issues appeared. (Cross Hist.)

People's Journal. Weekly. Established in 1871 as the successor to the *Workingmen's Journal.* Was not, strictly speaking, a labor paper after this change. (Banc.)

The Picket; also *The Union Picket.* July 1907–. Independent. (Banc.)

The Printer. 1859. Published by Local 21 of the Typographical Union. Only a few numbers were issued. (Cross Lab. Clar.)

Revolt. Weekly. May 1911–May 1912. Orientation: Socialist. Editors: Thomas J. Mooney, Austin Lewis, and others. (Banc.)

The Sand Lot. Published during the spring of 1879 by William Wellock and others, in the interests of the Workingmen's Party of California. (Cross Hist.)

The Settlers' and the Workingmen's Journal. Weekly. Began publication in the latter part of 1869. Succeeded by the *People's Journal* in 1871. (Banc.)

The Shop and Senate. Weekly. Founded by A. M. Winn in Jan. 1873. Both a labor journal and the organ of the Ecumenic Order of United Mechanics. Ceased publication in March 1874. Campaigned for an eight-hour law. (Banc.)

The Socialist. Weekly. 1895–1897. Succeeded by the *Social Economist.* (Banc.)

Special Bulletin. Approximately weekly. July 14, 1934–Nov. 14, 1935 (nos. 1–38). Orientation: Questions affecting labor as viewed by the employers. Published by the Industrial Association of San Francisco. Superseded by the *Anti-Communist Bulletin.* (U.C.B.)

Tom Mooney's Monthly. Monthly. Aug. 1920–Dec. 1922. Editor: Tom Mooney; acting editors: George T. Sayles and others. Independent. (Banc.)

Truth. Weekly and Monthly. Jan. 28, 1882–Oct. 1884. Editor: Burnette G. Haskell. Accepted by the San Francisco Trades Assembly as its official organ. A weekly until Jan. 1, 1884, when it became a monthly. (Banc.)

Truth in Small Doses. May 9–Sept. 3, 1886. Organ of the San Francisco Social League and Labor Lyceum. "Issued by the Women for the Men." (Banc.)

"Unemployment Reserves" Bulletin. Approximately monthly. 1935–1936. Published by the Industrial Association of San Francisco. (U.C.B.)

Union Labor Voice. 1903. Orientation: Labor in politics. (Cross Lab. Clar.)

Voice of the Federation. Weekly. June 14, 1935–Aug. 2, 1941. Official publication of the Maritime Federation of the Pacific. Absorbed by west coast office of the *Pilot.* (U.C.B.)

Voice of Labor. Weekly. 1893–1900. Editor: M. McGlynn. Official organ of the San Francisco Labor Council and the S. F. Building Trades Council. (Banc.)

Waterfront Worker. Irregular. 1932–1936. Variously sponsored: by a group of longshoremen; by a group of longshoremen with the cooperation of the Marine Workers Industrial Union; by members of the International Longshoremen's Association. (ILWU)

Weekly People's Press. Weekly. 1892. Orientation: Reform. (Banc.)

Western Worker. Semimonthly, weekly, and semiweekly. Jan. 1932–Dec. 1937. Orientation: Communist. Editors: Sam Darcy, George Morris, Lawrence Ross, Mike Quin. (U.C.B.)

White Labor Herald. 1889. Orientation: Anti-Chinese. Published by the Cigar Makers Union. (Cross Lab. Clar.)

LOS ANGELES

California Federationist. Semimonthly. Founded by the Typographical Union in 1894. Ceased publication in 1895. (Cross Lab. Clar.; Stimson)

The Citizen. Weekly. Appeared March 1, 1907, as successor to the *Union Labor News*. Merged with the *Labor Press* May 1, 1916. Editors: John Murray, Stanley Wilson. Owned and published by the labor unions of Southern California. (Banc.)

Evening Union. Daily. Founded July 11, 1885. Was a strike organ of the printers and ceased publication at end of the strike, Oct. 1885. (Stimson)

Farmer and Labor Review. Weekly. A merger in March 1893 of the *Labor Review* and the *California Farmer*. Ceased publication in March 1895. Had the endorsement of the Council of Labor for a time. (Stimson)

The Fraternity. Monthly and, from March 1902, a weekly. Published by the Printers' Protective Fraternity, a rival of the International Typographical Union; supported the Los Angeles *Times* in its fight against the ITU. (Stimson)

Industrial Age. Weekly. April 1892. Editors: Joseph Phillis, S. A. Collins. Was popularly regarded as the official organ of the Council of Labor but repudiated by it in July 1892 and soon after ceased publication. (Cross Lab. Clar.; Stimson)

Industrial Unionist. Weekly. 1937–1939. Organ of the Los Angeles Industrial Union Council. (U.C.B.)

Labor Press. Weekly. Jan. 21–April 28, 1916. Merged with the *Citizen* on May 1, 1916, to become the *Los Angeles Citizen*. Had endorsement of the

Central Labor Council, the Building Trades Council, and the Allied Printing Trades Council. (U.C.B.)

Labor Review. Weekly. Established in Nov. 1892, with the endorsement of the Council of Labor. Merged with the *California Farmer,* March 1893. (U.C.B.)

Labor World. Weekly. March 1896. Orientation: Reform. Editor: F. B. Colver. Changed to *Labor World and Silver Champion,* Oct. 1896. (Stimson)

Labor World and Silver Champion. Weekly. 1896–1897. Orientation: Reform. Editor: F. B. Colver. (Banc.)

Los Angeles Socialist. Weekly. Nov. 2, 1901–March 1905. Official publication of the Los Angeles Socialist Party. Published as *Common Sense* beginning Aug. 20, 1904. (Banc.)

The "Other" Printer. Daily. Launched by the Printers' Protective Fraternity Nov. 5, 1896, as an election campaign paper. (Stimson)

Publicity. Monthly. Issued in 1909 by the Los Angeles Typographical Union to further certain factional aims. Discontinued publication in 1910. (Stimson)

Southern California Labor Press. Weekly. Feb. 29, 1924–Feb. 27, 1928. Founded by the Los Angeles County Building Trades Council and District Council of Carpenters. Merged with the *Los Angeles Citizen.* (U.C.B.)

Union Labor. Weekly. 1914. Official publication of the Los Angeles Building Trades Council. (Banc.)

Union Labor News. Weekly. Founded in Jan. 1901 and sponsored by the Council of Labor. Succeeded by the *Citizen* in March 1907. (Stimson)

Union Printer. Appeared Aug. 8 or 9, 1890, as strike organ of the Typographical Union in its strike against the four daily newspapers of Los Angeles, and continued publication for several months. Was succeeded by the *Workman,* which was sponsored by the Council of Labor. (Cross Lab. Clar.; Stimson)

Union "Totem." Daily. Issued during the election campaign in 1896 by the Typographical Union in retaliation to the Printers' Protective Fraternity's *The "Other" Printer.* (Stimson)

Voice of Labor. Daily. Appeared from end of July to Sept. 1879 as election publication. Organ of the Workingmen's Party of California. (Stimson)

Workman. Succeeded the *Union Printer* in Nov. 1890. Semiweekly to weekly in Nov. 1891. Sponsored by the Council of Labor. Suspended publication in April 1892. (Stimson)

OAKLAND

Alameda County Union Labor Record. Weekly. 1918–Sept. 28, 1928. Publication of the Central Labor Council, Building Trades and Iron Trades Councils of Alameda County. Title varies. (U.C.B.)

California Labor Journal. Weekly. 1907– . Official organ of the American Labor Press Association. (Banc.)

Co-operative Journal. Weekly. 190? Publication of the Pacific Coast Co-operative Union. (Banc.)

The Industry. Weekly. 1894. Lasted only briefly. (Cross Lab. Clar.; Banc.)

Labor Advocate. 1888. Organ of the Knights of Labor and of the trade unions of Alameda County. Had a brief existence. (Cross Lab. Clar.)

Oakland Printer. 1894– . Published for a few years. (Cross Lab. Clar.)

The Pressman. 1891. Lasted only briefly. (Cross Lab. Clar.)

Socialist Voice. Weekly. 1904–1907. Published by Alameda County Socialist Party. (Banc.)

SAN DIEGO

The News. April 1897. Published by the printers as strike organ. (Cross Lab. Clar.)

San Diego Appeal. 1889. Published by the printers as strike organ. (Cross Lab. Clar.)

San Diego Union. 1888. Had a brief existence. (Cross Lab. Clar.)

VARIOUS

Altrurian. Berkeley; Altruria. Weekly and monthly. 1894–1896. Orientation: Cooperative, Socialist. Began publication in Berkeley on Oct. 6, 1894, moved to the colony after Nov. 22, 1894, publishing there weekly until Feb. 22, 1896. Became a monthly in May, and ceased publication in Nov. 1896. (Banc.)

American Citizen. San Raphael. Twice monthly. Aug. 2, 1935–June 21, 1937. Orientation: "For an American front of labor and industry." Editor: Henry R. Sanborn. (U.C.B.)

Associated Farmer. Fresno. 1937–1950. Published by the Associated Farmers of California. (U.C.B.)

L'Etoile des Pauvres et des Souffrants. Published monthly and irregularly at St. Helena, California, Jan.–July 1881, and at Cloverdale, California,

Aug. 1881–Oct. 1883. Orientation: "Organe du Communisme libérateur des peuples et de l'individu." Editor and publisher: Jules Leroux. (Banc.)

Farmer-Labor News. Modesto. Weekly. 1923–1959. Official publication of the Central Labor Council of Stanislaus County, Farmers' Educational and Cooperative Union, and the Central Labor Union of Merced. (U.C.B.)

Hollywood Atom. Hollywood. 1945. Published by the 15 local unions in the Hollywood Studio Strike Strategy Committee. (U.C.B.)

Humboldt News. Eureka. Weekly. July 4, 1925–Nov. 3, 1927. Published by the Eureka Federated Trades and Labor Council. Superseded *Labor News.* (U.C.B.)

Kaweah Commonwealth. Visalia. Weekly and monthly. Jan. 18, 1890–April 1892. Organ of the Kaweah Cooperative Colony. (Banc.)

Labor News. Eureka. Weekly. Feb. 1905–June 27, 1925. Published by the Eureka Trades Council, affiliated unions of Humboldt County, and the International Brotherhood of Woodsmen and Sawmill Workers. Superseded by *Humboldt News.* (Banc.)

Labor News. Long Beach. Weekly. 1920–1948? "Published by the labor movement of Long Beach." (U.C.B.)

Pasadena Labor News. Pasadena. Weekly. 1927–1928? Endorsed by the Pasadena Board of Labor and Pasadena Building Trades Council. (U.C.B.)

San Fernando Valley Labor News. San Fernando Valley. Weekly. 193?–194? Official publication of the San Fernando Valley Central Labor Council. (U.C.B.)

San Pedro Labor Gazette. San Pedro. Weekly. 1926–1928? Official organ of the Central Labor Council of San Pedro and Wilmington. (U.C.B.)

The Socialist. Sacramento. Weekly. 1899. (Banc.)

Stockton Labor Journal. Stockton. Weekly and semimonthly. 1922–1959. Endorsed by the San Joaquin Central Labor and Building Trades Councils. (U.C.B.)

The Tribune. Sacramento. Weekly. 190–? Endorsed by the Federated Trades and Building Trades Councils. (Banc.)

Union Labor News. Glendale. Weekly. 1925–1928. Title varies. (U.C.B.)

Union Labor News. Santa Barbara. Weekly. 1925–1928? Endorsed by the Central Labor Union of Santa Barbara and the Santa Barbara County Building Trades Council. (U.C.B.)

Western Comrade. Llano. Monthly. 1913. Orientation: Cooperative, Socialist. (Banc.)

EMPLOYER ASSOCIATIONS

Bahrs, George O. *The San Francisco Employers' Council*. Philadelphia: University of Pennsylvania Press, 1948. 39 pp.

States that the Employers' Council was organized in 1938 in response to the changed conditions created in San Francisco by the emergence of a strongly organized trade-union movement. Almon E. Roth, first president of the Council, is quoted as declaring that "The Council seeks to achieve a balance in industrial relations founded upon a collective employer strength comparable to the collective strength of organized labor."

Bonnet, Clarence E. *Employers' Associations in the United States: A Study of Typical Associations*. New York: Macmillan, 1922. 594 pp.

Contains a number of references to California and Pacific Coast employers' associations.

Chambers, Clarke A. *California Farm Organizations: A Historical Study of the Grange, the Farm Bureau and the Associated Farmers, 1929–1941*. Berkeley: University of California Press, 1952. 277 pp.

Intended to serve as a general history of the development of farm organizations and their role in fulfilling the economic, social, and political needs of California farm owners. Chaps. 4–12, pp. 31–114, however, are entirely devoted to the labor policies and labor activities of these organizations, with particular stress on the dominant role assumed by the Associated Farmers in the field of labor relations.

Koster, Frederick J. *Law and Order and the San Francisco Chamber of Commerce*. An address by the president of the San Francisco Chamber of Commerce. San Francisco, 1918. 16 pp.

Surveys the accomplishments of the Law and Order Committee. This committee had been organized, through the efforts of the Chamber, to provide assistance to the Waterfront Employers Union in meeting a strike of the San Francisco longshoremen in 1916.

"The La Follette Committee's Hearings in California," *Land Policy Review*, vol. 4, Jan. 1941, pp. 27–31.

"Below is a condensed guide for professional workers and others wishing to use this material."

Ryder, David Warren. "San Francisco's Fight for Industrial Freedom," *Review of Reviews*, vol. 75, Jan. 1927, pp. 82–85.

Tells of the defeat of the building trades strike in 1921, the organization of the

Industrial Association, and its introduction of the American Plan. Sees the defeat of the carpenters' strike in 1926 as beneficial to San Francisco's economic life.

U.S. Congress. Senate. Committee on Education and Labor. *Violations of Free Speech and Rights of Labor*. Hearings, 76th Cong., 3d sess. Washington, 1940.

Part 52

Testimony: Paul A. Dodd on the Los Angeles labor market, pp. 19004–15; J. W. Buzzell on the relations of the Los Angeles Central Labor Council with the Los Angeles Chamber of Commerce, pp. 19026–28.

Parts 56, 57, 58

Review of the activities of The Neutral Thousands, Southern Californians, Inc., and other similar organizations in Southern California dedicated to the open shop. Testimony: Paul Shoup on the employers' view, pp. 20907–20; J. W. Buzzell on organized labor's experiences with open-shop organizations, pp. 21321–34, 21446–48.

Part 60

Testimony: John F. Shelley on organized labor in San Francisco, pp. 21951–57; Paul Eliel on Industrial Association of San Francisco, pp. 21962–73, 21998–2000; Edward Vandeleur on union organization in California agriculture, pp. 22052–62; Theodore R. Rasmussen on civil liberties and the right to collective bargaining, pp. 22062–75.

Part 61

"Committee of 43," pp. 22309–17. Testimony: Paul Shoup, pp. 22379–89 (Exhibit 9529); Harry Bridges, pp. 22407–10 (Exhibit 9531).

———. ———. ———. *Violations of Free Speech and Rights of Labor*. Report of the Committee. "Employers' Associations and Collective Bargaining in California."

77th Cong., 2d sess., S. Rept. 1150. Washington, 1942.

Part 1. "General Introduction," pp. 1–62.

Defines the scope of the California inquiry and comments on its significance and bearing on current national issues.

Part 2. "Organized Anti-Unionism in California Industry Prior to the Passage of the National Labor Relations Act," pp. 63–152.

Reviews some of the history of California employer-employee relations and describes the policies and practices of employers' organizations in the strikes of the mid-1930's.

Part 4. "Employers' Associations and Their Labor Policies in California's Industrialized Agriculture," pp. 407–672.

Includes a study of "area" and "commodity" agricultural employers' organizations, and of their labor policy applications in the agricultural strikes of the 1930's.

78th Cong., 1st sess., S. Rept. 398. Washington, 1943.

Part 5. "The Organization of Resistance to Collective Bargaining in California, 1935–1939," pp. 699–781.

Includes a review of resistance to collective bargaining in nonagricultural industries and in the legislative field.

Part 6. "A Study of Employers' Associations in the Los Angeles Area, 1935–1939," pp. 789–1022.

Among the organizations considered are the Los Angeles Chamber of Commerce, Merchants and Manufacturers Association, The Neutral Thousands, and Southern Californians, Inc.

Part 7. "A Study of Labor Policies of Employers' Associations in the San Francisco Bay Area, 1935–1939," pp. 1029–1127.

Considers the activities of the Industrial Association, the Waterfront Employers Association, the Committee of 43, and the San Francisco Employers Council.

78th Cong., 2d sess., S. Rept. 398. Washington, 1944.

Part 8. "The Associated Farmers of California, Inc.; Its Reorganization, Policies and Significance, 1935–1939," pp. 1129–1617.

Considers the relationship of the Associated Farmers to the Industrial Association of San Francisco, the California State Chamber of Commerce, and Southern Californians, Inc., and its labor policies as exemplified by its activities in various agricultural strikes and in the field of labor legislation.

Part 9. "The Origin and Promotion of Recent Legislation in California, Limiting Labor's Civil Rights," pp. 1641–96.

Refers to promotion by employer groups of antipicketing ordinances and other similar legislation.

"California Fruit Growers," *Fortune,* vol. 14, July 1936, pp. 47–56.

Cross, Ira B. *Collective Bargaining and Trade Agreements in the Brewery, Metal, Teaming and Building Trades of San Francisco, California.* California Publications in Economics, vol. 4, no. 4. Berkeley: University of California Press, 1918. Chap. 2, "Employers' Associations in San Francisco," pp. 243–47.

Davis, Henry L. Annual addresses to the Manufacturers and Employers of California, 1893, 1894. San Francisco, 1893 and 1894. 7 and 8 pp.

Frank, H. W. "The Merchants and Manufacturers' Association," *Land of Sunshine,* vol. 6, April 1897, pp. 212–17

Hosmer, Helen. "Associated Farmers: Sowers of Fascism," *New Masses,* vol. 33, Oct. 10, 1939, pp. 17–20; Oct. 17, 1939, pp. 13–15.

———. "Who Are the Associated Farmers?" *The Rural Observer,* vol. 1, Special Issue, Sept.–Oct. 1938, pp. 2–19.

Institute for Propaganda Analysis. "The Associated Farmers," *Propaganda Analysis* (New York), vol. 2, Aug. 1, 1939, pp. 1–16.

Kirstein, George G. *Stores and Unions.* New York: Fairchild Publications, 1950. "Association Bargaining in San Francisco," pp. 137–40.

Lapham, Roger, and Paul Eliel. *San Francisco Employers Council—Organization, Policies and Objectives.* San Francisco, 1938. 25 pp.

Los Angeles Industrial Union Council, CIO. *Unions Mean Higher Wages: The Story of the La Follette Committee Hearings in Los Angeles.* Los Angeles, 1940. 31 pp.

Neuberger, Richard L. "Who Are the Associated Farmers?" *Survey Graphic,* vol. 28, Sept. 1939, pp. 517–21, 555–57.

Roth, Almon E. *Objectives of the San Francisco Employers Council.* Address before the Industrial Relations Council of the American Management Association, Chicago, Ill., Feb. 17, 1939. Chicago, 1939. 12 pp.

Seldes, George. *Witch Hunt: The Technique and Profits of Red Baiting.* New York: Modern Age Books, 1940. "Tom Joad, That Red," pp. 237–45.

Smith, William H. *Local Employers' Associations.* Berkeley: Institute of Industrial Relations, University of California, 1955. 72 pp

Special Libraries Association of San Francisco. *Trade Associations: A Preliminary Directory for Northern California,* by Jeannette Cyr Stern. [San Francisco] 1934. 38 pp.

Watson, John S. *Statement of Associated Farmers of California to the La Follette Civil Liberties Committee.* [San Francisco? 1940] 14 pp.

OPEN AND CLOSED SHOP

California State Federation of Labor. *The 44 Year Campaign to Destroy Civil Liberties in California.* History of the activities of the Merchants and Manufacturers Association of Southern California. San Francisco [1944?] 24 pp.

Outlines the efforts of the Merchants and Manufacturers Association to keep Los Angeles and Southern California an open-shop area. Among the activities listed are supplying strikebreakers to member companies and promoting antiunion legislation such as antipicketing and antiboycott ordinances.

A History of Organized Felony and Folly: The Record of Union Labor in Crime and Politics. New York, 1923. 104 pp.

A reprint of thirty-two articles which had originally appeared in the *Wall Street Journal* in 1922, on the issue of the open shop versus the closed shop. Four of the articles relate to California labor issues: "Uplifting the Press" refers to the bombing of the Los Angeles *Times;* "Abe Ruef's Paint Eaters" deals with the San Francisco graft prosecutions during the administration of Mayor Eugene E. Schmitz; "Union Defense of Mooney" gives a particular version of the case; "Dethronement of a Czar" deals with the administration of P. H. McCarthy, one-time mayor of San Francisco.

Palmer, Frederick. "San Francisco of the Closed Shop," *Hampton's Magazine,* vol. 26, Feb. 1911, pp. 217–30.

Describes the San Francisco scene at a time when the closed shop was supreme.

Ryder, David Warren. "The Unions Lose San Francisco," *American Mercury,* vol. 7, April 1926, pp. 412–17.

Contends that the unions met complete defeat after decades of power because they had used that power to the injury of the community at large.

Ryder, Warren. "The 'American Plan' in San Francisco," *Review of Reviews,* vol. 67, Feb. 1923, pp. 187–90.

Describes the American Plan in operation a year after it had been inaugurated, with the Industrial Association setting wage scales and conducting various trade training schools.

U.S. Congress. Senate. Commission on Industrial Relations. *Final Report and Testimony.* 64th Cong., 1st sess., S. Doc. 415. Washington, 1916. "Open and Closed Shop Controversy in Stockton, California," vol. 5, pp. 4771–909; "Open and Closed Shop Controversy in Los Angeles," vol. 6, pp. 5485–999.

Testimony: John P. Irish, secretary, Stockton Chamber of Commerce, pp. 4773–90; Anton Johannsen, general organizer, United Brotherhood of Carpenters and Joiners of America, pp. 4790–809; Harrison Gray Otis, publisher, Los Angeles *Times,* pp. 5487–93, 5518–36; F. J. Zeehandelaar, secretary, Merchants and Manufacturers Association, pp. 5493–518, 5839–45; L. W. Butler, secretary-treasurer, Central Labor Council, pp. 5665–73; Katherine P. Edson, commissioner, California Welfare Commission, pp. 5682–98; Job Harriman, attorney for organized labor, pp. 5796–818.

"The American Plan: A Special Section Containing Articles by Warren H. McBride, F. C. Metcalf, Paul Scharrenberg...," *Pacific Industries,* vol. 1, Feb. 1922, pp. 13–24.

Berke, Nathan R. "Local Right to Work Ordinances: A New Problem in Labor and Local Law," *Stanford Law Review,* vol. 9, July 1957, pp. 674–89. [See Ted Finman, below]

The California Crusaders. [History and program of California Crusaders, Northern Division] [San Francisco] 1935. 11 pp.

California Labor League for Political Education. *Secretary-Treasurer's Report to C.L.L.P.E. Pre-Primary Convention.* San Francisco, April 1958. " 'Right to Work' Issue in California, 1944 through March 31, 1958," pp. 12–22.

California State Federation of Labor. *Report on "The Right to Work" Defense Fund, July 1, 1957 to November 30, 1958.* San Francisco, 1958. 22 pp.

———. *Shall California Labor Be Free or Slave?* San Francisco [1917?] 8 pp.

———. *Slave Bill 877 and What It Means to You.* San Francisco [1942] 8 pp.

Citizens' Alliance of San Francisco. *Constitution and By-Laws.* San Francisco [1906?] 15 pp.

———. *A Few Things Done.* [San Francisco? 1904?] 22 pp. [Includes "Think It Out," by Herbert George, pp. 6–13]

Eliel, Paul. "San Francisco, a Free City," *Law and Labor,* vol. 12, March 1930, pp. 53–58; April 1930, pp. 83–89.

"Enforcement of 'American Plan' by Restraints upon Interstate Commerce in Building Materials Enjoined," *Law and Labor,* vol. 6, March 1924, pp. 64–65.

Finman, Ted. "Local 'Right to Work' Ordinances: A Reply," *Stanford Law Review,* vol. 10, Dec. 1957, pp. 53–75. [See Nathan Berke, above]

Fitch, John A. "Los Angeles, a Militant Anti-Union Citadel," *Survey,* vol. 33, Oct. 3, 1914, pp. 4–6.

Grady, Harry F. "The Open Shop in San Francisco," *Survey,* vol. 37, Nov. 25, 1916, pp. 192–94.

———. "A Rejoinder," *Survey,* vol. 37, March 24, 1917, pp. 717–18. [See Robert Lynch, below]

Industrial Association of San Francisco. *An Analysis of San Francisco's Present Economic Condition.* [San Francisco?] 1925. 12 pp.

———. *Report of the American Plan Open Shop Conference Held in San Francisco June 16–17–18, 1927.* [San Francisco, 1927] [17] pp.

Jacobson, Pauline. "Otis: Jehovah of Industrial Freedom." Series of articles in San Francisco *Bulletin,* Dec. 9, 16, 23, 30, 1911; Jan. 6, 20, 27, 1912.

Los Angeles County Labor Committee to Save Our State. *Save Our State from the Compulsory Open Shop.* Los Angeles [1958?] 47 pp.

Lynch, Robert Newton. "The Open Shop in San Francisco: A Reply," *Survey,* vol. 37, March 24, 1917, pp. 716–17. [See Harry Grady, above]

National Industrial Peace Association. *Industrial Peace.* [San Francisco] C. A. Murdock & Co., 1910. 32 pp.

Otis, Harrison Gray. *What the Course of "The Times" Shall Be.* Letter of General Otis to Mr. and Mrs. Chandler. [Los Angeles? 1917] 15 pp.

Ryder, Warren. "The 'American Plan' in San Francisco: An Excellent Remedy for Labor Troubles," *Barron's,* vol. 3, Sept. 24, 1923, pp. 3, 12.

"Shipowners' Association Maintaining Central Employment Agencies ...," *Law and Labor,* vol. 11, May 1929, pp. 99–101.

"Story of Forty-Year War for a Free City," Los Angeles *Times,* Oct. 1–31, Nov. 1–2, 1929. [Daily title of series varies]

Town Hall, Los Angeles. *Report on Proposition No. 18 ... to Be Submitted to the Electors of the State of California November 4, 1958.* Los Angeles, Oct. 1958. 50 pp.

LOYALTY PROGRAMS

Brown, Ralph S., Jr., and John D. Fassett. "Security Tests for Maritime Workers: Due Process under the Port Security Program," *Yale Law Journal,* vol. 62, July 1953, pp. 1163–1208.

Examines "the legal issues—the power of the government to deny private employment, the authorization of the Coast Guard to undertake this program, the adequacy of the standards and the procedures it employs. . . . " A number of the cases cited refer to screening procedures in Pacific Coast ports.

Committee Against Waterfront Screening. *The Case Against Waterfront Screening: Questions and Answers of Interest to Americans.* San Francisco [1956?] [15] pp.

Tells how waterfront screening started, how it has been applied, and how it has affected some two thousand waterfront workers. Included as footnotes are excerpts from a decision of the 9th U.S. Circuit Court of Appeals, October 26, 1956.

Federation for Repeal of the Levering Act. *California's New Loyalty: The Levering Act and the Program of the Federation for Repeal of the Levering Act.* San Francisco, 1950. 10 pp.

Reviews the major implications of the Levering Act for public employees.

Harper, Lawrence A. "Shall the Professors Sign?" *Pacific Spectator,* vol. 4, Winter 1950, pp. 21–29.

Discusses loyalty oaths, academic freedom, freedom in general, and tenure.

Horowitz, Harold W. "Loyalty Test for Employment in the Motion Picture Industry," *Stanford Law Review,* vol. 6, May 1954, pp. 438–72.

Reviews the nature and extent of the application of loyalty employment standards in the motion picture industry. Particularly noted is the influence of governmental investigations and pressures from non-industry groups on the application of these standards.

————. "Report on the Los Angeles City and County Loyalty Programs," *Stanford Law Review,* vol. 5, Feb. 1953, pp. 233–46.

Reviews the operation of the two loyalty programs and examines the essential differences between them. Attempts to evaluate the data obtained from the operation of the programs as a step toward the solution of such fundamental problems connected with governmental loyalty policies as the establishment of proper hearing procedures, the limitation of the scope of the programs, and the definition of standards of loyalty.

International Longshoremen's and Warehousemen's Union. *Union Busting, New Model: The Case Against the Coast Guard Screening Program.* San Francisco, 1951. 21 pp.

Maintains that the Coast Guard screening program is another form of the blacklist, which has often been used in the past to discourage trade-union organization among workers and which has been especially aimed at the militant and active elements among them. Citing Coast Guard screening hearings as proof, the claim is made that the International Longshoremen's and Warehousemen's Union is the special target of the screening program.

"Shepheard Says 'Reds' Are Threat to Port Security," *The Log,* Oct. 1952, pp. 47–48, 74, 77.

Comments by Admiral Shepheard, chief of the Coast Guard's Office of Merchant Marine Safety, on the MCS and the ILWU in relation to the Coast Guard's port security program.

United Defense Committee Against "Loyalty" Checks. *If We Remain Silent.* Los Angeles, 1949. 18 pp.

Examines the significance of loyalty checks required of Los Angeles workers under a city council ordinance. At the time, the constitutionality of such checks had been challenged in an appeal to the United States Supreme Court, the first such appeal to come before the Court.

American Civil Liberties Union of Northern California. *Crisis at the University of California.* A statement to the people of California. San Francisco, 1949. 9 pp.

———. *Crisis at the University of California.* A further statement to the people of California. San Francisco, 1950. 14 pp

California. Legislature. Assembly. Committee on Judiciary. *Loyalty Oaths.* Report of the Subcommittee. Assembly Interim Committee Reports, vol. 20, no. 7, 1957–59. Sacramento, 1959. 40 pp.

California. University. *University of California Security Manual.* Berkeley: University Security Office, 1957. 32 pp.

Cogley, John. *Report on Blacklisting.* Vol. 1, *Movies.* Vol. 2, *Radio–Television* [New York?] The Fund for the Republic, 1956. 312 and 287 pp.

The Fund for the Republic. Editorial comments on John Cogley's *Report on Blacklisting.* New York [1956?] [39] pp.

Horowitz, Harold W. "Legal Aspects of 'Political Blacklisting' in the Entertainment Industry," *Southern California Law Review,* vol. 9, April 1956, pp. 263–305.

Kantorowicz, Ernst H. *The Fundamental Issue: Documents and Marginal Notes on the University of California Loyalty Oath.* San Francisco: Parker Printing Co., 1950. 40 pp.

Kerby, Phil. "Hollywood Blacklist," *Frontier,* vol. 3, July 1952, pp. 5–7.

McCall, Mary C. "As a Matter of Fact," *Frontier,* vol. 3, May 1952, pp. 9–11, 26.

Matthews, J. B. "Did the Movies Really Clean House?" *American Legion Magazine,* Dec. 1951, pp. 12, 51–56.

Poe, Elizabeth. "The Hollywood Story," *Frontier,* vol. 5, May 1954, pp. 6–25.

Royle, Selena. "I Was Accused," *Frontier,* vol. 3, Aug. 1952, pp. 5–8.

Thomas, John, and others. "Teachers Under Attack," *Frontier,* vol. 5, Feb. 1954, pp. 10–14.

Trimble, Peter. "Thought Control on the Water Front," *Nation,* vol. 173, July 14, 1951, pp. 27–29.

SYNDICALISM

INDUSTRIAL WORKERS OF THE WORLD

Blaisdell, Lowell L. *The Desert Revolution, Baja California, 1911.* Madison: University of Wisconsin Press, 1962. 268 pp. Illustrated.

A documented history of the five-month revolutionary war fought by the forces of the Liberal Party of Mexico in Lower California. The California labor movement of that time, especially that of the left, was peculiarly involved in this conflict. The war was directed by Ricardo Flores Magón, leader of the Liberal Party, from the offices of the anarchist newspaper *La Regeneración* in Los Angeles; it was actively supported by the Socialist Party and other labor groups; and the Liberal Party's army, which had in its ranks many soldiers of fortune, also included a sizeable contingent of IWW members from California.

Brissenden, Paul F. *The I.W.W.: A Study of American Syndicalism.* Columbia University Studies in History, Economics and Public Law, no. 193. New York: Columbia University Press, 1919. 432 pp.

An historical and descriptive sketch of the background, birth, and first thirteen years of the IWW (1905–1917). Generally considered the most authoritative on the subject, the study is general in nature but references to IWW activity in California are sufficient to afford an adequate history of the organization in that area. The index is detailed and the bibliography may be the most exhaustive available for that period.

California. Commissioner to Investigate Disturbances in San Diego. *Report of Harris Weinstock, Commissioner ... to His Excellency Hiram W. Johnson, Governor of California.* Sacramento, 1912. 22 pp.

States that officials of the City and County of San Diego, in collusion with private citizens or vigilantes, had denied the right of free speech to alleged members of the IWW and other persons and had subjected them to extreme cruelties. Recommends that the State Attorney General institute criminal proceedings against officials and private citizens of San Diego who are found to have acted in violation of state laws.

Caughey, John W. *Their Majesties The Mob.* Chicago: University of Chicago Press, 1960. 214 pp.

A documentary history of the vigilante process in America during the last century. A number of the documents deal with California events, and two have direct reference to California labor: "Raid on the I.W.W. Hall," pp. 127–129, and "The Hollywood Technique," pp. 154–58.

Duff, Harvey. *The Silent Defenders: Courts and Capitalism in California.* Chicago: Industrial Workers of the World, 1919. 112 pp.

In December 1917 some fifty members of the Industrial Workers of the World were arrested in Sacramento, California, following a minor explosion at the governor's mansion. They were eventually prosecuted by the federal government for violating various wartime laws. Five of the defendants died in custody. Forty-three of those remaining refused counsel and chose to conduct a silent defense. This pamphlet, in the main, is the story of the trial and this unusual form of defense.

Gambs, John S. *The Decline of the I.W.W.* Columbia University Studies in History, Economics and Public Law, no. 361. New York: Columbia University Press, 1932. 268 pp.

The stated purpose of this study of IWW activity from 1917 to 1931 is to supplement Paul F. Brissenden's work on the organization's first thirteen years of existence. The numerous references to the IWW in California provide an interpretive summary of its activities there. The bibliography is probably the most complete on the subject for the period treated.

McGowan, Joseph A. *History of the Sacramento Valley.* New York: Lewis Historical Publishing Co., 1961. Vol. 2, chap. 43, "The 'Wobblies' and Public Apprehension," pp. 106–17.

Describes the conditions on the Durst Ranch which led to the Wheatland riot. The latter part of the chapter tells of Kelly's Army of the unemployed in Sacramento in 1914 and of its difficulties with the city authorities.

Parker, Carleton H. *The Casual Laborer and Other Essays.* New York: Harcourt, Brace and Howe, 1920. 199 pp.

In the spring of 1914 Professor Parker, then executive secretary of the California State Immigration and Housing Commission, was deputized by the federal government to investigate the Wheatland riot. The investigation of this incident prompted the professor to make a more thorough study of the casual worker and the IWW. These essays grew out of this study. An appendix contains the complete report of the Wheatland riot.

————. "The Wheatland Riot and What Lay in Back of It," *Survey,* vol. 31, March 21, 1914, pp. 768–70.

Comprises the report made by Parker, secretary of the California Commission of Immigration and Housing, to the U. S. Commission on Industrial Relations. The riot of migratory agricultural workers in 1913, in which four men were killed, is described, as are the conditions which sparked the riot. The report also treats of the role of the IWW in the incident.

Parker, Cornelia Stratton. *An American Idyll: The Life of Carleton H. Parker.* Boston: Atlantic Monthly Press, 1919. 190 pp.

Written by his wife a year after his death, the biographical sketch stresses Parker's interest in the migrant and casual laborers of California and other western states, and in the philosophy of the IWW, which was then the chief influence among these groups of workers.

San Francisco Labor Council. *San Diego Free Speech Controversy.* Report to the San Francisco Labor Council by Special Investigating Committee, headed by O. A. Tweitmoe and Paul Scharrenberg. San Francisco, 1912. 12 pp.

The committee, after assessing the evidence it has gathered, reports that the San Diego Chamber of Commerce and the business community generally have been actively supporting violence against members or alleged members of the Industrial Workers of the World, that a paid constabulary exists, and that organized vigilantes have committed assaults and atrocities against unarmed men. The police, according to the committee, are no less guilty, having cooperated with the vigilantes in deportations and having themselves committed acts of brutality.

Thompson, Fred, comp. *The I.W.W., Its First Fifty Years, 1905–1955: The History of an Effort to Organize the Working Class.* Chicago: Industrial Workers of the World, 1955. 203 pp.

Contains numerous scattered but significant references to IWW activity in California. Includes useful chapter bibliographies.

U.S. Congress. Senate. Commission on Industrial Relations. *Final Report and Testimony.* 64th Cong., 1st sess., S. Doc. 415. Washington, 1916. "The Seasonal Labor Problem in Agriculture," vol. 5, pp. 4911–5027.

Testimony: E. Clemens Horst, president, E. Clemens Horst Co., pp. 4922–32; Carleton H. Parker, executive secretary, California State Commission of Immigration and Housing, pp. 4932–36; George H. Speed, general organizer, IWW, pp. 4936–49.

Van Valen, Nelson. "The Bolsheviki and the Orange Growers," *Pacific Historical Review,* vol. 22, Feb. 1953, pp. 39–50.

Tells of the methods used by Southern California orange growers to break an IWW-led strike of orange workers in 1918.

Wedge, Frederick R. *Inside the I.W.W.* Berkeley, Calif.: Privately printed, 1924. 48 pp.

Refers to experiences during the 1923 IWW longshore strike in San Pedro, California.

American Civil Liberties Union. *The Truth about the I.W.W.* New York, 1922. "The Sacramento Trial," pp. 24–28, 44–45.

Bell, George L. "Wheatland Hop-Field Riot," *Outlook,* vol. 107, May 16, 1914, pp. 118–23.

Booth, Edward Townsend. "Wild West," *Atlantic Monthly,* vol. 126, Dec. 1920, pp. 785–88.

"California Injunction Against the I.W.W. Sustained by the Supreme Court of California . . . ," *Law and Labor,* vol. 6, Sept. 1924, pp. 240–43.

Cleland, Robert Glass. *California in Our Time.* New York: Knopf, 1941. Chap. 6, "Durst and Mooney," pp. 88–104.

"Conviction of 27 Starts General Strike in San Pedro," *Industrial Pioneer,* vol. 1, Aug. 1923, pp. 3–4.

"The Cossack Regime in San Diego," *Mother Earth,* vol. 7, June 1912, pp. 97–107.

"Country-Wide Free Speech Fights," *Mother Earth,* vol. 7, April 1912, pp. 46–49.

"The Curse of California," by Spectator, *Industrial Pioneer,* vol. 4, May 1926, pp. 33–38.

Delaney, Ed. "Wheatland: The Bloody Hop Field," *Industrial Pioneer,* vol. 2, Feb. 1925, pp. 34–36.

Downing, Mortimer. "The Case of the Hop Pickers," *International Socialist Review,* vol. 14, Oct. 1913, pp. 210–13.

Edwards, George. "Free Speech in San Diego," *Mother Earth,* vol. 10, July 1915, pp. 182–85.

Fisher, Harry. "Over Eight Hundred Hear Geo. Speed Expose the Truth about the San Pedro Raid," *Industrial Pioneer,* vol. 2, Aug. 1924, pp. 3–6, 43–44.

[Ford, Richard] "The People of the State of California, Respondent, Against Richard Ford (Otherwise Known as 'Blackie' Ford) and H. D. Suhr, Appellants. . . . " N.p. [1914] 4 vols. 1444 pp. Typewritten.

Gerhard, Peter. "The Socialist Invasion of Baja California, 1911," *Pacific Historical Review,* vol. 15, Sept. 1946, pp. 295–304.

Gilmore, Inez Haynes. "Marysville Strike," *Harper's Weekly,* vol. 58, April 4, 1914, pp. 18–20.

Goldman, Emma. *Living My Life.* New York: Knopf, 1931. Vol. 1, chap. 38, pp. 486–503. [San Diego free speech fights]

———. "The Outrage of San Diego," *Mother Earth* (San Diego ed.), vol. 7, June 1912, pp. 115–22.

Hill, Mary Anderson. "The Free Speech Fight at San Diego," *Survey,* vol. 28, May 4, 1912, pp. 192–94.

Parker, Carleton. "The California Casual and His Revolt," *Quarterly Journal of Economics,* vol. 30, Nov. 1915, pp. 110–26.

Plotting to Convict Wheatland Hop Pickers. Oakland, Calif.: The International Press [1913?] 28 pp.

Reitman, Ben L. "The Respectable Mob," *Mother Earth* (San Diego ed.), vol. 7, June 1912, pp. 109–14.

Ryder, David Warren. "California: Ashamed and Repentant," *New Republic,* vol. 51, June 1, 1927, pp. 41–44.

The Sage of La Jolla [pseud., Henry A. Adams] *History versus Histerics: An Open Letter to the Vigilantes and the I.W.W*. [Los Angeles? 1912?] [7] pp.

Schroeder, Theodore A. *Free Speech for Radicals.* New York: Free Speech League, 1916. Chap. 9, "History of the San Diego Free Speech Fight," pp. 116–90.

Shippy, Hartwell. "The Shame of San Diego," *International Socialist Review,* vol. 12, May 1912, pp. 718–23.

Sinclair, Upton. "Civil Liberties in Los Angeles," *Industrial Pioneer,* vol. 1, Aug. 1923, pp. 27–29.

"Solidarity Wins in Fresno," *International Socialist Review,* vol. 11, Apr. 1911, pp. 634–36.

Sterling, Jean. "Silent Defence in Sacramento," *Liberator,* vol. 1, Feb. 1919, pp. 15–17.

U.S. Federal Writers' Project. "The Industrial Workers of the World in California Agriculture." [Oakland? 1936?] 65 pp. Typewritten.

———. "Toilers of the World." [Oakland? 1936?] 21 pp. Typewritten.

Weintraub, Hyman. "The I.W.W. in California: 1905–1931." Unpublished M.A. thesis. University of California, Los Angeles, 1947. 328 pp.

Whitaker, Robert. "What Ails California?" *Industrial Pioneer.* vol. 2, Jan. 1925, pp. 8, 44; Feb. 1925, pp. 45–46.

Whitten, Woodrow C. "The Wheatland Episode," *Pacific Historical Review,* vol. 17, Feb. 1948, pp. 37–42.

Wilson, Ione Elizabeth. "The I.W.W. in California, with Special Reference to Migratory Labor (1910–1913)." Unpublished M.A. thesis. University of California, Berkeley, 1946. 79 pp.

Woehlke, Walter V. "Bolshevikis of the West," *Sunset,* vol. 40, Jan. 1918, pp. 14–16, 70–72.

———. "The I.W.W.," *Outlook,* vol. 101, July 6, 1912, pp. 531–36.

CRIMINAL SYNDICALISM LAW

California. District Courts of Appeal. *California Appellate Decisions.* San Francisco: Recorder Printing and Publishing Co., 1920–1922.

Vol. 33, no. 1599. Crim. no. 891, First Appellate District, Division One, Oct. 18, 1920, pp. 346–56.

An appeal by James P. Malley from a judgment of the Superior Court, San Francisco, of conviction of violating the Criminal Syndicalism Act.

Vol. 33, no. 1609. Crim. no. 727, Second Appellate District, Division Two, Nov. 24, 1920, pp. 594–604.

An appeal by N. Steelik from a judgment of the Superior Court of Los Angeles County of conviction of criminal syndicalism.

Vol. 34, no. 1629. Crim. no. 937, First Appellate District, Division One, Feb. 4, 1921, pp. 414–20.

An appeal by John C. Taylor from a judgment of the Superior Court of Alameda County of conviction of criminal syndicalism.

Vol. 38, no. 1756. Crim. no. 907, First Appellate District, Division One, April 25, 1922, pp. 26–27.

An appeal by Charlotte A. Whitney from a judgment of the Superior Court of Alameda County of conviction of violating the Criminal Syndicalism Act.

Vol. 38, no. 1785. Crim. no. 523, Third Appellate District, Aug. 4, 1922, pp. 743–49.

An appeal by Walter Wismer from a judgment of the Superior Court of Sacramento County of conviction of violating the Criminal Syndicalism Act.

Vol. 38, no. 1785. Crim. no. 609, Third Appellate District, Aug. 4, 1922, pp. 750–58.

An appeal by James Roe from a judgment of the Superior Court of Sacramento County of conviction of violating the Criminal Syndicalism Act.

Vol. 39, no. 1822. Crim. no. 637, Third Appellate District, Dec. 11, 1922, pp. 633–36.

An appeal by J. A. Casdorf and Earl Firey from a judgment of the Superior Court of Sacramento County of violation of the Criminal Syndicalism Act.

California. Governor, 1923–1927 (Friend W. Richardson). *Case of Charlotte A. Whitney.* [Sacramento, 1925] 14 pp.

Convicted in February 1920 on charges of violating the Criminal Syndicalism Act of California, Miss Whitney fought for a reversal of the conviction and won support from various quarters. This report, released under the signature of Governor Richardson of California, is a review of the issues in the case prepared from court records and other sources and was apparently intended to serve as a negative reply to many requests for executive clemency.

———. Governor, 1927–1931 (Clement C. Young). *The Pardon of Charlotte Anita Whitney.* Sacramento, 1927. 15 pp.

The governor of California pardons Miss Whitney, who had been convicted in February 1920 of violating the California Criminal Syndicalism Act. Here, in the full text of the pardon message, the governor reviews the facts of the case which determined his decision.

Chafee, Zechariah, Jr. *Free Speech in the United States.* Cambridge: Harvard University Press, 1954. Chap. 10, "Criminal Syndicalism," pp. 326–54.

Examines the legal implications of the injunction issued against the IWW by a California Superior Court in 1923 and its relationship to the California Criminal Syndicalism Act. The author questions the legal propriety of the injunction and notes that its purpose—the destruction of the IWW by circumventing trial by jury—was not realized. By 1930 Communists, whom the author appears to consider the successors to the IWW, were being prosecuted under the Criminal Syndicalism Act. This examination is followed by a brief review of the prosecution and conviction of Anita Whitney under the Act in 1919–20. The author then analyzes the U.S. Supreme Court's decision in 1927 to uphold the conviction, giving particular consideration to the sharp disagreement of Justices Brandeis and Holmes with the reasoning of the majority on freedom of speech and its application to the Syndicalism Act.

Christensen, Otto. *Statement Submitted to the Attorney General of the United States, Concerning the Present Status of the I.W.W. Cases.* Chicago: Hawkins and Loomis Co. [1922?] 42 pp.

Includes discussion of the Sacramento convictions.

"Criminal Syndicalism Statutes Before the Supreme Court," *University of Pennsylvania Law Review and American Law Register,* vol. 76, Dec. 1927, pp. 198–203.

Observes that of the questions occupying the Court in relation to the statutes, the principal one was whether they violated the constitutional guarantee of free speech.

Dowell, Eldridge Foster. *A History of Criminal Syndicalism Legislation.* Baltimore: Johns Hopkins Press, 1939. Chap. 4, "Attempts to Moderate or Repeal the Criminal Syndicalism Laws: California, 1921–1933," pp. 122–27.

An appendix contains the text of the California Criminal Syndicalism Act.

International Labor Defense. *Free the Imperial Valley Prisoners.* Appeal to the United States Supreme Court by the seven workers convicted of criminal syndicalism in Imperial Valley, California, June 14, 1930. New York: Workers Library Publishers, 1932. 48 pp.

The seven workers, in an informal appeal, ask the Supreme Court to reverse their conviction, contending that it violated their basic constitutional rights. They seek to prove that no evidence of even a single act of actual violence was submitted at their trial and that they were convicted only for trying to organize a union among Mexican and Filipino agricultural and American packing-shed workers who in January and February 1930 had spontaneously struck to improve their economic conditions.

Quin, Michael. *The C.S. Case Against Labor: The Story of the Sacramento Criminal Syndicalism Railroading.* San Francisco: International Labor Defense, Northern California District [1935?] 31 pp.

A report of the trial in 1935 of eighteen men and women for violation of the California Criminal Syndicalism Act. The trial climaxed the opposition to a wave of trade-union organization and strike actions in the California agricultural fields in 1933 and 1934. The case, which attracted widespread attention, resulted in the conviction of eight of the defendants.

Richmond, Al. "Anita Whitney—Communist," *Political Affairs,* vol. 34, April 1955, pp. 44–54.

A biographical sketch of Anita Whitney as a social worker, suffragette leader, and active participant in militant labor movements. Her prosecution under the California Criminal Syndicalism Act is given some prominence.

Solow, Herbert. *Union Smashing in Sacramento: The Truth about the Criminal Syndicalism Trial.* With prefatory notes by Samuel S. White, of the San Francisco Joint Board of the International Ladies' Garment Workers Union, and Travers Clement, co-author of "Rebel America." New York: National Sacramento Appeal Committee, 1935. 31 pp.

An account of the efforts made by the Cannery and Agricultural Workers Industrial Union in the early 1930's to gain improved working conditions and higher wages for California agricultural workers and the opposition to these efforts by the employers, headed by the Associated Farmers. This opposition, violent at times, was climaxed by the arrest in 1934 of eighteen leaders of the union and their indictment for violation of the California Criminal Syndicalism Act. The account describes the trial and the conviction of eight of the defendants, and particularly emphasizes the methods used to influence the jury. In an appendix the National Sacramento Appeal Committee, which was representing Norman Mini, one of the defendants, refers to differences with the International Labor Defense, representing the other defendants.

"Activities of the I.W.W. Enjoined in California; Membership Forbidden...," *Law and Labor,* vol. 5, Oct. 1923, pp. 272–74.

American Civil Liberties Union. California Committee. *California Attacked by One of Her Own Laws!* [San Francisco, 1925?] 8 pp.

Ballantine, Henry W. "Injunction: Extension of Criminal Equity; Criminal Syndicalism Punishable as Contempt of Court," *California Law Review,* vol. 13, Nov. 1934, pp. 63–68.

The California Crusaders. *The California Criminal Syndicalism Law: A Factual Analysis.* San Francisco, 1936. 30 pp.

Callahan, Daniel F. "Criminal Syndicalism and Sabotage," *Monthly Labor Review,* vol. 14, April 1922, pp. 803–12.

Chafee, Zechariah, Jr. "California Justice," *New Republic,* vol. 36, Sept. 19, 1923, pp. 97–100.

Clement, Travers. "Red Baiters' Holiday in Sacramento," *Nation,* vol. 140, March 13, 1935, pp. 306–8.

Cohen, Myer, ed. *Selected Supreme Court Decisions.* New York: Harper, 1937. "Whitney v. California," pp. 16–20.

de Ford, Miriam Allen. "An Injury to All," *Overland,* vol. 82, Dec. 1924, pp. 536–37, 575.

[Dolsen, James H.] *The Defense of a Revolutionist by Himself.* Story of the trial of James H. Dolsen. San Francisco: By the author [1920?] 112 pp.

Flynn, Elizabeth Gurley. *Daughters of America: Ella Reeve Bloor—Anita Whitney.* New York: Workers Library Publishers, 1942. 15 pp.

Gartz, Mrs. Kate (Crane). *More Letters.* (Third Series.) Long Beach, Calif.: By Mary Craig Sinclair [1927?] 151 pp.

Gendel, Martin. "Criminal Law: Criminal Syndicalism; Red Flag Law: History of Enforcement in California," *California Law Review,* vol. 19, Nov. 1930, pp. 64–69.

General Defense Committee. *California, the Beautiful and Damned.* Chicago [1927?] 31 pp.

Hichborn, Franklin. *The Case of Charlotte Anita Whitney.* N.p., 1920. 12 pp.

"Injunctions to Restrain Criminal Acts," *University of Pennsylvania Law Review and American Law Register,* vol. 73, Jan. 1925, pp. 185–90.

"An Interesting Revelation of I.W.W. Methods," *Law and Labor,* vol. 4, Dec. 1922, pp. 340–42.

Labor Defense League, San Francisco. *Citizens of California! Especially of the Bay Cities. Do You Wish to Be Known as Approving the Arrest and Conviction of...Miss Charlotte Anita Whitney...?* [San Francisco, 1920?] [8] pp.

McGregor, Helen A. "Criminal Syndicalist Act: Constitutional Law: Validity of the Act under the Free Speech Clause," *California Law Review,* vol. 10, May 1922, pp. 512–18.

Mini, Norman. "The California Dictatorship," *Nation,* vol. 140, Feb. 20, 1935, pp. 224–26.

Oakes, Edwin Stacey. *The Law of Organized Labor and Industrial Conflicts.* Rochester, N.Y.: Lawyers Co-operative Publishing Co., 1927.

Chap. 12, "Criminal Anarchy—Criminal Syndicalism—Sabotage," pp. 160–99.

"The Pardon of Anita Whitney," *New Republic,* vol. 51, Aug. 10, 1927, pp. 310–13.

"Personal Knowledge of Unlawful Character of Organization Must Be Proved to Sustain Conviction . . . ," *Law and Labor,* vol. 6, May 1924, pp. 134–35.

Richmond, Al. *Native Daughter: The Story of Anita Whitney.* San Francisco: Anita Whitney 75th Anniversary Committee, 1942. Chap. 6, "The Case of Anita Whitney," pp. 90–140.

"The Sacramento Criminal Syndicalism Cases," *International Juridical Association Bulletin,* vol. 4, Nov. 1935, pp. 4–6.

Symes, Lillian. "California, There She Stands," *Harper's,* vol. 170, Feb. 1935, pp. 360–68.

Whitten, Woodrow C. "Criminal Syndicalism and the Law in California, 1919–1927." Unpublished Ph.D. dissertation. University of California, Berkeley, 1946. 275 pp.

———. "The Trial of Charlotte Anita Whitney," *Pacific Historical Review,* vol. 15, Sept. 1946, pp. 286–94.

Wilson, Lawrence. "California Convicts Itself," *Christian Century,* vol. 52, April 17, 1935, pp. 506–8.

LABOR CASES

McNAMARA BROTHERS

Adamic, Louis. *Dynamite: The Story of Class Violence in America.* New York: Viking, 1931. Part 4, "The McNamara Affair," pp. 179–253.

Discusses the bombing of the Los Angeles *Times* building in 1910 against the background of the California and national trade-union movement as represented by the AFL. Noting the common use of dynamite by AFL unions against aggressive antiunion employers, the author asserts that the bombing of the Los Angeles *Times* was planned and directed by top San Francisco AFL officials as part of a plan to organize Los Angeles. He contends that Samuel Gompers was aware of the guilt of the McNamaras and that top AFL leaders must have known of the plan to have them plead guilty. The outcome of the McNamara affair, he suggests, robbed the AFL of its militant spirit and dealt the rapidly rising socialist movement both in Los Angeles and nationally a decisive blow.

Ainsworth, Ed. *History of the Los Angeles Times.* [Los Angeles, 1941?] 42 pp.

"The Great Struggle," pp. 15–18, tells of the *Times'* difficulties with the Typographical Union, beginning in 1887. "The Bombing," pp. 21–28, is an account of the bombing of the *Times* building in 1910.

American Federation of Labor McNamara Ways and Means Committee. "A Statement to the American Public on the McNamara Case," *American Federationist,* vol. 19, Jan. 1912, pp. 17–23.

The committee consisted of Samuel Gompers and other national officers of the AFL. The statement seeks to explain and justify the AFL's participation in the defense of the McNamara brothers before their admission of guilt in the bombing of the Los Angeles *Times.*

Baillie, Hugh. *High Tension: The Recollections of Hugh Baillie.* New York: Harper, 1959. Chap. 2, "Rogers and Darrow," pp. 10–27.

A veteran reporter writes about his first important assignment—covering the two trials of Clarence Darrow in 1912 and 1913 on charges of attempted bribery of prospective jurors for the trial of the McNamara brothers, who had been indicted for the bombing of the Los Angeles *Times* building in 1910.

Burns, William J. *The Masked War.* The story of a peril that threatened the United States by the man who uncovered the dynamite conspirators and sent them to jail. New York: Doran, 1913. 328 pp.

The annotated reports of the Burns Detective Agency operatives and Burns's own investigations, convictions, and observations are arranged to form a connected narrative. They are offered as evidence of the guilt of J. B. McNamara and the complicity of J. J. McNamara and other officials of the International Association of Bridge and Structural Iron Workers in the Los Angeles *Times* and other bombings.

Cohn, Alfred, and Joe Chisholm. *"Take the Witness!"* New York: Stokes, 1934. Chaps. 22–24, pp. 195–225.

Tells of attorney Earl Rogers' part in preparing the prosecution's case against the McNamara brothers and of his role as chief counsel in the defense of Clarence Darrow on charges of jury bribery in the McNamara case. The authors lay claim to exclusive information which for the first time explains why the McNamara brothers unexpectedly pleaded guilty. The Darrow trial is presented in a manner to emphasize Earl Rogers' skill.

Darrow, Clarence. *The Story of My Life*. New York: Scribner, 1932. Chaps. 21–22, "The McNamara Case," "Lights and Shadows," pp. 172–91.

The chief defense counsel for the McNamara brothers recalls some of the key incidents in the case and in his own defense against charges of jury bribery. Prominent in the recollections is an attempt to explain the motives and circumstances that prompted him to advise the McNamaras to change their plea to guilty.

Debs, Eugene V. "The McNamara Case and the Labor Movement," *International Socialist Review,* vol. 12, Jan. 1912, pp. 397–401.

Condemns the officials of the AFL, including Samuel Gompers, for joining the employers in denouncing the McNamaras; defines the approach of the Socialist Party in situations that involve class conflict; and stresses some of the questions in the case which he contends have not been sufficiently dealt with.

Geisler, Jerry (as told to Pete Martin). *The Jerry Geisler Story*. New York: Simon & Schuster, 1960. "Earl Rogers and the Bar Examination," pp. 269–80; "Defending Darrow," pp. 285–88.

Speaks of his minor part in the San Francisco graft prosecution cases and in the defense of Darrow in the McNamara case.

Gompers, Samuel. "The McNamara Case," *American Federationist,* vol. 18, June 1911, pp. 433–50.

States labor's position on violence, the reasons why union men could not have been implicated in the explosion of the Los Angeles *Times* building, and why labor must join in the defense of the McNamara brothers.

———. *President Gompers' Report to the 31st Convention of the AFL.* Washington, D.C., 1911. 60 pp.

Includes an account of the action taken by the convention on the McNamara case (pp. 51–55).

"Larger Bearings of the McNamara Case," *Survey,* vol. 27, Dec. 30, 1911, pp. 1413–36.

> The entire issue is devoted to the McNamara case. Among the contributors are Victor L. Berger, Louis D. Brandeis, Robert L. Hoxie, W. B. Dickson, J. Howard Melish, Edwin R. Seligman, Meyer London, Samuel McCune Lindsay, and Lincoln Steffens. Includes a petition sent to President Taft calling for the setting up of a federal commission on industrial relations

Lawler, Oscar. "The Bombing of the Los Angeles Times: A Personal Reminiscence," *Claremont Quarterly,* vol. 6, Winter 1959, pp. 25–32.

> The attorney representing the Merchants and Manufacturers Association in the prosecutions resulting from the bombing of the Los Angeles *Times* building in 1910 recalls some of the incidents surrounding the bombing and the trial of the McNamara brothers. He refers particularly to two phases of the defense strategy: alleged "feelers" suggesting a plea of guilty by J. B. McNamara and dismissal of charges against J. J. McNamara, thus avoiding involvement of the International Association of Bridge and Structural Iron Workers; and the sudden pleas of guilty by both defendants. The suggested explanation of the change of plea is that Clarence Darrow hoped thereby to avoid prosecution for alleged jury tampering.

McManigal, Ortie E. *The National Dynamite Plot.* Los Angeles: Neale Co., 1913. 91 pp.

> On April 12, 1911, McManigal and J. B. McNamara were arrested in Detroit, Michigan, by Burns detectives for complicity in the Los Angeles *Times* bombing. McManigal soon afterward turned state's evidence. Here he offers his version of the part he and other principals played in the *Times* and other bombings.

Mayo, Morrow. *Los Angeles.* New York: Knopf, 1933. Part 3, pp. 139–99.

> The story of the drive for the open shop in Los Angeles, the bombing of the *Times* building, and the events which followed it is retold in a dramatic and popular vein. A novel approach to the McNamara case is introduced, expressing doubts that J. B. McNamara's confession was bona fide or that he had actually placed the bomb.

O'Higgins, Harvey J. "The Dynamiters: A Great Case of Detective William J. Burns," *McClure's Magazine,* vol. 37, Aug. 1911, pp. 346–64.

> Another version of Burns's clever detective work in developing the case against the McNamara brothers in the bombing of the Los Angeles *Times.*

Palmer, Frederick. "Otistown of the Open Shop," *Hampton's Magazine,* vol. 26, Jan. 1911, pp. 29–44.

> Maintains that the militant advocacy of the open shop by Otis and the Merchants and Manufacturers Association had much to do with creating an enmity that came to a climax in the bombing of the Los Angeles *Times.*

Perlman, Selig, and Philip Taft. *History of Labor in the United States, 1896–1932.* Vol. 4, *Labor Movements.* New York: Macmillan, 1935. Chap. 26, "Dynamite and the Public," pp. 318–25.

Sees the bombing of the Los Angeles *Times* in 1910 as the culmination of a long and bitter war between the International Association of Bridge and Structural Iron Workers and the Erectors' Association, dominated by the United States Steel Corporation, rather than a reckless dynamite plot, as it appeared to the outside world. The authors do not accept the view, often expressed, that the McNamaras' confession put an end to the militancy of the American Federation of Labor, citing later developments to support their belief that it did not.

Robinson, William Wilcox. *Lawyers of Los Angeles: A History of the Los Angeles Bar Association and of the Bar of Los Angeles County.* Los Angeles: Ward Ritchie Press, 1959. Chap. 8, "Bombs and Bribery," pp. 131–54.

Contains references to General Otis' feud with organized labor in Los Angeles and an outline of the story surrounding the conviction of the McNamara brothers for the bombing of the Los Angeles *Times* and its aftermath, including an account of Lincoln Steffens' famous "compromise" and a description of the trials of Clarence Darrow for attempted bribery of McNamara jurors.

St. Johns, Adela Rogers. *Final Verdict.* New York: Doubleday, 1962. Chaps. 48–62, pp. 367–458.

An account by the daughter of attorney Earl Rogers of his participation in the prosecution of the McNamara brothers for the bombing of the Los Angeles *Times* and of his later role as chief defense counsel in the prosecution of Clarence Darrow for attempted bribery. The author's recollections of Darrow are less than flattering.

Schroeder, Theodore A. "The McNamaras: Martyrs or Criminals?" *Forum,* vol. 54, Sept. 1915, pp. 329–36.

Analyzes some of the psychological factors involved in forming value judgments of martyrs and criminals and how they apply to the McNamara brothers.

Steffens, Lincoln. *The Autobiography of Lincoln Steffens.* New York: Harcourt, Brace, 1931. Part 4, chaps. 4–7, "Dynamite," "Settling the Dynamiters' Case," "The Churches Decide Against Christianity," "I Become a Goat," pp. 659–701.

The renowned muckraker describes how he tried to get the golden rule accepted in the McNamara case and how he almost succeeded. He tells of getting the cooperation of some of the most prominent men in Los Angeles, including General Otis and Harry Chandler of the Los Angeles *Times,* Clarence Darrow, chief counsel for the McNamara brothers, and even the McNamaras themselves. But he implies that the chain was evidently not complete because, though the McNamaras kept to their bargain, the prosecution did not. Chap. 7 tells how he was denounced for his golden-rule role and his part in the Darrow trials for alleged jury bribery.

Stimson, Grace Heilman. *The Rise of the Labor Movement in Los Angeles.* Berkeley: University of California Press, 1955. Chaps. 21–22, "The 'Crime of the Century,'" "Reactions and Aftermath," pp. 366–419.

A vivid account of the bombing of the Los Angeles *Times* building on October 1, 1910, and the significant events which followed it. The varied reactions to the bombing, the frantic search for the guilty, the arrest of Ortie McManigal and the McNamara brothers, the confession by McManigal, and the preparations for the trial are climaxed by the sudden pleas of guilty by the McNamaras and the stunned reaction of the labor movement. Serving as an anticlimax is an account of the two trials of Clarence Darrow on bribery charges and the arrest and trials of Matthew Schmidt and David Kaplan.

Stone, Irving. *Clarence Darrow for the Defense: A Biography.* New York: Doubleday, Doran, 1941. Chaps. 8–9, "This Is War," "Prisoner's Dock," pp. 248–343.

A master popularizer retells the story of the McNamara brothers and the bombing of the Los Angeles *Times* building in 1910. Told through the medium of fiction biography, the story adds up to an unusual interpretation of the available facts in the McNamara case and Clarence Darrow's role in it.

U.S. Commission on Industrial Relations. *The National Erectors' Association and the International Association of Bridge and Structural Iron Workers,* by Luke Grant. Washington, 1915. 192 pp.

Describes the organization and development of the two organizations and the nature of their labor relations. The growth of the open-shop war initiated by the National Erectors Association is traced, as is the war's culmination in the conviction of the McNamara brothers for the bombing of the Los Angeles *Times* and in the dynamite conspiracy trials involving the top officials of the union. An appendix contains copies of agreements reached at times between the two organizations and the constitution and bylaws of the Erectors Association.

U.S. Congress. Senate. Commission on Industrial Relations. *Final Report and Testimony.* 64th Cong., 1st sess., S. Doc. 415. Washington, 1916. "Labor and the Law," vol. 11, pp. 10451–928.

Testimony: Anton Johannsen, general organizer, United Brotherhood of Carpenters and Joiners of America, pp. 10667–704.

Weinberg, Arthur N., ed. *Attorney for the Damned.* Foreword by Justice William O. Douglas. New York: Simon and Schuster, 1957. "They Tried to Get Me," pp. 491–531.

Clarence Darrow's summation to the jury while on trial for alleged bribery of jurors in the McNamara case not only serves as a refutation of the charges against him but, because of the nature of the trial, also adds to knowledge of the facts in that case.

Baker, Robert Munson. "Why the McNamaras Pleaded Guilty to the Bombing of the Los Angeles Times." Unpublished M.A. thesis. University of California, Berkeley, 1949. 113 pp.

Berkman, Alexander. "Labor on Trial," *Mother Earth,* vol. 10, July 1915, pp. 166–68.

———. "The Schmidt-Caplan Defense," *Mother Earth,* vol. 10, Aug. 1915, pp. 208–11.

Bohn, Frank. "The Passing of the McNamaras," *International Socialist Review,* vol. 12, Jan. 1912, pp. 401–4.

Burns, William J. (as told to editors of *McClure's*). "How Burns Caught the Dynamiters," *McClure's,* vol. 33, Jan. 1912, pp. 325–29.

Cleland, Robert Glass. *California in Our Time.* New York: Knopf, 1941. Chap. 5, "Dynamite," pp. 67–87.

Fitch, John A. "The Dynamite Case," *Survey,* vol. 29, Feb. 1, 1913, pp. 607–17.

Gompers, Samuel. "A.F. of L. and the Iron Workers," *Survey,* vol. 29, Feb. 1, 1913, pp. 621–23.

———. *Seventy Years of Life and Labor.* New York: Dutton, 1925. 2 vols. Vol. 2, chap. 32, "Violence," pp. 174–93.

Haywood, William D. "Get Ready," *International Socialist Review,* vol. 11, June 1911, pp. 725–29.

Hunt, Rockwell D. *California's Stately Hall of Fame.* Publications of the California History Foundation, no. 2. Stockton: College of the Pacific, 1950. "Joseph Lincoln Steffens, Arch-enemy of Special Privilege," pp. 505–10.

Johannsen, Anton, Clarence Darrow, and Mother Jones. *The True History of the Famous McNamara Case.* Kansas City, Mo.: Carpenters Local 61 [1915?] 32 pp.

"Labor's Illuminating Moment," *Craftsman,* vol. 21, Jan. 1912, pp. 451–53.

"The Los Angeles Conspiracy Against Organized Labor," *International Socialist Review,* vol. 11, Nov. 1910, pp. 262–66.

Miller, Richard Connelly. "Otis and His Times: The Career of Harrison Gray Otis of Los Angeles." Unpublished Ph.D. dissertation. University of California, Berkeley, 1961. "Trial by Chemistry," pp. 397–416; chap. 13, "The Solidification of the Stiffs," pp. 417–86.

Nadeau, Remi. *Los Angeles from Mission to Modern City.* New York: Longmans, Green, 1960. Chap. 10, "A Suitcase Full of Dynamite," pp. 121–41.

Newmark, Marco R. *Jottings in Southern California History.* Los Angeles: Ward Ritchie Press, 1955. "Great Journalist—Harrison Gray Otis," pp. 103–5. [A thumbnail biographical sketch]

"On the Road," *Mother Earth,* vol. 10, Sept. 1915, pp. 238–42.

Owen, William C. "The Los Angeles Explosion," *Mother Earth,* vol. 5, Dec. 1910, pp. 310–15.

"Rally to the Defense of Caplan and Schmidt," *Mother Earth,* vol. 10, July 1915, pp. 168–72.

Schmidt, Matthew A. "Address before His Executioner in the Court of Los Angeles," *Mother Earth,* vol. 10, Feb. 1916, pp. 397–99.

Searing, Richard Cole. "The McNamara Case: Its Causes and Results." Unpublished M.A. thesis. University of California, Berkeley, 1952. 132 pp.

Steffens, Joseph Lincoln. *The Letters of Lincoln Steffens.* Edited by Ella Winter and Granville Hicks. Introductory notes and a memorandum by Carl Sandburg. New York: Harcourt, Brace, 1938. 2 vols. Vol. 1, pp. 273–363 (scattered); vol. 2, pp. 773–1049 (scattered).

Taft, Philip. *The A.F. of L. in the Time of Gompers.* New York: Harper, 1957. Chap. 17, "Steel and the McNamaras," pp. 272–88.

Tichenor, Henry M. *A Wave of Horror.* Rip-Saw Series no. 8. St. Louis, Mo.: Rip-Saw Publishing Co., n.d. 31 pp.

Woehlke, Walter V. "The End of the Dynamite Case—Guilty," *Outlook,* vol. 99, Dec. 16, 1911, pp. 903–8.

MOONEY-BILLINGS

Adamic, Louis. *Dynamite: The Story of Class Violence in America.* New York: Viking, 1931. Part 5, chap. 26, "The Mooney-Billings Frame Up," pp. 264–77.

States that the disclosures following the Mooney-Billings trials, pointing to widespread use of perjured testimony, had convinced many that Mooney and Billings had been framed and that aggressive open-shop elements in San Francisco, headed by the utility corporations, had initiated the frame-up. Maintains that efforts to free Mooney and Billings failed because the executive and legal machinery of California was manipulated by big business interests to keep them in prison, out of fear that their release would give workers a sense of victory and encourage an attack on the open shop.

Burke, Robert E. *Olson's New Deal in California.* Berkeley: University of California Press, 1953. Chap. 5, "The End of the Mooney Case," pp. 48–58.

Briefly reviews the Mooney case and tells of the pardoning of Mooney by Governor Culbert L. Olson. Describes the varied reactions to the pardon and comments on Mooney's last years.

Duffus, R. L. *The Tower of Jewels: Memoirs of San Francisco.* New York: Norton, 1960. Chap. 5, "Preparedness Day, 1916," pp. 128–65.

The writer's unhurried reminiscences of years spent on the staff of Fremont Older's *Bulletin* include an account of the Preparedness Day bombing and the prosecution of Mooney and Billings that followed it.

Goldberg, Louis P., and Eleanore Levenson. *Lawless Judges*. New York: Rand School Press, 1935. "Mooney and Billings Case," pp. 201–8.

An analysis of the legal basis of two decisions of the California Supreme Court in the Mooney case: its denial of an appeal for a new trial and its refusal in 1930 to recommend a pardon for Mooney and Billings.

Hays, Arthur Garfield. *Trial by Prejudice*. New York: Covici-Friede, 1933. Chap. 2, "Mooney and Billings," pp. 153–248.

Examines the character of the witnesses and the nature of their testimony in the trials which followed the San Francisco Preparedness Day parade bombing on July 22, 1916, and reviews the post-trial history of the Mooney-Billings case to 1932.

Hopkins, Ernest Jerome. *What Happened in the Mooney Case*. New York: Brewer, Warren and Putnam, 1932. 258 pp.

A newspaperman who covered the San Francisco Preparedness Day bombing and the prosecutions resulting from it maintains that all the proof of the guilt or innocence of Tom Mooney is not to be found in the prosecution record. He believes that much of this proof is rather to be found in an examination of the period preceding the bombing and in the post-trial developments. He examines in some detail the war with Mexico and its effect on Mexican nationals in San Francisco, the war in Europe and its impact on various national and local groups, the partisan passions aroused by widespread labor-capital strife, and the gradual disclosure after the trials of many evidences of perjury and subornation of perjury. He concludes that a study of all these factors points to a miscarriage of justice.

In the Matter of the Application Made on Behalf of Thomas J. Mooney for a Pardon. Decision of Hon. James Rolph, Jr., Governor of the State of California, together with the report of Hon. Matt I. Sullivan, former Chief Justice of the Supreme Court of the State of California, and special adviser to the governor in the above entitled proceeding. Sacramento: State Printing Office, 1932. 92 pp.

Governor Rolph denies the application of Tom Mooney for a pardon in a brief statement which also serves as an introduction to the report on which this decision was mainly based. The major portion of the report is concerned with the activities and political and economic beliefs of Mooney before the Preparedness Day bombing, as well as miscellaneous matters in the years after Mooney's conviction. The rest of the report deals with the prosecution record.

Marcantonio, Vito. *We Accuse: The Story of Tom Mooney*. New York: International Labor Defense, 1938. 31 pp.

Stating that a new generation had grown up since Tom Mooney and Warren Billings were convicted and imprisoned for the San Francisco Preparedness Day bombing in 1916 and that it should know the story of their imprisonment, the author reviews the highlights in the record of the case. References to Mooney and Billings as trade-union organizers among utility workers, the election of C. M. Fickert as San Francisco District Attorney, and his relations with the utility companies are followed by a review of the bombing, the arrests, trials, developments pointing to the questionable character of the witnesses and their testimony, federal investigations, actions by various governors and courts, the second trial of Mooney in 1933, and a pending appeal to the United States Supreme Court in 1938.

The Mooney-Billings Report. Suppressed by the Wickersham Commission. New York: Gotham House, 1932. 243 pp.

An extensive examination of the legal proceedings in the series of cases generally known as the "Mooney-Billings Case" but including the Rena Mooney, Israel Weinberg, and Edward D. Nolan cases. Among the more important features of the report are a brief retelling of the bomb explosion; a general history of the trials, appeals, and applications for executive clemency; and an analysis of the conduct of the prosecution preceding, during, and following the trials. The analysis includes the preliminary investigation of the explosion, the methods used in identifying witnesses, the role and use of the press, the character of the prosecution witnesses and the prosecution's relationship to them, alleged suppression of evidence, and a treatment of the Oxman affair.

Mooney Molders Defense Committee, Tom. *Justice Raped in California.* San Francisco, 1917. 47 pp.

Contends that the prosecution and conviction of Tom Mooney and Warren K. Billings for the bombing of the Preparedness Day parade in San Francisco, July 22, 1916, was a deliberate frame-up by antilabor elements in retaliation for the activities of these two men in behalf of labor. Claims that many of the prosecution witnesses had been proven to be of questionable reliability and guilty of perjury, accuses District Attorney C. M. Fickert and his assistant, E. A. Cunha, of having masterminded the frame-up, and intimates bribery and attempts at bribery. Of particular interest are the numerous contemporary photographs of persons and places referred to in the text.

――――. *Labor Leaders Betray Tom Mooney.* San Francisco, 1931. 50 pp.

Accuses California and national AFL leaders of betraying Tom Mooney and Warren Billings. Claims that they have not only failed actively to seek their pardon, but on the contrary have conspired to keep them behind bars. Statements and acts of such AFL leaders as William Green, Matthew Woll, Paul Scharrenberg, P. H. McCarthy, A. W. Brouillet, Michael Casey, John O'Connell, and others are offered as proof of the claim.

――――. *Tom Mooney's Message to Organized Labor, His Friends and Supporters, and All Liberal and Progressive Voters of California.* San Francisco, 1938. [29] pp.

Urges support of State Senator Culbert L. Olson, candidate for governor of California in the 1938 election. Included with the message is the text of a resolution introduced in the California State Senate March 16, 1937, calling for a full pardon for Tom Mooney and Senator Olson's extended remarks on it.

Refregier, Anton. *Prisoner 31921.* The story of the Mooney case told in pictures. With an introduction by Theodore Dreiser. New York: International Labor Defense [1934?] 32 pp.

Full-page drawings, accompanied by explanatory notes, illustrate key incidents in the Mooney story.

"Report on the Mooney Dynamite Cases in San Francisco, Submitted by President Wilson's Mediation Commission," *Official Bulletin,* U.S. Committee on Public Information, January 28, 1918, pp. 14–15.

This was the first federal investigation into the Mooney case. The report comments on the atmosphere of industrial conflict surrounding the case and on the role of utilities detective Martin Swanson in the Mooney arrests and prosecutions. It considers Oxman's testimony at the trial as decisive and suggests the need of a new trial as a result of the post-trial revelation that Oxman had attempted to suborn perjury. Recommends presidential intervention.

Swanson, Martin. *Theodore Roosevelt and the Mooney Case.* San Francisco, 1921. 32 pp.

Contains two letters: one is from Theodore Roosevelt to Felix Frankfurter, counsel for the Mediation Commission appointed by President Wilson to review the Mooney–Billings prosecutions; the other is from Martin Swanson, who helped prepare the prosecutions, to Mercer Green Johnston, past Rector of Trinity Church, Newark, New Jersey.

Symes, Lillian. "Our American Dreyfus Case: A Challenge to California Justice," *Harper's,* vol. 162, May 1931, pp. 641–52.

Points to the similarity between the Dreyfus case of France and the Mooney–Billings case as reflected in the parallel methods of manufactured evidence, perjured testimony, and involvement of people in high places. Reviews some of the generally accepted facts in the case, giving special emphasis to the parts played by such acknowledged open-shop advocates as the utility corporations, the San Francisco Chamber of Commerce, and the District Attorney of San Francisco, Charles M. Fickert, whom Miss Symes links with the United Railroads.

Wells, Evelyn. *Fremont Older.* New York: Appleton-Century, 1936. Chaps. 21–23, "Mooney," "A Newspaper Tragedy," "Mooney Again," pp. 289–336.

The story of Fremont Older's long and intimate connection with the Mooney case told against the background of his activity as editor of the San Francisco *Bulletin* and later of the *Call.* The account emphasizes Older's earlier belief that Mooney was guilty and his later realization that Mooney was the victim of perjured testimony when the Oxman letters came to light. The *Bulletin* was the first to publish these letters, and the sensational Densmore Report was published in the *Call.*

Williams, Brad. *Due Process.* The fabulous story of criminal lawyer George T. Davis and his thirty-year battle against capital punishment. New York: Morrow, 1960. 336 pp.

George T. Davis was one of the Tom Mooney defense attorneys during Mooney's last years in prison. The author assigns a considerable role to Davis in the defense of Mooney and in making his pardon by Governor Olson possible. The early chapters of the biography are given over almost entirely to the Mooney case.

American Civil Liberties Union. *The Story of Mooney and Billings at a Glance.* New York [1937?] [8] pp.

Berkman, Alexander. "Legal Assassination," *Mother Earth,* vol. 11, Oct. 1916, pp. 635–39.

———. "The Life and Death Struggle in San Francisco," *Mother Earth,* vol. 11, Dec. 1916, pp. 698–701.

[Billings, Warren K.] "Warren K. Billings, the Story of a Rebel." A biographical interview conducted by Corrine L. Gilb for the Institute of Industrial Relations Oral History Project, University of California, Berkeley. Jan.–March 1957. 376 pp. Typewritten.

Blackstone, Robert. *By Their Deeds.* Drawings by Joy Postele. New Orleans: Mooney Defence Committee of Dixie, 1937. 27 pp.

Bruce, John. *Gaudy Century: The Story of San Francisco's Hundred Years of Robust Journalism.* New York: Random House, 1948. Chap. 40, "The Preparedness Day Parade," pp. 274–82.

California. Legislature. Senate. *Consideration of Assembly Concurrent Resolution No. 18 [Mooney pardon resolution], as Recorded in the Senate Journals of March 16 and 17, 1937.* Sacramento, 1938. 28 pp.

California Mooney-Billings Committee. *The Story of Mooney and Billings.* San Francisco, 1929. 22 pp.

Carrasco, H. C. *Eulogy of Tom Mooney.* Delivered at the dedication of the Tom Mooney Labor School, San Francisco, Aug. 2, 1942. San Francisco, 1942. 8 pp.

———. *A San Franciscan Tells the Story of the Mooney Case.* San Francisco: Railway Employees' Committee for the Release of Thomas J. Mooney [1935?] 30 pp.

Clement, Travers. "Mooney," *American Mercury,* vol. 17, May 1929, pp. 26–33.

Cockran, Bourke. *The Mooney Case.* Address at Washington, D.C., July 28, 1918; and a Memorial to President Wilson submitted by a labor delegation through the Hon. Bourke Cockran. San Francisco: International Workers Defense League [1918?] 31 pp.

————. *To the Commissioners Appointed by the President to Investigate the Conditions under Which Thomas J. Mooney Was Convicted of Murder* ... San Francisco, 1917. 58 pp.

de Ford, Miriam Allen. "California's Disgrace: How and why Tom Mooney was framed; including a complete history of the world-famous case from 1916 to 1933." N.p., 1938. 187 pp. Typewritten.

————. *They Were San Franciscans.* Caldwell, Ida.: Caxton Printers, 1941. Chap. 8, "Last of the Tolstoyans: Fremont Older," pp. 212–34.

Eastman, Crystal. "The Mooney Congress," *Liberator,* vol. 1, March 1919, pp. 19–24.

Fitch, John A. "The San Francisco Bomb Cases," *Survey,* vol. 38, July 17, 1917, pp. 305–12.

————. "The Strange Case of Tom Mooney," *Survey Graphic,* vol. 24, Dec. 1935, pp. 586–90.

Frost, Richard Hindman. "The Mooney Case." Unpublished Ph.D. dissertation. University of California, Berkeley, 1960. 737 pp. [Note: Mr. Frost is at present writing a comprehensive documented history of the Mooney case. Its materials are being drawn primarily from legal documents and from newspaper and manuscript collections, including the Mooney papers in the Bancroft Library. The Stanford University Press is planning its publication for 1965.]

Goldman, Emma. *Living My Life.* New York: Knopf, 1931. 2 vols. Vol. 2, pp. 573–92. [Tom Mooney]

————. "Stray Thoughts," *Mother Earth,* vol. 11, Sept. 1916, pp. 615–22.

Haldeman-Julius, Marcet. *The Amazing Frame-up of Mooney and Billings.* How California has stolen thirteen years from these labor leaders. Girard, Kans.: Haldeman-Julius Publications, 1931. 113 pp.

Hindman, Jay A. "The Mooney Case," *American Law Review,* vol. 52, Sept.–Oct., 1918, pp. 743–46.

Hunt, Henry T. *The Case of Thomas J. Mooney and Warren K. Billings.* Abstract and an analysis of record before Governor Young of California. New York: National Mooney-Billings Committee, 1929. 444 pp.

————. "Mooney and Billings," *New Republic,* vol. 58, April 10, 1929, pp. 219–23.

International Workers Defense League. *Excerpts from the Press Concerning the Preparedness Parade Murders in San Francisco.* Prepared for the attention of the President's Investigating Committee. San Francisco, 1917. 46 pp.

———. *Justice and Labor in the Mooney Case*. San Francisco, 1919. 19 pp.

"Is Mooney Guilty?" *Commonwealth,* vol. 14, March 1, 1938, pp. 47–54.

Johnston, James A. *Prison Life Is Different*. Boston: Houghton Mifflin, 1937. Chap. 23, "Mooney, Billings, the McNamara Brothers, and Other Dynamiters," pp. 224–36.

"Lynch Jury in San Francisco Convicts Thomas Mooney," *Mother Earth,* vol. 12, March 1917, pp. 11–14.

McGurrin, James. *Bourke Cockran: A Free Lance in American Politics*. New York: Scribner, 1948. Chap. 20, "The World War—Tom Mooney," pp. 289–303.

McNutt, Maxwell. *Significant Facts Concerning the Cases [Mooney-Billings]: Before the Special Commission appointed by the President of the United States*. San Francisco: Pernau Publishing Co., 1917. 96 + xlv pp.

———. *Before the Governor of the State of California: Petition for Pardon of Thomas J. Mooney*. San Francisco: Pernau-Walsh Printing Co., 1918. 92 pp. + Addenda, 167 pp.

———. *Before the Governor of the State of California: Reply of Thomas J. Mooney to Brief Filed by District Attorney of the City and County of San Francisco Against Petition for Pardon*. San Francisco: Pernau-Walsh Printing Co., 1918. 30 pp.

Minor, Robert. *The Frame-Up System: Story of the San Francisco Bomb*. San Francisco: International Workers Defense League, 1916. 16 pp.

———. "The San Francisco Bomb," *Mother Earth,* vol. 11, Sept. 1916, pp. 608–12.

Montgomery, Roger. "Did Mooney Plant the Bomb?" *in* Roger Sherman Loomis, ed., *Freshman Readings*. Boston: Houghton Mifflin, 1925. Pp. 433–39.

Mooney Defense Committee of Southern California. *Justice Is Waiting*. Los Angeles, 1930. 31 pp.

Mooney Molders Defense Committee, Tom. *Just-ice for Tom Mooney*. San Francisco [1931?] 10 pp.

———. *Pardon Tom Mooney—Innocent*. San Francisco, 1930. 30 pp.

———. *The Story of Tom Mooney, Molder and Miner's Son,* by a star labor reporter. San Francisco [192–?] 7 pp.

———. *A Voice from a Living Grave*. San Francisco, 1930. 30 pp.

National Mooney-Billings Committee. *The Scandal of Mooney and Billings*. The decisions of the California Supreme Court, the Advisory Pardon Board, and Governor Young denying pardons to Mooney and Billings. New York, 1931. 62 pp.

Nolan, Ed. *The Preparedness Day Tragedy*. Oakland: *The World,* 1916. 15 pp.

Nye, Gerald P. *Justice for Tom Mooney*. Washington: Government Printing Office, 1929. 30 pp.

Ocana, Floreal. *El Proceso del Capitalismo: Tom Mooney, Otra Victima de la Barbarie Americana*. Barcelona: Ediciones de "La Revista Blanca" [1931?] 32 pp.

Olin, John M. *Review of the Mooney Case*. Its relation to the conduct in this country of Anarchists, I.W.W. and Bolsheviki. [Madison, Wis.? 1919?] 104 pp.

Schall, Thomas D. "Why Is Mooney in Prison?" *Plain Talk,* vol. 4, May 1929, pp. 513–27.

Spangler, Colin Irving. "Frame-Up or Square Deal?" *Sunset,* vol. 38, May 1917, pp. 28–29, 90–92.

U.S. Congress. House. *Connection of Certain Department of Labor Employees with the Case of Thomas J. Mooney*. 66th Cong., 1st sess., H. Doc. 157. Washington, 1919. Part 1, "The Mooney Case: A Report Addressed to the Secretary of Labor by J. B. Densmore, Director General of Employment." 90 pp. Part 2, "Exhibit B: Meeting of the Grand Jury of the City and County of San Francisco, State of California." 68 pp.

———. ———. Committee on the Judiciary. *Tom Mooney*. Hearings before Subcommittee No. 1 on H.J. Res. 297. 75th Cong., 3d sess., Serial 18. Washington, 1938. 154 pp.

Walker, J., Aaron Sapiro, Cyrus B. King, and Frank P. Walsh. *A Review of the Facts in the Case of Thomas Mooney for Consideration by His Excellency, Hon. James Rolph, Jr., Governor of California*. Dec. 1, 1931. 56 pp.

Zimmerman, Charles S. *Mooney and Billings Must Be Freed!* Radio address, Station WEVD, July 29, 1936. New York: Dressmakers' Union, Local 22, ILGWU, 1936. 14 pp.

BRIDGES

Biddle, Francis. *In Brief Authority*. Garden City, N.Y.: Doubleday, 1962. Chap. 19, "Harry Bridges—Communist?" pp. 296–307.

Tells how, shortly after he had been appointed U.S. Attorney General, he was faced with the difficult decision whether to deport Bridges as a Communist. In 1941 Judge Sears had ruled that he was deportable. Biddle allowed Sears' decision to go before the Board of Immigration Appeals for review. The Board reversed Sears in January 1942, holding that the record did not sustain his findings. Biddle, however, sustained Judge Sears and ordered Bridges' deportation.

Bridges Defense Committee, Harry. *Dean Landis Speaks on the Case of Harry Bridges.* San Francisco [1939?] 15 pp.

Annotated excerpts from the report of James MacCauley Landis, Dean of Harvard Law School and special trial examiner in the deportation hearing of Harry Bridges in 1939. The excerpts refer, in the main, to the testimony and character of the chief prosecution witnesses, Stanley M. Doyle, Harper Knowles, John J. Keegan, Raphael P. Bonham, Laurence A. Milner, and John L. Leech. Also included are excerpts from the testimony of Harry Bridges.

———. *Harry Bridges.* Who he is, what he has been doing in the labor movement, why he is on trial for deportation! San Francisco [1939?] 12 pp.

The scheduled deportation hearing before Dean Landis in 1939 is viewed against the background of the struggle of the Pacific Coast maritime workers for trade-union organization and improved economic conditions and against company union-ism. Biographical references tell of Bridges' early days as seaman and longshore-man, his role in the organization and leadership of the Pacific Coast maritime strikes of 1934 and 1936–37, and his part in organizing workers in industries away from the waterfront. The charge of Communism is reviewed and some of the scheduled witnesses at the impending hearing are discussed.

Bridges-Robertson-Schmidt Defense Committee. *The Law and Harry Bridges.* San Francisco, 1952. [26] pp.

A review and legal history of the official and unofficial hearings, trials, and congres-sional actions to 1952 in the efforts to deport Harry Bridges. Those included are the investigations by the San Francisco Police Department and Federal Immigra-tion Service in 1934, congressional measures in 1936 and 1937, the Landis hearing in 1939, the Allen and Hobbs bills in Congress in 1940, the Sears hearing in 1941, and the Bridges–Robertson–Schmidt trial of 1949. The last is dealt with in some detail.

Dies, Martin. *The Trojan Horse in America.* New York: Dodd, Mead, 1940. Chap. 13, "An Australian Communist Controls American Ship-ping," pp. 176–95.

The chairman of the U.S. House of Representatives committee investigating un-American activities contends that Harry Bridges is a Communist. As proof, he cites Bridges' associations with known and suspected Communists and his state-ments at the deportation hearings before Dean Landis.

Hallinan, Vincent. *A Lion in Court.* New York: Putnam, 1963. Chaps. 13–14, "The Case Which Changed My Life," "The Bridges Trial," pp. 227–77.

The widely known attorney tells of the circumstances that prompted him to assume the role of chief defense counsel in the 1950 trial of Harry Bridges when he was being tried for irregularities allegedly committed by him and others in applying for citizenship. The author describes some of the extraordinary episodes of that trial, characterizing the tactics of the government prosecutors as questionable, the position of the presiding judge as dubious, and the testimony of the prosecution witnesses as perjurious.

Huberman, Leo. *Storm over Bridges*. Illustrated by Giacomo Patri. San Francisco: Harry Bridges Defense Committee, 1941. 89 pp.

Reviews the hearing in 1941 to deport Harry Bridges and compares it with a previous hearing in 1939. After considering the similarity of motives, type of witnesses, and testimony of the two hearings, the author concludes that the inspector in this hearing, Judge Charles B. Sears, must come to the same conclusion as did Dean Landis in 1939 and dismiss all charges against Bridges.

Hyman, Alvin D. "The Front Page: Harry Bridges on the Stand," *in* William Hogan and William German, eds., *The San Francisco Chronicle Reader*. New York: McGraw-Hill, 1962. Pp. 279–86.

Covers two of the many days when Bridges appeared on the witness stand to defend himself against a charge of perjury in applying for citizenship. The days were February 8 and 9, 1950.

International Longshoremen's and Warehousemen's Union, C.I.O. *Because a Man Stood Up for Human Rights*. What the late Mr. Justice Frank Murphy said about the first three frame-up attempts against Harry Bridges. Introduction by Louis Goldblatt, secretary-treasurer, ILWU. San Francisco, 1949. 20 pp.

The full text of the concurring opinion of U.S. Supreme Court Justice Murphy in the Court's action reversing a lower court decision and holding a warrant for the deportation of Harry Bridges, issued by the Attorney General in 1942, to be unlawful. The Court's decision, as expressed in the opinion of Justice Murphy, was based on the Bill of Rights and on fundamental principles of American jurisprudence.

―――――. *The Everlasting Bridges Case*. San Francisco, 1955. 14 pp. Illustrated.

Summarizes all attempts to deport Harry Bridges up to 1955. The summary includes an investigation in 1934 and 1935 by the District Director of Immigration and Naturalization in San Francisco, an investigation by a congressional committee in 1936, an investigation by the Solicitor of the Department of Labor in 1937, hearings in 1938 and 1939, the Allen and Hobbs congressional bills in 1940, the hearing in 1941, Attorney General Biddle's deportation order in 1942, and the trial of Bridges, Robertson, and Schmidt in 1949. The occasion for the summary was a new trial scheduled to begin on June 20, 1955.

Konvitz, Milton R. *Civil Rights in Immigration*. Ithaca, N.Y.: Cornell University Press. 1953. "The Case of Harry Bridges," pp. 114–22.

A chronological summary of the case.

Minton, Bruce, and John Stuart. *Men Who Lead Labor.* Drawings by Scott Johnston. New York: Modern Age Books, 1937. Chap. 7, "Harry Bridges, Voice of the Rank and File," pp. 172–202.

A brief biographical sketch of Bridges' early years in Australia is followed by a description of waterfront conditions in San Francisco in the twenties and early thirties, Bridges' participation in attempts to revive the longshore union during that period, his rise to leadership in 1933 and 1934, and his activity as a Pacific Coast labor leader to the time of the affiliation of the longshore union with the CIO.

Perkins, Frances. *The Roosevelt I Knew.* New York: Viking, 1946. Pp. 312–19. [Harry Bridges]

Describes her involvement, as Secretary of Labor, in the efforts to deport Bridges and tells of President Roosevelt's advice to her on the problem.

[Sears, Charles B.] U.S. Immigration and Naturalization Service, Department of Justice. File No. 55973/217. *In the Matter of Harry Renton Bridges: Memorandum of Decision.* Washington, 1941. 187 pp.

Following the Landis decision in 1939, Congress amended the deportation statute so that it would more clearly apply to Bridges. As the Immigration and Naturalization Service was then part of the Department of Justice, having been transferred there from the Department of Labor in 1940, Attorney General Robert Jackson appointed Judge Sears as a special examiner to take evidence against Bridges. With the aid of the new statute and some new witnesses Judge Sears ruled that he was deportable.

Trumbo, Dalton. *Harry Bridges.* A discussion of the latest efforts to deport Civil Liberties and the rights of American labor. Los Angeles: League of American Writers, 1941. 28 pp.

Written against the background of west coast waterfront labor history and previous attempts to deport Bridges, this presents the 1941 deportation hearing as a denial of guaranteed civil liberties and a misuse of legislative and legal procedures to destroy the effectiveness of an honest and able representative of labor.

Ward, Estolve E. *Harry Bridges on Trial.* New York: Modern Age Books, 1940. 240 pp.

An effective dramatization of the 1939 deportation hearing of Harry Bridges before Dean Landis. Testimony of the numerous prosecution and defense witnesses affords a broad review of Pacific Coast maritime history and personalities of the 1930's. Bridges' responses to exhaustive questioning at the hearing form a composite autobiography, telling of his early home background, his activities as sailor, longshoreman, and waterfront leader, and the nature of his trade-union and political convictions.

American Committee for Protection of the Foreign Born. *The Supreme Court on the Bridges Case.* Concurring opinion of Justice Frank Murphy. Introduction by Carol King. [New York] 1945. 15 pp.

Anderton, John E. *The Nationality Status of Harry Renton Bridges: An Opinion*. [San Francisco, 1950?] 33 pp.

"The Bridges Case in the Circuit Court of Appeals," *Lawyers Guild Review,* vol. 4, June-July 1944, pp. 25–27.

"The Bridges Deportation Bill," *Lawyers Guild Review,* vol. 1, Oct. 1940, pp. 5–8.

Bridges-Robertson-Schmidt Defense Committee. *The Record*. San Francisco[1950?] 94 pp. (" ... the verbatim record of the Federal Court trial of Messrs. Bridges, Robertson and Schmidt from the point of the opening statements of counsel up to and through the contempt citation and sentence of six months in jail against Defense Counsel Vincent Hallinan.")

"Dean Landis Reports in Bridges Case," *American Bar Association Journal,* vol. 26, Feb. 1940, p. 194.

"The End of the Bridges Case and After," *Lawyers Guild Review,* vol. 6, Jan.-Feb. 1946, pp. 424–26.

Hafner, Jeannette. "Note and Comment—the Bridges Deportation Bill," *Oregon Law Review,* vol. 22, Dec. 1942, pp. 88–95.

Harper, Fowler. "The Crusade Against Bridges," *Nation,* vol. 174, April 5, 1952, pp. 323–26.

Harry Bridges Victory Committee. *Biddle's Private War Against Harry Bridges*. [New York, 1945?] [12] pp.

Huberman, Leo. *Citizenship for Harry Bridges, Production Soldier*. Harry Bridges Victory Committee [New York, 1942] 23 pp.

"In Re Harry Bridges," *Yale Law Journal,* vol. 52, Dec. 1942, pp. 108–29.

The Key. Special edition on Harry Bridges. Los Angeles, May 22, 1950.

[Landis, James McCauley] *In the Matter of Harry Renton Bridges*. Findings and conclusions of the Examiner. Washington: Government Printing Office, 1939. 152 pp.

Murray, Philip. *The Harry Bridges Case*. A foreword to the famous dissenting opinion of Judge William Healy and Judge Francis Garrecht of the U. S. Circuit Court of Appeals for the Ninth District. San Francisco: Harry Bridges Victory Committee, 1945. 16 pp.

National Federation for Constitutional Liberties. *600 Prominent Americans Ask President to Rescind Biddle Decision*. New York, 1942. 32 pp.

Neuberger, R. L. "Bad-Man Bridges," *Forum,* vol. 101, April 1939, pp. 195–99.

Pressman, Lee. *Harry Bridges, Petitioner, Against I. F. Wixon, as District Director, Immigration and Naturalization Service, Department of Jus-*

tice. *On Certiorari to the United States Circuit Court of Appeals for the Ninth Circuit.* Brief for Harry Bridges. Supreme Court of the U.S., October Term 1944. [New York, 1944] 123 pp.

"The Second Bridges Hearing," *International Juridical Association Bulletin,* vol. 10, March 1942, pp. 93, 97–104.

Smith, Louise Pettibone. *Torch of Liberty: Twenty-five Years in the Life of the Foreign Born in the U.S.A.* New York: Dwight-King Publishers, 1959. Pp. 188–200.

The Story of the 18 Year Plot to Frame Harry Bridges. Special Supplement, *March of Labor* [1953] 11 pp.

KING–RAMSAY–CONNER

Huberman, Leo. *Free These Three.* San Francisco: King–Ramsay–Conner Defense Committee [1941?] [6] pp.

Gives the essential facts in the murder of marine engineer George W. Alberts on March 22, 1936, of which two officials and a rank-and-file member of the Marine Firemen's Union were convicted. Views are briefly expressed on the trial judge, the jury, and the nature of the evidence and trial procedures.

International Labor Defense. *"Equal Justice," Yearbook of the Fight for Democratic Rights, 1936–1937.* Prepared by Louis Colman. New York, 1937. 104 pp.

Tells of the activities of the ILD to obtain pardons for Thomas J. Mooney, Warren K. Billings, J. B. McNamara, and Matt Schmidt, and its participation in the King–Ramsay–Conner and Modesto cases and the Sacramento syndicalism trials.

King–Ramsay–Conner Defense Committee. *Not Guilty!* San Francisco [1936] 15 pp.

Describes the murder of chief marine engineer George W. Alberts on March 22, 1936, in Alameda, California, and the indictment for the murder five months later of Earl King, secretary of the MFOWW, Ernest G. Ramsay, secretary of the Fish Reduction Workers' Union and former MFOWW patrolman, and three others. Concluding sections accuse Earl Warren, Alameda County District Attorney, of prejudicing the position of the accused men by issuing inflammatory statements to the press, and link the indictments with pending negotiations for new contracts between the Pacific Coast maritime unions and the maritime employers.

———. *The Ship Murder: The Story of a Frame-up.* San Francisco [1937] 23 pp.

A review of the circumstances surrounding the murder of George W. Alberts, the prosecution and conviction of Earl King, Ernest G. Ramsay, and Frank J. Conner for the crime, and Alameda County District Attorney Earl Warren's part in the case. Evidence is offered to show that much of the court testimony was perjured, the jury hand-picked, and the presiding judge biased.

————. *Punishment Without Crime.* San Francisco [1940] 23 pp.

Maintains that the imprisonment of Earl King, Ernest Ramsay, and Frank Conner for the murder of George W. Alberts is part of a plan to nullify the gains of the Pacific Coast maritime workers by destroying their leadership. To support this contention, reviews the activities in the case of the "unholy three," Harper L. Knowles, Stanley M. Doyle, and John J. Keegan, their relationship to certain shipping interests, and their involvement in the 1939 deportation hearing of Harry Bridges before Dean Landis.

MODESTO

California. Legislature. Assembly. Modesto Defendants Committee. *Majority and Minority Reports on the Modesto Defendants, Pursuant to Assembly Resolution Adopted January 21, 1935.* 52d sess. Sacramento, 1937. 19 pp.

The majority of the committee, after investigation, concluded that James F. Scrudder and George Brazelton, as Standard Oil of California undercover agents, had engineered the stealing of the dynamite as a provocation, and that the record showed evidence of perjury and subornation of perjury. It recommended pardon for the defendants and changes in the state laws relating to participation of private corporations in criminal prosecutions and in prosecutions for public offenses involving labor disputes or arising out of labor disputes. The minority of the committee disagreed with all the major conclusions of the majority and opposed all its recommendations.

Joint Marine Modesto Defense Committee. *The Modesto Frame-up.* San Francisco, 1935. 35 pp.

An account of a labor case associated with the Pacific Coast oil tanker strike of 1935. On the evening of April 20, 1935, eleven men, some of them members of the tanker strike committee, were arrested outside the town of Patterson, California, after dynamite had been found in one of the two cars they were riding in. One of the eleven men was found to be a Standard Oil of California detective, another an informer for the San Francisco police department. The remaining nine men were later tried and convicted of illegal possession of dynamite. The contention is made in this review of the case that the dynamite was planted by agents of the oil companies as part of a campaign to prejudice the position of the unions with the public.

————

California. Legislature. Assembly. Special Committee Appointed to Investigate Charges of Perjury and Subornation of Perjury Growing Out of the Conviction of Nine Modesto Defendants in the 1935 Dynamite Plot Case. "Transcript of Proceedings, Commencing February 17, 1937. Held at San Francisco, California and San Quentin State Prison." 2 vols. San Francisco: Foster and Mingins [1937] 1266 pp. Typewritten.

NATIONAL AND RACIAL MINORITIES

GENERAL

California. Bureau of Labor Statistics. *Thirteenth Biennial Report, 1907–1908*. Sacramento, 1908. "Oriental Statistics," pp. 201–20.

Includes statistics on hours and wages of Chinese and Japanese workers in San Francisco stores and factories owned by their nationals.

————. State Board of Control. *California and the Oriental: Japanese, Chinese and Hindus*. Report to Governor William D. Stephens. Sacramento, 1920. 231 pp.

In a letter submitting the report to U.S. Secretary of State Bainbridge Colby, Governor Stephens states that its contents are the result of "painstaking search for the facts," and on the basis of these facts urges the passage of an act excluding further Japanese immigration. Although the report treats also of Chinese and Hindus, its main concern is Japanese labor competition in California and particularly Japanese assumption of land ownership on a large scale.

"California United Against Asiatic Immigration," *The White Man* ("Organ of the Movement for Asiatic Exclusion"), vol. 1, Aug. 1910, pp. 9–21.

This collection of letters, extracts from speeches, and interviews with political candidates includes statements by Walter Macarthur, Hiram Johnson, U. S. Webb, and Julius Kahn.

Cleland, Robert Glass. *California in Our Time*. New York: Knopf, 1947. Chap. 13, "Aliens and Nomads," pp. 242–64.

A discussion of the Japanese and Mexican minorities, the refugees from the "dust bowl," and the problems they posed for California in the first part of the twentieth century. Describes the numerous legislative measures taken against the Japanese, the general acceptance of the Mexican laborer in agricultural areas and the changed attitude toward him when he took steps to improve his economic conditions, and the still largely unsolved problems of the migrants from the drought areas of the western and southern states.

Greer, Scott. *Last Man In: Racial Access to Union Power*. Glencoe, Ill.: Free Press, 1959. 189 pp.

A study, couched in the language of the professional sociologist, of the inner life of twenty-one Los Angeles local unions in which half of the membership consists of ethnic minority groups, mostly Negro and Mexican. Some of the questions studied are the type of jobs allotted to the minorities, the nature and degree of participation by the minority groups in the affairs of the locals, and the problem of representation of these groups in leadership positions. Chap. 7 examines locals in which the question of race is an immediate issue.

Palmer, Albert W. *Orientals in American Life.* New York: Friendship Press, 1934. 212 pp.

Contains an annotated book list, pp. 202–8.

U.S. Work Projects Administration. *History of Journalism in San Francisco.* 7 vols. San Francisco, 1939–40. Vol. 7, Part 2, "Social Consciousness," pp. 31–71.

Representative editorials from the press on the Indians, Chinese, Japanese, unemployment, and trade unions, among others.

Asiatic Exclusion League of North America. *Proceedings of the First International Convention, Seattle, Washington, Feb. 3, 4, 5, 1908.* San Francisco: Organized Labor, 1908. 92 pp.

Berry, John Thomas. "Fair Employment Practice in California: A Study of the Groups and Pressures Influencing Opinion on This Issue." Unpublished M.A. thesis. University of California, Berkeley, 1952. 138 pp.

Blanpied, Charles W., comp. *A Humanitarian Study of the Coming Immigration Question on the Pacific Coast, Being a Digest of the Pacific Coast Congress of 1913.* San Francisco, 1913. 63 pp.

California. Bureau of Labor Statistics. *Ninth Biennial Report, 1899–1900.* Sacramento, 1900. "Alien Labor in California," pp. 15–35.

———. ———. *Eleventh Biennial Report, 1903–1904.* Sacramento, 1904. "Numbers and Condition of Chinese and Japanese in California," pp. 72–78.

———. Fair Employment Practices Commission. *First Annual Report, September 18, 1959–December 31, 1960.* Sacramento, 1961. 37 pp.

California Labor Federation. *Statement before the United States Commission on Civil Rights.* Hearings, San Francisco, Jan. 27, 1960. San Francisco: California Labor Federation, Committee on Civil Rights, 1960. 18 pp.

The College Woman's Club of San Diego. *Pathfinder Social Survey of San Diego.* San Diego, 1914. "Industrial Conditions—Foreign Population," pp. 31–35.

Council for Civic Unity of San Francisco. *Employment Practices in Private Industry in San Francisco Affecting Minority Group Applicants and Employees.* Testimony before San Francisco Board of Supervisors, Jan. 30, 1957. [San Francisco, 1957] 43 pp.

Greer, Scott A. "Participation of Ethnic Minorities in the Labor Unions of Los Angeles County." Unpublished Ph.D. dissertation. University of California, Los Angeles, 1952. 413 pp.

Hewes, Laurence I. *Intergroup Relations in San Diego.* San Francisco: American Council on Race Relations, 1946. 35 pp.

Hume, Samuel. *The Square Deal in the Pacific.* A presentation of the arguments in favor of a modification of the United States Immigration Act of 1924, the elimination of the Discriminatory Exclusion Clause, Section 13-c, and the extension of the quota system to China, Japan, and other Asiatic countries. An address delivered before the Commonwealth Club of San Francisco. Berkeley: California Council on Oriental Relations [1933?] 26 pp.

Jones, Chester Lloyd. "The Legislative History of Exclusion Legislation," *Annals of the American Academy of Political and Social Science,* vol. 34, Sept. 1909, pp. 351–59.

McKenzie, Roderick Duncan. *Oriental Exclusion.* The effect of American immigration laws, regulations, and judicial decisions upon the Chinese and Japanese on the American Pacific Coast. Seattle: University of Washington Press, 1927. 200 pp.

Mellor, M. L. "Fair Employment Practices: Legislation Trends and Proposals," *California Law Review,* vol. 38, Aug. 1950, pp. 515–24.

Nadeau, Remi. *Los Angeles from Mission to Modern City.* New York: Longmans, Green, 1960. Chap. 17, "Angels, First and Second Class," pp. 238–51.

Record, Wilson. *Minority Groups and Intergroup Relations in the San Francisco Bay Area.* Berkeley: Institute of Governmental Studies, University of California, 1963. 48 pp.

Reynolds, Charles N. "Oriental–White Race Relations in Santa Clara County, California." Unpublished Ph.D. dissertation. Stanford University, 1927. 396 pp.

San Francisco. Board of Supervisors. *Fair Employment Practices Ordinance, City and County of San Francisco, 1957.* [San Francisco, 1957] 23 pp.

———. Commission on Equal Employment Opportunities. *Final Report.* San Francisco, 1960. 30 pp.

San Jose State College. Student Committee. *Interracial Prejudices in San*

Jose, California, 1950. San Jose, 1951. "Labor Unions," pp. 33–39; "Employment," pp. 70–80.

Smith, William E. *The Second Generation Oriental in America.* Honolulu: Institute of Pacific Relations [1927] 36 pp.

U.S. Federal Writers' Project. "Oriental Labor Unions and Strikes—California Agriculture." [Oakland? 1938?] 27 pp. Typewritten.

U.S. War Manpower Commission, Region 12. *Surveys of Total Employment and Unemployment of Non-whites in Selected Establishments.* [San Francisco, 1943]

Waldron, Gladys Hennig. "Anti-foreign Movements in California, 1919–1929." Unpublished Ph.D. dissertation. University of California, Berkeley, 1956. 316 pp.

Winn, Frank. "Labor Tackles the Race Question," *Antioch Review,* vol. 3, Feb. 1943, pp. 341–61.

Yoell, A. E. "Oriental vs. American Labor," *Annals of the American Academy of Political and Social Science,* vol. 34, Sept. 1909, pp. 347–56.

Young, John P. "The Support of the Anti-Oriental Movement," *Annals of the American Academy of Political and Social Science,* vol. 34, Sept. 1909, pp. 231–38.

CHINESE

Andrews, Elisha Benjamin. *The History of the Last Quarter Century in the United States, 1870–1895.* New York: Scribner, 1896. Vol. 1, chap. 13, "Domestic Events during Mr. Arthur's Administration," pp. 343–90.

Part of the chapter (pp. 356–81) discusses the Chinese question in California and "Kearneyism."

Andrews, John B. "Chinese Exclusion," *in* John R. Commons and Associates, *History of Labor in the United States.* New York: Macmillan, 1918. Vol. 2, pp. 146–51.

Reviews the two dominant issues that occupied the California labor movement in the late 1860's, the eight-hour day and the rising problem of Chinese labor competition, and comments on the relationship of these issues to the national labor movement.

Archbald, John. *On the Contact of Races: Considered Especially with Relation to the Chinese Question.* San Francisco: Towne & Bacon, 1860. 41 pp.

Argues that the opposition to the Chinese is basically due to "narrow prejudice, arising from limited knowledge." The objections that the Chinese are coolies, and that their competition deprives white labor of employment and reduces its wages, are rejected by the author. He emphasizes, however, that despite his objection to exclusion of the Chinese, he does not consider them equal to the white man.

Bates, Mrs. D. B. *Incidents on Land and Water, or Four Years on the Pacific Coast.* Boston: Libby and Co., 1858. Chap. 24, "Peculiarities of John Chinaman...," pp. 263–70.

A character sketch of the writer's Chinese servant, in itself unimportant but reflecting the more tolerant attitude toward the Chinese of that period.

Beadle, J. H. *The Undeveloped West, or Five Years in the Territories.* Philadelphia: National Publishing Co., 1873. Chap. 17, "John," pp. 313–25.

Considers the oft repeated charges against the Chinese—that they cheapen labor, that they will overrun the country, that they degrade labor—and finds them unfounded.

Bowles, Samuel. *Across the Continent: A Summer's Journey to the Rocky Mountains, the Mormons, and the Pacific States.* Samuel Bowles and Company, Springfield, Mass. New York: Hurd and Houghton, 1866. Chap. 23, "The Chinese on the Pacific Coast," pp. 238–54.

Sympathetically describes the varied occupations of the Chinese, and maintains that the jealousy and prejudice of the ignorant white laborer, particularly the Irish laborer, are the basis of opposition to them. "The new state, to be built upon manufactures and agriculture, is seen to need their cheap labor."

California. Bureau of Labor Statistics. *Second Biennial Report, 1885–1886.* Sacramento, 1887. Chap. 4, "Chinese Labor and Chinese Mode of Living," pp. 80–117.

Includes the report of a special committee appointed by the San Francisco Board of Supervisors to investigate San Francisco's Chinatown.

————. Legislature. Senate. *Governor's Annual Message to the Legislature of the State of California, 1855 Session.* Doc. no. 1. Sacramento: B. B. Redding, State Printer, 1855. Item 22, "Asiatic Immigration," pp. 31–36.

Invites the attention of the Legislature "To this Growing Evil" and contends that the states have the constitutional power to exclude undesirable groups.

Coolidge, Mary Roberts. *Chinese Immigration.* New York: Holt, 1909. 531 pp.

Generally considered to be the most authoritative treatment of the Chinese question in the United States and particularly in California, the study rejects most of the assumptions and claims that many writers on the problem have wholly or in part accepted: "coolyism," labor competition with the white man, the menace of overimmigration, and the inability of the Chinese to assimilate. Mrs. Coolidge offers extensive documentation to support her position, maintaining that the

Chinese question has been used as a political football by unprincipled politicians, as a scapegoat by labor leaders to avoid facing up to basic economic ills, and as a mask for the general desire to keep the wealth of California in "white hands." Special consideration is given to treatment of the Chinese issue by Congress and the California Legislature, including an analysis of the report in 1876 of the U.S. Congress Joint Special Committee to Investigate Chinese Immigration and of the California Senate's Address and Memorial to the Congress in 1877.

————. "Chinese Labor Competition on the Pacific Coast," *Annals of the American Academy of Political and Social Science,* vol. 34, Sept. 1909, pp. 340–50.

Discusses the reasons for the early acceptance of the Chinese and later objection to them, and examines some of the generally accepted fallacies about the Chinese as laborers.

Davis, Winfield J. *History of Political Conventions in California, 1849–1892.* Publications of the California State Library, no. 1. Sacramento, 1893. Chap. 33, "1886: Anti-Chinese Conventions—Memorial to Congress. ..."

Tells of the state convention of anti-Chinese societies and includes the anti-Chinese memorial it addressed to the President and Congress.

Dillon, Richard H. *The Hatchet Men: The Story of the Tong Wars in San Francisco's China Town.* New York: Coward, McCann, 1962. Chap. 5, "Sand Lots and Pick Handles," pp. 99–127.

Another version of some of the violent acts against the Chinese in the 1870's in which some of the San Francisco unemployed played a part.

Eaves, Lucile. *A History of California Labor Legislation.* Berkeley: The University Press [1910] Chaps. 3–6, "California Legislation for the Exclusion and Regulation of the Chinese, 1852–1867," "Federal Relations with the Chinese, 1840–1871," "California Legislation for the Exclusion and Regulation of the Chinese, 1867–1880," "Federal Legislation Regulating Chinese Immigration, 1871–1902," pp. 105–96.

States that legislation dealing with Chinese labor follows a specific pattern: ordinances or orders of local authorities, state laws aiming to discourage or diminish immigration by special taxation or curtailment of political and civil rights, and federal legislation regulating immigration. It is noted that these measures reflect marked periods of development: the years before 1867, when opposition to the Chinese was limited and not well organized; the late sixties and the seventies, when strong and well-organized opposition influenced the adoption of radical measures by both the State of California and the federal government; and the period after the enactment of the federal exclusion law of 1882. It is also noted that many local communities often depended on extralegal actions rather than on legislative measures and that many state laws, though obviously violating the federal constitution, remained operative for long periods of time before they were declared unconstitutional.

Farwell, Willard B. *The Chinese at Home and Abroad*. Together with the report of the special committee of the Board of Supervisors of San Francisco on the condition of the Chinese quarter of that city. San Francisco: A. L. Bancroft & Co., 1885. Chaps. 6–7, "Chinese Labor for the Development of California," "The Points of View," pp. 72–93.

Also appended is a survey of Sacramento's Chinatown (Part 2, pp. 97–114).

Gray, Arthur A. *History of California from 1542*. New York: Heath, 1934. Chap. 23, "The Chinese in California," pp. 397–408; chap. 26, "Turbulent Times," pp. 438–47.

Intended for high school reading.

Helper, Hinton Rowan. *The Land of Gold: Reality Versus Fiction*. Baltimore: Published for the author by Henry Taylor, 1855. Chap. 7, "The Chinese in California," pp. 86–96.

Presents an unflattering description of the appearance, habits, and occupations of the Chinese and then poses the question: "Is this Chinese immigration desirable?" After some speculation the writer supplies his own answer: "... there is no chance of making anything of them either in the way of trade or labor."

Kerr, J. G. *The Chinese Question Analyzed*. A lecture delivered at the YMCA, Nov. 13, 1877. San Francisco: Privately printed, 1877. 24 pp.

Argues that the usual objections brought against the Chinese—including the claim "that they work cheap and live cheap"—are not valid enough to be used as a basis for their exclusion from the United States.

Kung, S. W. *Chinese in American Life: Some Aspects of Their History, Status, Problems, and Contributions*. Seattle: University of Washington Press, 1962. Chap. 3, "Free Immigration (1820–82)," pp. 64–79.

Provides a broad review of the Chinese question in California, with emphasis on its economic aspects, to the passage of the first Chinese Immigration Restriction Act in 1882.

McGowan, Joseph A. *History of the Sacramento Valley*. New York: Lewis Historical Publishing Co., 1961. Vol. 1, chap. 25, "The Chinese," pp. 321–33.

Sketches the history of the Chinese in the Sacramento Valley from the completion of the intercontinental railroad to World War I. Many of the thousands of Chinese engaged in the construction of the railroad found jobs in agriculture and in the service industries of the valley. As in other parts of California, feeling against the Chinese ran high during the depression of the 1870's, resulting in violence against them in such centers as Chico, Redding, and Vacaville. Only a few remained in the valley after World War I when the mines had been worked out, the levees built, and agriculture in great measure mechanized.

McLeod, Alexander. *Pigtails and Gold Dust.* Caldwell, Ida.: Caxton Printers, 1947. Chap. 5, "Chinese-American Coolie Trade," pp. 71–85.

Describes the trade in Chinese contract labor to the Americas which flourished
after the abandonment of the African slave traffic and which is believed to have
brought some of the first Chinese labor to California.

Norton, Frank H. "Our Labor-System and the Chinese," *Scribner's
Monthly,* vol. 2, May 1871, pp. 61–70.

Regards Chinese labor as beneficial and necessary in the development of our resources because of our labor system which encourages the native-born American
to look down on menial labor. The writer notes that if for no other reason than
that of breaking up the unions, "the advent of Chinese labor should be hailed with
warm welcome by all who have the true interests of labor and the laboring classes
at heart."

Perlman, Selig. "The Anti-Chinese Agitation in California," *in* John R.
Commons and Associates, *History of Labor in the United States.* New
York: Macmillan, 1918. Vol. 2, chap. 5, pp. 252–68.

Describes the widespread unemployment in California in the late 1870's, the discontent of the unemployed, the problem of Chinese labor competition, the formation and fortunes of the Workingmen's Party of California, and the intense anti-
Chinese agitation which by 1880 had assumed national proportions and which in
1882 was climaxed by the passage by Congress of the Chinese Exclusion Act.

Phelan, James D. *Addresses.* San Francisco: Cubry & Co., 1901. "Debate
on the Chinese Question with Imperial Chinese Consul, Ho Yow," pp.
49–62.

Phelan argues against relaxation of the Chinese Exclusion Act, basing his opposition chiefly on the contention that past experience has proven Chinese labor competition to be detrimental to white California labor.

Sandmeyer, Elmer Clarence. *The Anti-Chinese Movement in California.*
Urbana, Ill.: University of Illinois Press, 1939. 127 pp.

After analyzing the conditions in China which influenced the Chinese to emigrate,
and the lure of gold and the demand for labor that made California their destination, the author traces the beginnings, growth, and bases of anti-Chinese agitation.
He observes that although such factors as racial differences and political considera-
tions influenced this agitation, the chief factor was economic competition. Local,
state, and national legal measures aimed at restriction of Chinese immigration or
at complete exclusion are outlined. The author stresses the role of organized labor
in the campaign for exclusion, noting that the Chinese became a problem at a
time when organized labor's power was growing and when it was trying to improve working conditions. Also commented on are the groups opposed to exclusion,
particularly those interested in the China trade.

————. "California Anti-Chinese Legislation and the Federal Courts: A
Study in Federal Relations," *Pacific Historical Review,* vol. 5, Sept.
1936, pp. 189–211.

Examines the extensive California state and municipal anti-Chinese legislation and shows how, generally, it was in conflict with provisions of the U.S. Constitution, the Burlingame Treaty, and the Civil Rights Act.

Schrieke, B. *Alien Americans: A Study in Race Relations*. New York: Viking, 1936. Chap. 1, "The Chinese in California," pp. 3–22.

Reviewing the differing patterns of anti-Chinese feeling and activity in California history, the author, a Dutch social anthropologist, suggests that they were always related to changes in economic conditions. In the labor vacuum of 1851–1859 the Chinese was accepted, even welcomed, when he showed a willingness to perform the more menial and laborious tasks. In the years between 1859 and 1900, when labor surpluses were common, he was under constant attack. Since then, again reflecting changed economic conditions, agitation against him has become almost nonexistent.

Seward, George F. *Chinese Immigration in its Social and Economical Aspects*. New York: Scribner, 1881. 420 pp.

Written by a former United States minister to China, the book is divided into four parts or approaches to the question. Part 1 deals mainly with the controversial question of the actual number of Chinese in the United States. Part 2 points to the benefits derived by California from Chinese labor: the building of the western part of the continental railroad quickly and at a minimum cost, reclamation of swamp lands, and the contributions of Chinese workers in mining, fruit culture, manufacturing, and domestic service. Part 3 lists and rejects the often expressed objections to the Chinese. Part 4 treats of the widespread fears of overflowing Chinese immigration.

Sienkiewicz, Henry. *Portrait of America: Letters of Henry Sienkiewicz*. Edited and translated by Charles Morley. New York: Columbia University Press, 1959. Letter 12, "The Chinese in California," pp. 247–66.

The renowned Polish author, who lived in California in 1876 and 1877, writes of his keen interest in the California Chinese. He observed the forms of their religious worship, their cultural life, and particularly their economic position, and describes the numerous tasks they perform in the city and country. An eyewitness to a number of anti-Chinese acts, he discusses the reasons for the intense and widespread agitation against the Chinese at the time.

Soulé, Frank, John H. Gihon, and James Nisbet. *The Annals of San Francisco*. New York: Appleton, 1854. Part 2, chap. 20, "1852: The Chinese in California ...," pp. 378–90.

An early statement of objections to the Chinese in California, the principal one being their "coolie" status. The authors contend that "He should be driven from competition with free white labor, or his labor should be confined to certain inferior kinds of work...."

Stimson, Grace Heilman. *Rise of the Labor Movement in Los Angeles*. Berkeley: University of California Press, 1955. Chap. 5, "Union against the Chinese," pp. 60–67.

Deals with the revival in Los Angeles of the dormant anti-Chinese movement in 1885 and 1886. Sparked by the importation of Orientals for construction work on the Santa Fe Railroad, the anti-Chinese agitation was first taken up by the independently organized Anti-Chinese Union, and later continued, on the initiative of the Typographical Union, by the Trades Council and the Knights of Labor.

Stone, W. W. "The Knights of Labor on the Chinese Labor Situation," *Overland,* vol. 7, March 1886, pp. 225–30.

An official of the Knights of Labor states the reasons for the organization's opposition to the use of Chinese labor.

U.S. Congress. House. *Causes of General Depression in Labor and Business.* Investigation by a Select Committee of the House of Representatives. 46th Cong., 2d sess., Misc. Doc. 5. Washington, 1879. "Testimony Taken at San Francisco: Land Monopoly and Chinese Immigration," pp. 238–365.

The investigation seeking to ascertain the effect of Chinese immigration on industry, agriculture, and labor in California heard testimony, in part, by the following: T. B. Shannon, collector of customs, port of San Francisco; Loring Pickering, newspaper editor and publisher; J. C. Gorman, surveyor; J. V. Webster, farmer; B. C. Duffy, cigar manufacturer; J. O'Sullivan, printer; T. B. O'Brien, miner; and the Rev. Otis Gibson, missionary to the Chinese.

———. ———. *Mining Statistics West of the Rocky Mountains.* 42d Cong., 1st sess., Ex. Doc. 10. Washington, 1871. "Introductory," pp. 1–8.

Discusses Chinese labor in the mines.

Whitney, James A. *The Chinese and the Chinese Question.* New York: Thompson & Moreau, 1880. 87 pp.

Reviews some elements in Chinese history that are allegedly related to Chinese immigration to the United States, points to some negative results of Chinese labor competition in California, and reasons that the Burlingame Treaty should be repealed.

Williams, Samuel Wells. *Chinese Immigration.* A paper read before the Social Science Association. New York: Scribner, 1879. 48 pp.

Maintains that the chief arguments of those who have denounced the Chinese have been based on a distortion of fact and an exaggeration of evils which are often the result of the ill treatment the Chinese have been subjected to. Ridicules many of the numerous laws and legal restrictions that have been enacted against the Chinese and touches on the significance of the Chinese question as an issue in the conflict between capital and labor and in the field of politics.

An Address from the Workingmen of San Francisco to Their Brothers Thruout the Pacific Coast. San Francisco, 1888. 24 pp.

[Allison, O.] *Some of the Evils of California.* San Francisco: S. W. Raveley, 1881. 29 pp.

Ayers, James J. *Chinese Exclusion.* Speech at Constitutional Convention, Dec. 9, 1878. Los Angeles: Evening Express Newspaper and Printing Co., 1878. 13 pp.

Bancroft, Hubert Howe. *History of California.* San Francisco: The History Co., 1890. 7 vols. Vol. 7, chap. 14, "Chinese, the Labor Agitation, and Politics," pp. 335–69.

Bee, Fred A. *The Other Side of the Chinese Question.* Memorial to the people of the United States and the Honorable Senate and House of Representatives. Testimony of California's leading citizens. San Francisco: Woodward and Co., 1886. 76 pp.

Bennet, H. C. *Chinese Labor.* Lecture delivered before the San Francisco Mechanics' Institute, in reply to the Hon. F. M. Pixley. San Francisco, 1870. 41 pp.

Blackwood, Wm. C. "A Consideration of the Labor Problem," *Overland,* vol. 3, May 1884, pp. 449–60.

Bonner, John. "A Chinese Protest Against Exclusion," *Californian Illustrated,* vol. 5, April 1894, pp. 603–10.

Bouvé, Clement L. *A Treatise on the Laws Governing the Exclusion and Expulsion of Aliens in the United States.* Washington, D.C.: John Byrne and Co., 1912. Appendix B, "Laws Relating to the Admission of Chinese into the United States"; Appendix C, "Regulations Governing the Admission of Chinese into the United States," pp. 797–845.

Brace, Charles Loring. *The New West: or California in 1867–1868.* New York: Putnam, 1869. Chaps. 16–17, "The Chinese," pp. 209–27.

Brooks, B. S. *Brief of the Legislation and Adjudication Touching the Chinese Question, Referred to the Joint Commission of Both Houses of Congress.* San Francisco: Women's Co-operative Printing Union, 1877. 104 pp.

———. *Matters to Be Considered in Connection with the Question of the Advantage of Chinese Labor.* [San Francisco? 1877?] 13 pp.

———. *Opening Statement before the Joint Committee of the Two Houses of Congress on Chinese Immigration.* San Francisco, 1876. 33 pp.

Brooks, Charles Wolcott. "The Chinese Labor Problem," *Overland,* vol. 3, Nov. 1869, pp. 407–19.

California. Legislature. Assembly. Committee on Mines and Mining Interests. *Report of Committee, Session of 1856.* Sacramento, 1856. 16 + 6 pp.

————. ————. Senate. *Chinese Immigration: The Social, Moral and Political Effect of Chinese Immigration.* Testimony taken before a committee of the Senate. Sacramento, 1876. 173 pp.

————. ————. ————. *Chinese Immigration: Its Social, Moral and Political Effect.* Report to the California State Senate. Sacramento, 1878. 302 pp.

California Chinese Exclusion Convention. *For the Re-enactment of the Chinese Exclusion Law.* California's Memorial to the President and the Congress of the U.S. San Francisco: James H. Barry, 1901. 11 pp.

————. *Proceedings, San Francisco, November 21 and 22, 1901.* San Francisco: James H. Barry, 1901. Addresses by Walter Macarthur, pp. 98–102; Rev. Peter C. Yorke, pp. 104–9.

Corlett, William W. *The Labor Question as Affected by Chinese Immigration.* Speech in House of Representatives, Jan. 25, 1879. Washington, 1879. 24 pp.

de Ford, Miriam Allen. *They Were San Franciscans.* Caldwell, Ida.: Caxton Printers, 1941. Chap. 7, "Chinese and Dynamite: Dennis Kearney and Burnette Haskell," pp. 188–211.

[Densmore, G. B.] *Description of Chinese Life in San Francisco: Their Habits, Morals and Manners.* Illustrated by Voegtlin. San Francisco: Pettit & Russ, 1880. 122 pp.

Fisher, Walter M. *The Californians.* London: Macmillan, 1876. Chap. 4, "Their Chinese," pp. 50–68.

Frost, Jennett Blakeslee. *California's Greatest Curse.* San Francisco: Joseph Winterburn & Co., 1879. Sec. 1, "The Chinese Question," pp. 9–24.

Fuller, Varden. "The Supply of Agricultural Labor as a Factor in the Evolution of Farm Organization in California." Unpublished Ph.D. dissertation. University of California, Berkeley, 1939. Chap. 4, "Chinese Labor: Intensive Cultivation in an Area of Sparse Population," pp. 93–147.

George, Henry. "The Chinese on the Pacific Coast" (letter to New York *Tribune,* May 1, 1869), *in* Henry Josiah West, ed., *The Chinese Invasion.* San Francisco: Bacon & Co., 1873. Pp. 24–41.

Gibson, Rev. O. *Chinaman or White Man, Which?* Lecture in reply to Father Buchard. San Francisco: Alta California Printing House, 1873. 30 pp.

Goodenough, Rev. S. "Foes of Labor," *California Review* (Oakland), vol. 1, Oct. 1893, pp. 34–40.

Healy, Patrick J. *Some Reasons Why an Exclusion Act Should Not Be Passed.* San Francisco, 1902. 16 pp.

Hittell, John S. "Benefits of Chinese Immigration," *Overland,* vol. 7, Feb. 1886, pp. 120–24.

Hittell, Theodore H. *History of California.* San Francisco: N. J. Stone & Co., 1886–1897. 4 vols. Vol. 4, chaps. 9–11, pp. 567–640. [Chinese]

Kinley, Joseph Macy. *Remarks on Chinese Immigration; Remarks on Chinese Labor.* San Francisco: C. H. Street, 1877. 13 pp.

Layres, Augustus. *Both Sides of the Chinese Question.* Or a critical analysis of the evidence for and against Chinese immigration, as elicited before the Congressional Commission; also a review of Senator Sargent's report; with an appendix concerning a widespread conspiracy against the Chinese. San Francisco: A. F. Woodbridge, 1877. 16 pp.

Loomis, A. W. "How Our Chinamen Are Employed," *Overland,* vol. 2, March 1869, pp. 231–40.

McLeod, Alexander. *Pigtails and Gold Dust.* Caldwell, Ida.: Caxton Printers, 1947. Chap. 7, "The China Boys in the Kitchen," pp. 100–10.

McWilliams, Carey. "Cathay in Southern California," *Common Ground,* vol. 6, Autumn 1945, pp. 31–38.

O'Meara, James. "The Chinese in Early Days," *Overland,* vol. 3, May 1884, pp. 477–81.

Palmer, Albert. "Chinese Americans," *in* Francis J. Brown and Joseph Slabey Roucek, eds., *Our Racial and National Minorities.* New York: Prentice-Hall, 1937. Pp. 463–71.

Paul, Rodman W. "The Origin of the Chinese Issue in California," *Mississippi Valley Historical Review,* vol. 25, Sept. 1938, pp. 181–96.

Powderly, Terence Vincent. *Thirty Years of Labor, 1859–1889.* Columbus, Ohio: Excelsior Publishing House, 1889. Pp. 412–27 [on the Chinese question]

Roach, Philip A. "Minority Report of Select Committee on Contracts for Foreign Labor, California Senate, March 20, 1852," *in* Henry Josiah West, ed., *The Chinese Invasion.* San Francisco: Bacon & Co., 1873. Pp. 17–24.

Ryer, Washington M. *The Conflict of Races.* San Francisco: P. J. Thomas, 1886. 80 pp.

Sheldon, Francis E. "The Chinese Immigration Discussion," *Overland,* vol. 7, Feb. 1886, pp. 113–19.

Shen, Tzo-Chien. *What "Chinese Exclusion" Really Means*. New York: China Institute in America, 1942. 58 pp.

Sherwin, H. "Observations on the Chinese Laborer," *Overland,* vol. 7, Jan. 1886, pp. 91–99.

Spier, Robert F. G. "Food Habits of Nineteenth-Century Chinese," *California Historical Society Quarterly,* vol. 37, June 1958, pp. 129–36.

Starr, M. B. *The Coming Struggle*. Or what the people on the Pacific Coast think of the coolie invasion. San Francisco: Bacon & Co., 1873. 115 pp.

Stegner, Wallace, and the Editors of *Look. One Nation*. Boston: Houghton Mifflin, 1945. "The Americanization of Chinatown," pp. 69–94.

Stout, Arthur B., *Chinese Immigration and the Physiological Causes of the Decay of a Nation*. San Francisco: Agnew & Deffebach, 1862. 26 pp.

U.S. Congress. Senate. Joint Special Committee. *Report of the Joint Special Committee to Investigate Chinese Immigration*. 44th Cong., 2d sess., Rept. 689. Washington, 1877. 1281 pp.

U.S. Department of Commerce and Labor. *The Laws, Treaty and Regulations Relating to the Exclusion of Chinese from the United States*. Arranged for the use of officers of the Bureau of Immigration. Washington, 1903. 94 pp.

Wellborn, Mildred. "The Events Leading to the Chinese Exclusion Acts," Historical Society of Southern California, *Annual Publications,* vol. 9, pts. 1–2, 1912–1913, pp. 49–58.

Whipple, Leon. *The Story of Civil Liberty in the United States*. New York: Vanguard Press, 1927. "Persecution of the Chinese," "The Japanese Question," pp. 197–209.

Woltor, Robert. *A Short and Truthful History of the Taking of California and Oregon by the Chinese in the Year A.D. 1889, by a Survivor*. San Francisco: A. L. Bancroft and Co., 1882. 82 pp.

JAPANESE

American Council on Race Relations. *Facts about Japanese Americans*. Prepared by Setsuko Nishi. Chicago, 1946. 34 pp.

Deals with Japanese Americans immediately preceding, during, and immediately following World War II. Includes considerable reference to employment problems of California Japanese Americans.

Jordan, David Starr. "The Japanese Problem in California," *Out West,* vol. 26, March 1907, pp. 224–30.

Accepts restrictions on the immigration of Japanese laborers into the United States as the least evil among a choice of evils.

Pajus, Jean. *The Real Japanese California.* Berkeley: James J. Gillick Co., 1937. Chaps. 1–2, "From the Beginning to the Gentleman's Agreement of 1907," "From the Gentleman's Agreement of 1907 to the Exclusion Act of 1924," pp. 1–30.

Reviews early Japanese immigration, consisting mostly of unskilled laborers, into California, the bearing of the Hawaiian Islands on this immigration, and the growth of opposition to further Japanese immigration.

Schrieke, B. *Alien Americans.* New York: Viking, 1936. Chap. 2, "The Japanese in California," pp. 23–45.

Shows that the Japanese were readily accepted to fill the gap in the labor supply caused by the exclusion of the Chinese in the eighties and nineties, and by 1900 had secured a monopoly of labor in the California agricultural industries. This acceptance was soon followed by opposition, with organized labor playing an important part in its organization.

Smith, Bradford. *Americans from Japan.* Philadelphia: Lippincott, 1948. Chap. 18, "Making a Living," pp. 234–43.

Sketches the changing patterns in the economic life of the Japanese on the Pacific Coast as they adjusted themselves to racial prejudice and restrictive laws and ordinances. Special reference is made to the economic problems of the Nisei.

tenBroek, Jacobus, Edward N. Barnhart, and Floyd W. Matson. *Prejudice, War and the Constitution: Japanese American Evacuation and Resettlement.* Berkeley: University of California Press, 1954. "The Workers," pp. 32–43.

In their search for the origins of the anti-Japanese bias that made the harsh treatment of Japanese Americans acceptable to the American people during World War II, the authors find that organized labor in California can be credited with the dubious honor of having pioneered in developing that bias. They point to the thirty years of anti-Japanese agitation by the labor press and the organization, under trade-union sponsorship, of such bodies as the Japanese and Korean Exclusion League and the Anti-Jap Laundry League.

U.S. Congress. House. Select Committee on National Defense Migration. 77th Cong., 2d sess. Washington, 1942. Part 29. San Francisco Hearing. "Problems of the Evacuation of Enemy Aliens and Others from Prohibited Military Zones."

Testimony of Louis Goldblatt, secretary, California State Industrial Union Council, on the interest and attitude of labor unions in the evacuation of Japanese from coastal areas, pp. 11178–90.

Vanderbilt, Cornelius, Jr., comp. *The Verdict of Public Opinion on the Japanese-American Question.* A symposium founded on Peter B. Kyne's novel, "The Pride of Palomar." New York: Privately printed [1921?] 62 pp.

Consists of comments on the Japanese question by many prominent Americans in answer to a request from Vanderbilt.

Anti-Jap Laundry League. *Pacific Coast Convention, San Francisco, December 6, 1908.* San Francisco, 1908. 70 pp.

Barnhart, Edward N. *Japanese-American Evacuation and Resettlement.* Catalog of material in the Main Library. Berkeley: University of California, 1958. 177 pp.

Bercovici, Konrad. *On New Shores.* Illustrated by Norman Borchardt. New York: Century Co., 1925. Chap. 16, "The Japanese in the United States," pp. 252–69.

Boddy, Manchester E. *Japanese in America.* Los Angeles: Manchester E. Boddy, 1921. Chaps. 5–6, "Japanese Population in California," "Standards of Wages and Working Hours," pp. 78–102.

Brown, Alice M. *Japanese in Florin, California.* N.p. [1913?] 7 pp.

Buell, Raymond Leslie. "The Development of the Anti-Japanese Agitation in the United States," *Political Science Quarterly,* vol. 37, Dec. 1922, pp. 605–38.

Burnight, Ralph T. *The Japanese in Rural Los Angeles County.* Sociological Monograph no. 16. Los Angeles: Southern California Sociological Society, 1920. 16 pp.

California. Bureau of Labor Statistics. *Seventh Biennial Report, 1895–1896.* Sacramento, 1896. "Japanese Labor," pp. 101–126.

———. University. Bureau of Guidance and Placement. *A Study of the Vocational Experiences of University of California Alumni of Japanese Ancestry,* by George Yasukochi. A National Youth Administration project. Berkeley, 1941. 20 pp.

Culberson, Charles A. *Exclusion of Japanese Coolies and Laborers.* Remarks in the Senate of the United States, Feb. 16, 1907. Washington, 1907. 8 pp.

Edwards, Percy L. "The Industrial Side of the Alien Land Law Problem," *Overland,* vol. 62, Aug. 1913, pp. 190–200.

Fuller, Varden. "The Supply of Agricultural Labor as a Factor in the Evolution of Farm Organization in California." Unpublished Ph.D. dissertation. University of California, Berkeley, 1939. Chap. 5, "Farm Organization Based on Chinese Labor Perpetuated through a period of Labor Scarcity by the Japanese," pp. 148–90.

Gulick, Sidney. *The American-Japanese Problem.* New York: Scribner, 1914. Appendix B, "A Summary by Labor Commissioner J. D. MacKenzie of the Report of the Special State Investigation of 1909 of the Japanese in California," pp. 316–23.

Harada, Tasuku, ed. *The Japanese Problem in California.* Answers of representative Americans to questionnaire printed for private circulation. San Francisco [1922?] 94 pp.

Hunt, Rockwell D. "California and the Japanese Question," *Overland,* vol. 83, April 1925, pp. 147–48, 172–73, 192; May 1925, pp. 195–96, 206, 218.

Irish, John P. "Reasons for Encouraging Japanese Immigration," *Annals of the American Academy of Political and Social Science,* vol. 34, Sept. 1909, pp. 294–300.

Iyenaga, T., and Kenoske Sato. *Japan and the California Problem.* New York: Putnam, 1921. Chap. 8, "Facts about the Japanese in California— Farmers and Alien Land Laws," pp. 120–47.

Japanese Association of America. *Statistics Relative to Japanese Immigration and the Japanese in California.* Rev. ed. San Francisco, 1921. 13 pp.

Japanese and Korean Exclusion League. *Japanese Immigration: Occupations, Wages,...* Compiled from U.S. Government reports and reports of the California Bureau of Labor Statistics. San Francisco: Organized Labor, 1907. 16 pp.

Johnsen, Julia E., comp. *Japanese Exclusion.* Vol. 3, no. 4, *The Reference Shelf.* New York: Wilson, 1925. 134 pp. [Bibliography, pp. 15–31]

Katayama, S. "California and the Japanese," *International Socialist Review,* vol. 14, July 1913, pp. 31–32.

Kawakami, Kiyoshik. *Asia at the Door.* New York: Revell, 1914. Chap. 8, "Hewers of Wood and Drawers of Water," pp. 131–44.

———. "The Japanese Question," *Annals of the American Academy of Political and Social Science,* vol. 93, Jan. 1921, pp. 81–88.

Macarthur, Walter. "Review of Exclusion History," *Annals of the American Academy of Political and Social Science,* vol. 93, Jan. 1921, pp. 38–42.

McClatchy, V. S. *Japanese Immigration and Colonization.* Brief prepared for consideration of the State Department. Sacramento: News Printing and Publishing Co., 1921. 109 pp.

McWilliams, Carey. *Prejudice: Japanese-Americans, Symbol of Racial Intolerance.* Boston: Little, Brown, 1944. Chap. 2, "The California-Japanese War (1900–1941)," pp. 14–72.

Matsui, Shichiro. "Economic Aspects of the Japanese Situation in California." Unpublished M.A. thesis. University of California, Berkeley, 1922. 117 pp.

Millis, H. A. *The Japanese Problem in the United States.* New York: Macmillan, 1915. Chap. 3, "The Japanese in Western Cities: Their Work and Business," pp. 50–78; chap. 5, "The Japanese as Agricultural Laborers in California," pp. 103–30.

Noguchi, Yone. *Japan and America.* Tokyo: Keio University Press; New York: Orientalia, 1921. "Open Letter to the Californians," pp. 60–66.

"Quota or Exclusion for Japanese Immigration?" *Transactions of the Commonwealth Club of California,* vol. 27, Dec. 1932, pp. 285–336.

Radamaker, John A. "Japanese Americans," *in* Francis J. Brown and Joseph Slabey Roucek, eds., *Our Racial and National Minorities.* New York: Prentice-Hall, 1937. Pp. 472–93.

Rowell, Chester. "Japan and the Kin of Balboa," *Survey,* vol. 47, Oct. 29, 1921, pp. 172–75.

St. Ignatius College. Junior Philistorian Debating Society. *Resolved, That Japanese Coolie Labor Should be Excluded from Continental United States.* Affirmative side of debate, May 4, 1908. San Francisco: James H. Barry, 1908. 16 pp.

Scharrenberg, Paul. "The Attitude of Organized Labor Toward the Japanese," *Annals of the American Academy of Political and Social Science,* vol. 93, Jan. 1921, pp. 34–38.

Steiner, Jesse Frederick. *The Japanese Invasion: A Study of the Psychology of Inter-Racial Contacts.* Chicago: A. C. McClurge and Co., 1917. Chap. 7, "The Reaction of the Japanese to American Economic Conditions," pp. 112–29.

Strong, Edward K., Jr. *The Second Generation Japanese Problem.* Stanford University Press, 1934. Chap. 1, "The Problem," pp. 1–32; chap. 9, "Occupation," pp. 208–24.

U.S. Bureau of Agricultural Economics. *The Japanese in California Agriculture,* by Lloyd H. Fisher and Ralph L. Nielson. Berkeley, 1942. 30 pp.

U.S. Commission on Immigration and Education. *Report on Immigration.* Washington, 1901. Part 4, "Special Report on Chinese and Japanese Labor in the Mountain and Pacific Coast States," pp. 745–801.

U.S. Congress. House. Committee on Immigration and Naturalization. *Japanese Immigration.* Hearings, 66th Cong., 2d sess. Washington, 1921. Hearings in California, parts 1–3, pp. 3–1056.

Weisend, William Frederick. "The Anti-Japanese Movement in California." Unpublished M.A. thesis. University of California, Berkeley, 1931. 159 pp.

Young, John P. "The Support of the Anti-Oriental Movement," *Annals of the American Academy of Political and Social Science,* vol. 34, Sept. 1909, pp. 231–38.

MEXICAN

California. Governor C. C. Young's Mexican Fact-Finding Committee. *Mexicans in California.* Sacramento, 1930. 214 pp.

A four-part report on the condition of the Mexican population in California. Parts 1 and 2 include a statistical analysis of Mexican immigration into California and the effect on such immigration of the limitation laws of 1921 and 1924; an estimate of the number of Mexicans employed in manufacturing and other industries, and the wages paid to them; a review of Mexican labor unions and an account of the strike of the Mexican cantaloupe workers in the Imperial Valley in 1928. Part 3 contains information on the preference of farm operators for various kinds of labor and their views concerning Mexican labor; and a comparison of wages and output of different groups of laborers including Mexicans. Part 4 is a study of social welfare problems of Mexicans, with emphasis on the southern California area, including Los Angeles County.

Clark, Margaret. *Health in the Mexican-American Culture: A Community Study.* Berkeley: University of California Press, 1959. Chap. 4, "Making a Living," pp. 73–95.

Sal Si Puedes, a Spanish-speaking community in the San Jose area of California, is the object of the study. Investigation revealed that "The economic problems of Sal Si Puedes residents are acute; but they stem not from unwillingness to work but rather from poor job opportunities, low wages and seasonal periods of unemployment"; and that all members of the average family have to share in the task of making a living. Also examined are the types of employment such a family engages in, its yearly income, how this income is spent, and how it tides over periods of unemployment.

Galarza, Ernesto. *Strangers in Our Fields.* Washington, D.C.: Joint United States–Mexico Trade Union Committee, 1956. 80 pp.

A survey of Mexican contract agricultural labor in the United States. A review of the background of the bracero program and a description of the mechanics of recruitment of the Mexican nationals are followed by an investigation of their rights under the international and the individual work agreements and the extent to which these rights are honored in practice. This part of the survey was made on site in a number of California work camps and included an examination of earnings, housing, food, transportation, insurance, the role of the labor contractor, administration and enforcement of the agreements, and the degree of worker representation.

McLean, Robert N. "Mexican Workers in the United States," *Proceedings, National Conference of Social Work, 56th Annual Session, June 26–July 3, 1929.* Chicago: University of Chicago Press, 1930. Pp. 531–38.

A Los Angeles social work director makes some observations on the problems of the Mexican worker in the Southwest, with special emphasis on California. States that he is generally in demand for certain unskilled work and that agriculture will remain dependent on his labor. Suggests that the approach to the question of the Mexican worker should reflect the understanding that he is here to stay.

Taylor, Paul S. *Mexican Labor in the United States—Imperial Valley.* University of California Publications in Economics, vol. 6, no. 1. Berkeley: University of California Press, 1928. Pp. 1–94.

Reviews the growth of the Mexican labor force in the Imperial Valley of California against the background of the valley's general economic and labor history. The rapid change-over from extensive crops in the early part of the century to intensive crops in later decades is shown to have brought to the Imperial Valley, in succession, Japanese, Hindu, Negro, Filipino, Chinese, Korean, and Mexican agricultural labor. The Mexican, proving the most adaptable, remained and in time comprised a third of the valley's population. Included is an account of the first attempts at trade-union organization and economic action by the Mexican agricultural workers and the growers' reaction to them. Numerous statistical tables accompany the text.

———. *Mexican Labor in the United States—Migration Statistics, III.* University of California Publications in Economics, vol. 12, no. 2. Berkeley: University of California Press, 1933. Pp. 11–22.

A statistical study of the northward and southward movement in California of Mexican agricultural workers during the period 1927–1929, as measured at California check points. The movement is shown to be related to crop harvests and to be sharply seasonal in character. Also included is a brief comparative study of migration of Negroes. Statistical tables, a graph, and an area map accompany the text.

Ward, Stuart R. "The Mexican in California," *Transactions of the Commonwealth Club of California,* vol. 21, March 1926, pp. 4–10.

Reviews some of the factors that have encouraged Mexican immigration into the United States and particularly into California. Among the factors cited are the Johnson Immigration Act of 1924 slowing immigration from Europe, a demand for the Mexican's services in the more menial jobs of industry, and the attitude of agricultural interests that his labor is indispensable to agriculture.

Bogardus, Emory S. *The Mexican in the United States.* Los Angeles: University of Southern California Press, 1934. Chap. 5, "Labor and Industry," pp. 37–45.

Burnhill, James. "The Mexican People in the Southwest," *Political Affairs,* vol. 32, Sept. 1953, pp. 43–52.

California. Bureau of Labor Statistics. *Twenty-Second Biennial Report, 1925–1926.* Sacramento, 1926. "Report on the Mexican Labor Situation in the Imperial Valley," pp. 113–27.

————. Department of Employment. *Mexican Nationals in California Agriculture, 1942–1959.* Sacramento, 1959. 36 pp.

California Development Association. *Survey of the Mexican Labor Problem in California.* [San Francisco? 1926?] 24 pp.

Coalson, George O. "Mexican Contract Labor in American Agriculture," *Southwestern Social Science Quarterly,* vol. 33, Dec. 1952, pp. 228–38.

Communist Party, U.S.A. "The Mexican-Americans—Their Plight and Struggles." Resolution on party work among the Mexican-American people, 14th National Convention, Aug. 3, 1948. In *Political Affairs,* vol. 28, May 1949, pp. 71–80.

Cramp, Kathryn, Louise F. Shields, and Charles A. Thomson. *Study of the Mexican Population in Imperial Valley.* New York: Council of Women for Home Missions, 1926. 25 pp.

Edson, George T. *Mexican Labor in the California Imperial Valley.* N.p., 1927. 7 pp.

Fuller, Varden. "The Supply of Agricultural Labor as a Factor in the Evolution of Farm Organization in California." Unpublished Ph.D. dissertation. University of California, Berkeley, 1939. Chap. 7, "The Mexicans and Filipinos in California Agriculture," pp. 215–88.

Gamio, Manuel. *The Mexican Immigrant: His Life Story.* Autobiographic documents collected by Manuel Gamio. Chicago: University of Chicago Press, 1931. 288 pp.

————. *Mexican Immigration to the United States.* Chicago: University of Chicago Press, 1930. Chap. 3, "The Mexican Immigrant Wage Earner," pp. 30–50.

Griffith, Beatrice. *American Me.* Boston: Houghton Mifflin, 1948. Sec. 2, chap. 2, "Mexican Jobs," pp. 112–23.

Heller Committee for Research in Social Economics, and Constantine Panunzio. *How Mexicans Earn and Live.* A study of the incomes and expenditures of one hundred Mexican families in San Diego, California. Cost of Living Studies, no. 5. Berkeley: University of California Press, 1933. 114 pp.

Johns, Bryan Theodore. "Field Workers in California Cotton." Unpublished M.A. thesis. University of California, Berkeley, 1948. 177 pp.

Joint United States-Mexico Trade Union Committee. United States Section. *Statement on the Mexican Contract Labor Program.* Washington, 1958. 8 pp.

"Labor and Social Conditions of Mexicans in California," *Monthly Labor Review,* vol. 32, Jan. 1931, pp. 83–89.

McWilliams, Carey. "California and the Wetback," *Common Ground,* vol. 9, Summer 1949, pp. 15–20.

"Mexican Immigration," *Transactions of the Commonwealth Club of California,* vol. 21, March 1926, pp. 1–34.

Pan-American Union. Division of Labor and Social Information. *Mexican War Workers in the United States.* The manpower recruiting program and its operation. By Robert C. Jones. Washington, 1945. 46 pp.

Salinas, Jose Lazaro. *La Emigración de Braceros.* Mexico, D.F.: "Cauh Temoc," 1955. 204 pp.

Scruggs, Otey M. "The Bracero Program under the Farm Security Administration, 1942–1943," *Labor History,* vol. 3, Spring 1962, pp. 149–68.

———. "Evolution of the Mexican Farm Labor Agreement of 1942," *Agricultural History,* vol. 34, July 1960, pp. 140–49.

Spaulding, Charles B. "The Mexican Strike at El Monte, California," *Sociology and Social Research,* vol. 18, July–Aug. 1934, pp. 571–80.

Stegner, Wallace, and the Editors of *Look. One Nation.* Boston: Houghton Mifflin, 1945. Chap. 5, "Okies in Sombreros: Migrant Mexican Crop-workers," pp. 95–116.

Topete, Jesus. *Aventuras de un Bracero.* Mexico, D.F.: Editora Gráfica Moderna, S.A., 1961. 120 pp. (First edition 1948)

Tuck, Ruth D. *Not with the Fist: Mexican-Americans in a Southwest City.* New York: Harcourt, Brace, 1946. 234 pp.

U.S. Bureau of Employment Security. Farm Placement Service. *Information Concerning Entry of Mexican Agricultural Workers into the United States* ... Washington [1952?] 14 pp.

U.S. Bureau of Labor Statistics. *Money Disbursements of Wage Earners and Clerical Workers in Five Cities in the Pacific Coast Region, 1934–36.* Washington, 1939. "Mexican Families in Los Angeles," pp. 85–109.

U.S. Congress. House. Committee on Immigration and Naturalization. *Seasonal Agricultural Laborers from Mexico.* Hearings, 69th Cong., 1st sess. Washington, 1926. 345 pp.

U.S. Federal Writers' Project. "Organization Efforts of Mexican Agricultural Workers." [Oakland? 1938?] 30 pp. Typewritten.

"Wetbacks: Can the States Act to Curb Illegal Entry?" *Stanford Law Review,* vol. 6, March 1954, pp. 287–323.

FILIPINO

Bogardus, Emory S. "Foreign Migrations within United States Territory: The Situation of the Filipino People," *Proceedings,* National Conference of Social Work, 56th Annual Session, June 26–July 3, 1929. Chicago: University of Chicago Press, 1930. Pp. 573–79.

Examines the Filipino immigration problem and offers recommendations toward solving it. The objections to continued Filipino immigration, particularly those of Pacific Coast organized labor, are reviewed and some of them are considered valid. However, instead of outright exclusion, methods of controlled immigration are suggested.

Buaken, Manuel. *I Have Lived with the American People.* Caldwell, Ida.: Caxton Printers, 1948. 358 pp.

Manuel Buaken, the son of a Filipino Methodist Episcopal minister, arrived in San Francisco in 1927 on his way to Princeton University, where he was to study for the ministry on a divinity scholarship. He decided, however, to forgo the scholarship and remained in California to acquire a general education on his own resources. To realize his goal he had to accept the lot of the Filipino laborer in California. His book is an autobiographical account of ten years of that experience.

Burma, John H. *Spanish-Speaking Groups in the United States.* Durham, N.C.: Duke University Press, 1954. Chap. 5, "Filipino Americans," pp. 138–55.

Outlines the Filipino Americans' economic problems and living conditions, the special discriminatory practices they are subject to, and their future prospects. Notes that despite the brevity of the migratory period, by 1930 some 45,000 had taken up residence on the mainland of the United States, most remaining on the west coast.

Lasker, Bruno. *Filipino Immigration to the Continental United States and to Hawaii.* Published for the American Council, Institute of Pacific Relations. Chicago: University of Chicago Press, 1931. Chaps. 6–8, "Economic Problems for the United States," "Economic Problems of the Filipino Immigrants," pp. 41–91; chap. 20, "Policies and Programs: On the Mainland of the United States," pp. 298–319.

This study was commissioned by the American Council with the hope that its findings would afford a basis for profitable discussion in the then current movement for the exclusion of Filipinos from the United States, a movement that was being spearheaded by organized labor. In the cited chapters the author notes that only on the Pacific Coast is Filipino economic competition a problem, and he concludes that even in this area competition, in the sense of undercutting American wage standards, is limited. The problems of the Filipinos, such as limited ability, occupational discrimination, and exploitation by employers, contractors, and agents, are reviewed in Chap. 8. Appendix E, pp. 358–65, describes the vigilante type of violence committed against Filipino agricultural workers in Watsonville, and discusses some preceding incidents which may have touched off the violence.

Sargent, Aaron M. "Survey of Filipino Immigration: Report of Immigration Section," *Transactions of the Commonwealth Club of California,* vol. 24, Nov. 1929, pp. 312–20.

Maintains that the rapid increase in Filipino immigration, particularly into California, is due to the intervention of agricultural interests seeking a source of cheap labor to take the place of Orientals who had become scarce because of exclusion laws. Contends that the Filipino does not remain in the rural areas but is attracted to the cities, where he adds to unemployment or replaces white workers because of lower standards, and where, in addition, he becomes a social problem because he is unassimilable. Immigration controls are suggested to lessen the problem.

Scharrenberg, Paul. "California Labor and the Filipinos," *Transactions of the Commonwealth Club of California,* vol. 24, Nov. 1929, pp. 349–53.

The author, secretary-treasurer of the California State Federation of Labor, contends that the Filipino has replaced native California workers in many trades because he is willing to work for lower wages. States that organized labor sees Filipino competition as a national as well as a state problem and supports pending legislation seeking to exclude the Filipino.

Anthony, Donald E. "Filipino Labor in Central California," *Sociology and Social Research,* vol. 16, Nov.–Dec. 1931, pp. 149–56.

Bogardus, Emory S. *Anti-Filipino Race Riots.* A report made to the Ingram Institute of Social Science, San Diego. San Diego, 1930. 29 pp.

California. Department of Industrial Relations. *Facts about Filipino Immigration into California.* Special Bull. no. 3. Sacramento, 1930. 76 pp.

Carrasco, H. C. *The Filipino in California.* Address under auspices of the Filipino Community of Salinas Valley, Calif. Aug. 2, 1940. San Francisco, 1940. 13 pp.

"Filipino Immigration." *Transactions of the Commonwealth Club of California,* vol. 24, Nov. 1929, pp. 308–78.

Fuller, Varden. "The Supply of Agricultural Labor as a Factor in the Evolution of Farm Organization in California." Unpublished Ph.D. dissertation. University of California, Berkeley, 1939. Chap. 7, "The Mexicans and Filipinos in California Agriculture," pp. 215–88.

Provido, Generoso Pacificar. "Oriental Immigration from an American Dependency." Unpublished M.A. thesis. University of California, Berkeley, 1931. 87 pp.

Rodo, Trinidad A. "Filipino-American Contacts: A Tentative Outline for the Materials Collected in a Sociological Survey." [Seattle? 1938?] 17 pp. Typewritten.

Stegner, Wallace, and the Editors of *Look. One Nation*. Boston: Houghton Mifflin, 1945. "The Filipino in America," pp. 19–44.

U.S. Congress. House. Committee on Immigration and Naturalization. *Hearings on Exclusion of Immigration from the Philippine Islands*. 71st Cong., 2d sess. Washington, 1930. Testimony of Andrew Furuseth, pp. 234–38.

————. ————. ————. *Return [of] Unemployed Filipinos to Philippine Islands*. 72d Cong., 2d sess., H. Rept. 1926. Washington, 1933. 8 pp.

U.S. Federal Writers' Project. "Unionization of Filipinos in California Agriculture." [Oakland? 1939?] 14 pp. Typewritten.

NEGRO

Bass, Charlotta A. *Forty Years: Memoirs from the Pages of a Newspaper*. Los Angeles: Privately printed, 1960. 198 pp. 36 pls.

An account of forty years of participation by a Los Angeles Negro newspaper, *The California Eagle,* in efforts to secure civil and economic rights for the Los Angeles Negro community. Chaps. 8, 11, 14, 25, and 62 include significant material on the past and present problems of the Los Angeles Negro worker.

Beasley, Delilah. "Slavery in California," *Journal of Negro History,* vol. 3, Jan. 1918, pp. 33–44.

Tells of the contest between the pro-slavery and anti-slavery groups in California immediately after its conquest by the United States, the defeat of the pro-slavery group at the Constitutional Convention, and the successful outcome of the struggle by anti-slavery legislators in Congress to admit California into the Union as a free state.

Bradley, Booker. "San Francisco's Waterfront Leadership," *Sepia,* Oct. 1960, pp. 45–48. Photographs by Harry L. Cox.

A brief account of Negroes among the officials of the International Longshoremen's and Warehousemen's Union and on the supervisory staffs on the docks.

Bratt, Charles. "Race Relations on the Pacific Coast—Profiles: Los Angeles," *Journal of Educational Sociology,* vol. 19, Nov. 1945, pp. 179–86.

Warns that the Los Angeles County Negro worker may face difficulties in the immediate postwar period. Having failed to become integrated in stable civilian employment and having succeeded in gaining only partial skills, the Negro war worker will have an employment problem. The housing shortage, already acute, is not likely to improve; and race relations, traditionally bad in Los Angeles, may be expected to worsen. Among the suggestions recommended to meet these problems is a closer alliance with the large Los Angeles Mexican minority.

Colored Citizens of California. *Proceedings of the Convention, Sacramento, October 25, 27, 28, 1865.* San Francisco: Office of the "Elevator," 1865. 28 pp.

A statistical report, pp. 12–14, and a report of the Committee on Industrial Pursuits, p. 20, contain information on the participation of California Negroes in various occupations.

Eaves, Lucile. *A History of California Labor Legislation.* Berkeley: The University Press [1910] Chap. 2, "Slave or Free Labor in California," pp. 82–104.

A record of the conflict between the pro- and anti-slavery forces in California during the years immediately following the American occupation. Notes that although the first Constitutional Convention in 1849 adopted an anti-slavery declaration without debate or a dissenting vote, pro-slavery and anti-Negro elements tried to gain their ends by other means, such as the McCarver amendment at the convention, legislative efforts to exclude Negroes, an effort to divide the state, and the passage of the Fugitive Slave Law.

Hansen, Woodrow James. *The Search for Authority in California.* Oakland: Biobooks, 1960. Chap. 26, "The Second Week—The Bill of Rights: Social and Political Ideals," pp. 113–17; chap. 30, "McCarver's Free Negro Amendment," pp. 131–34; chap. 35, "The Fifth Week—Resolution of the Banking, Free-Negro, and Indian Questions," pp. 151–54.

An account of the debate at the first California Constitutional Convention on the provision to prohibit slavery in California, and the more bitterly debated provision to prohibit the immigration of free Negroes into the state.

Helper, Hinton Rowan. *The Land of Gold: Reality Versus Fiction.* Baltimore: Published for the author by Henry Taylor, 1855. Chap. 19, "The Digger Indians and Negroes," pp. 268–79.

Discounts the Indian's usefulness as a laborer and provides a description of Negro life in California.

James, Joseph. "Race Relations on the Pacific Coast—Profiles: San Francisco," *Journal of Educational Sociology,* vol. 19, Nov. 1945, pp. 166–78.

Examines the occupational and race-relations patterns of the small San Francisco Negro community before World War II and the fundamental changes in these patterns resulting from the fivefold growth of the community during the war. These changes—a critical shortage in housing and recreation facilities, increasing problems in employment and trade-union relations, and, most serious of all, an abrupt change in public attitudes—are considered with a view to finding both immediate and longer-range postwar solutions.

Johnson, Charles S. "Negro Workers in Los Angeles Industries," *Opportunity,* vol. 6, Aug. 1928, pp. 234–40.

Analyzes the occupations and wages of the Negro worker in Los Angeles and shows how they are affected and determined by various types of discriminatory practices. Of special interest are references to the Negro's economic competition with the Mexican population and his share of membership in the local trade unions.

Keene, R. J. "Waterfront Screening," *Sun Reporter* (S.F.), Jan. 12, 19, 26, Feb. 2, 9, 1952.

Tells how Negro maritime workers on the Pacific Coast are affected by the U.S. Coast Guard port security screening procedures.

Mann, Horace. *New Dangers to Freedom and New Duties for Its Defenders: A Letter to His Constituents.* Boston: Redding and Co., 1850. 32 pp.

Contains references to attempts in Congress to extend slavery to California.

National Negro Congress. Los Angeles Council. *Jim Crow in National Defense.* [Los Angeles, 1940?] 28 pp.

Deals with discriminatory practices against Negro workers in the aircraft industry of southern California.

"Negro Problem Worries Coast," *Business Week,* Dec. 23, 1944, pp. 32–44.

"Far West's war industries have made it important for the first time, and part of the trouble is its newness. Union rules and community efforts will count heavily in any solution."

Record, C. Wilson. "The Chico Story: A Black and White Harvest," *Crisis,* Feb. 1951, pp. 95–101, 129–31, 133.

What happens when migrant Negro farm workers are introduced for the first time into a predominantly white community.

Savage, W. Sherman. "The Negro on the Mining Frontier," *Journal of Negro History*, vol. 30, Jan. 1945, pp. 30–46.

Asserts that historical evidence shows that the Negro, both as a slave and as a free man, was an important factor in the gold mines, serving not only as laborer but also as independent prospector or claim owner.

Weaver, Robert C. *Negro Labor: A National Problem.* New York: Harcourt, Brace, 1946. "A West Coast Version," pp. 171–81.

Tells how union and employer opposition prevented for a time the upgrading of Negroes in the Los Angeles transit system during World War II despite an extreme shortage of transit personnel. Negotiations lasting almost two years brought no positive results, and it was only after decisive intervention by the federal government in 1944 that upgrading of Negroes to operators and similar jobs was begun.

YWCA, American Missionary Association, Julius Rosenwald Fund. *The Negro War Worker in San Francisco: A Local Self Survey.* San Francisco, 1944. 98 pp.

A survey made during World War II of the features and problems of San Francisco's mushrooming Negro community. Text and statistical tables clarify the results of extensive surveys covering such aspects as the Negro family group, housing, education, delinquency, and employment. Pages 16–19 analyze Negro occupational patterns and trade-union affiliation. Chap. 7 examines problems of Negro wartime employment, including employer and union practices and attitudes, and concludes with recommendations touching on current and future problems of the San Francisco Negro worker.

American Council on Race Relations. *Negro Platform Workers*. Chicago, 1945. "A West Coast Variation," pp. 21–35.

Babow, Irving, and Edward Howden. *A Civil Rights Inventory of San Francisco*. Part 1, "Employment." San Francisco: Council for Civic Unity of San Francisco, June 1958. 352 pp.

Barbour, W. Miller. *An Exploratory Study of Socio-Economic Problems Affecting the Negro-White Relationship in Richmond, California*. New York: United Community Defense Services, 1952. Sec. 1, "Social and Economic Setting: Population and Income; Employment; Unions," pp. 1–16.

Beasley, Delilah L. *The Negro Trail Blazers of California*. Los Angeles, 1919. Chap. 9, "Slavery in California, Together with Freedom Papers," pp. 66–97.

Bond, J. Max. "The Negro in Los Angeles." Unpublished Ph.D. dissertation. University of Southern California, 1936. Chap. 4, "Occupations," pp. 158–200.

California. Division of Fair Employment Practices. *Negro Californians*. San Francisco, 1963. 34 pp.

"California Freedom Papers," *Journal of Negro History,* vol. 3, Jan. 1918, pp. 45–54.

Cayton, Horace R. "New Problem for the West Coast." Articles in Chicago *Sun,* Oct. 14–16, 1943.

Claiborne, M. C. *Achievements of the Negro in California*. [Berkeley] Berkeley Interracial Committee, 1945. 21 pp.

"Colored California," *Crisis,* vol. 6, Aug. 1913, pp. 192–95.

Council of Social Agencies and Community Chest, Oakland. *Study of Social and Economic Conditions Affecting the Local Negro Population,* by J. Harvey Kerns. Oakland, 1942. 31 pp.

Davison, Berlinda. "Educational Status of the Negro in the San Francisco Bay Region." Unpublished M.A. thesis. University of California, Berkeley, 1921. Chap. 1, "The Negro in the San Francisco Bay Region," pp. 1–24.

Dunimay, Clyde A. "Slavery in California after 1848," *American Historical Association Annual Report,* vol. 1 (of two), 1905, pp. 243–48.

East Bay Council of the Arts, Sciences and Professions. *Negro Professional in Bay Area Social Agencies, June 1, 1954.* Berkeley [1954?] [9] pp.

Friedman, Ralph. "The Negro in Hollywood," *Frontier,* vol. 9, July 1958, pp. 15–20.

Hill, Herbert. *No Harvest for the Reaper.* The story of the migratory agricultural worker in the United States. New York: National Association for the Advancement of Colored People [1959?] 47 pp. Illustrated.

Levene, Carol. "The Negro in San Francisco," *Common Ground,* vol. 9, Spring 1949, pp. 10–17.

McEntire, Davis A., and J. T. Arnopol. "Postwar Status of Negro Workers in the San Francisco Area," *Monthly Labor Review,* vol. 70, June 1950, pp. 612–17.

McWilliams, Carey. "Jim Crow Goes West." Articles in *PM,* April 24–26, 1945. [Also, condensed, in *Negro Digest,* vol. 3, Aug. 1945, pp. 71–74]

———. *Report on Importation of Negro Labor to California.* Los Angeles: California Division of Immigration and Housing, 1942. 9 pp.

National Urban League. *Negro Membership in American Labor Unions.* New York: Alexander Press, 1930. "Los Angeles, California," pp. 142–45.

Reynolds, Marian Hobart. "Instances of Negro Slavery in California." [Cambridge, Mass., 1914] [13] pp. Typewritten.

"The San Francisco Experiment: A Self Survey as a Basis for Action," *Fisk University Social Science Institute Monthly Summary,* vol. 1, May 1944, pp. 10–12.

Stripp, Fred. "The Relationships of the San Francisco Bay Area Negro-American Worker with the Labor Unions Affiliated with the American Federation of Labor and the C.I.O." Unpublished Th.D. dissertation. Pacific School of Religion, Berkeley, 1948. 305 pp.

U.S. Federal Writers' Project. "Labor in California Cotton Fields." [Oakland? 1938?] "The Negro," pp. 62–65. Typewritten.

Weaver, Robert C. "Negro Employment in the Aircraft Industry," *Quarterly Journal of Economics,* vol. 59, Aug. 1945, pp. 597–625.

Weiss, Myra Tanner. *Vigilante Terror in Fontana: The Tragic Story of O'Day Short and His Family.* Los Angeles: Socialist Workers Party, 1946. 20 pp.

INDIAN

Browne, J. Ross. "The Indian Reservations of California," *in* W. W. Beach, *Indian Miscellany*. Albany, N.Y.: J. Munsell, 1877. Pp. 303–22.

Condemns the white man's exploitation and general treatment of the California Indian and ridicules the federal government's efforts to alleviate his condition.

Caughey, John Walton, ed. *The Indians of Southern California in 1852*. The B. D. Wilson report and a selection of contemporary comment. San Marino, Calif.: Huntington Library, 1952. 154 pp.

Written by the federal subagent for Indians in Southern California, the report aims to establish that a well organized reservation system, along with other constructive programs, could revive the more practical and desirable features of the old mission system. The report is generally considered valuable not only because it described the condition of the Indians who at that time comprised the majority of the population in that area, but also because, as a contemporary newspaper observed, it reflected the general condition of that part of California in those days. Pages ix–xxxiv contain the editor's introduction to the report.

Cook, Sherburne Friend. *The Conflict between the California Indian and White Civilization. III: The American Invasion, 1848–1870*. Ibero-Americana: 23. Berkeley: University of California Press, 1943. "Labor," pp. 46–75.

Observes that of all the labor systems the Spanish had introduced into the Americas, the peonage system best suited the California Indian's condition, but that under American rule certain influences combined to destroy the preëminence of the peonage system and force the Indian into the free labor market. The study examines these influences and the Indian's reaction to the free labor system.

——. *Diet Adaptation among California and Nevada Indians*. Berkeley: University of California Press, 1941. 59 pp.

Studies the gradual loss by the Indian of his native food supply, his eventual almost total acceptance of the white man's food, and the fundamental change in the Indian's economic relationship to the white civilization this change of diet resulted in.

Hough, John C. "Charles Henry Brinley: A Case Study in Rancho Supervision," *Historical Society of Southern California Quarterly*, vol. 40, June 1958, pp. 174–79.

An examination of labor-management relations on an American-owned rancho in California shortly after the American conquest. The following memorandum from Brinley, the rancho administrator, to his employer is revealing: "Send someone to attend the auction that usually takes place at the prison on Mondays and buy me five or six Indians."

American Friends Service Committee. *Indians of California, Past and Present*. San Francisco, 1957. 36 pp.

Browne, J. Ross. *The Indians of California*. San Francisco: Colt Press, 1944. 73 pp. [First published in 1864]

Davis, Carlyle C. "Ramona, the Ideal and the Real," *Out West,* vol. 19, Dec. 1903, pp. 575–96.

Ellison, Joseph. *California and the Nation, 1850–1869*. University of California Publications in History, no. 16. Berkeley: University of California Press, 1926.

Knoop, Anna Marie. "The Federal Indian Policy in the Sacramento Valley, 1846–1860." Unpublished M.A. thesis. University of California, Berkeley, 1941. Chap. 2, "Sutter's Indian Policy in the Sacramento Valley, 1839–1846," pp. 10–34.

Robinson, W. W. *The Indians of Los Angeles: Story of the Liquidation of a People*. Los Angeles: Glen Dawson, 1952. 43 pp.

[San Diego County] *Fact-Finding Study of Social and Economic Conditions of Indians of San Diego County, California*. [San Diego, 1932] 126 pp.

Underhill, Ruth. *Indians of Southern California*. Photographs by Velino Herrera. Sherman Pamphlets, no. 2. Lawrence, Kans.: U.S. Office of Indian Affairs, Haskell Institute [1941?] "History," pp. 57–67.

Williamson, M. Burton. "The Mission Indians on the San Jacinto Reservation," Historical Society of Southern California, *Annual Publications,* vol. 7, pts. 2–3, 1907–1908, pp. 134–43.

VARIOUS MINORITIES

Ayers, James J. *Gold and Sunshine: Reminiscences of Early California*. Boston: Richard G. Badger, 1922. Chaps. 5–6, "The Chilean War in Calaveras County—A Thrilling Chapter of Unwritten History," "Obvious Observations upon the Bloody Episode," pp. 46–69.

An account of an armed clash between Chilean and American miners in 1849. Involved was the claim that the Chilean settlement was made up of headmen and their peons who were in fact equivalent to slaves. This claim was followed by a demand that a law prohibiting Americans from the southern states from taking up claims for their slaves be applied to the Chileans.

Bjork, Kenneth O. *West of the Great Divide: Norwegian Migration to the Pacific Coast, 1847–1893*. Northfield, Minn.: Norwegian-American Historical Association, 1958. Chap. 2, "Argonauts in California," pp. 22–73; chap. 4, "A San Francisco Story," pp. 151–77.

Letters of immigrants and the pages of the immigrant and homeland press tell how economic depression in Norway and the lure of gold brought thousands of Norwegians to California. Most of them remained to work at the trades or to follow business pursuits after the gold fever had passed, and they were later joined by many more from both the homeland and the established colonies in the Midwest. Of the Scandinavians he met in San Francisco in 1870, the Rev. Christian Hvistendahl is quoted as writing: "Most of the people are seamen and craftsmen."

Massarik, Fred. *A Report on the Jewish Population in Los Angeles.* Los Angeles: Jewish Community Council, 1953. 126 pp.

An annotated statistical review of the activities and interests of the Jewish population of Los Angeles. Pages 33–39 are devoted to statistical tables on employment by occupation and industry for Greater Los Angeles. Pages 92–98 are devoted to tables containing similar information for specific geographic areas within Greater Los Angeles.

————. *A Report on the Jewish Population of Los Angeles, 1959.* Los Angeles: Research Service Bureau, Jewish Federation–Council of Greater Los Angeles, 1959. Chap. 6, "Ways to Make a Living," pp. 20–27.

Analyzes survey data showing the occupational and industrial distribution and the employment status of Jewish wage earners in Los Angeles. Indicates that the data, compared to those of a similar survey made in 1951, reflect significant changes in the occupational and industrial distribution patterns of the Jewish wage earners.

Moment, Samuel. "A Study of San Francisco Jewry, 1938," *in* Sophia M. Robison, ed., *Jewish Population Studies.* Jewish Social Studies Publication no. 3. New York: Conference on Jewish Relations, 1943. Chap. 10, pp. 160–82.

Includes data on employment, occupations, and the professions.

Mukerji, Dhan Gopal. *Caste and Outcast.* New York: Dutton, 1923. Part 2, "In California Fields," pp. 264–82.

A University of California Hindu student relates his experiences as a member of a group of Hindu agricultural workers, harvesting field crops.

Radin, Paul. *The Italians of San Francisco: Their Adjustment and Acculturation.* Monograph no. 1. Introduction and Part 1, Abstract from the SERA Project 2-F2-98 (3-F2-145): Cultural Anthropology [San Francisco?] 1935. 111 pp.

States that the primary object of the study is to determine the action of certain processes relative to the Italian population in San Francisco during the period 1890–1930. The study includes an investigation of the composition of the Italian population, which showed a predominance of workers, and an examination of the fishing industry, which was the chief occupation of these workers. Illustrative autobiographies are included.

Altrocchi, Julia Cooley. "The Spanish Basques in California," *Catholic World,* vol. 146, Jan. 1938, pp. 417–24.

Austin, Leonard. *Around the World in San Francisco: A Guide to Unexplored San Francisco.* San Francisco: Fearon Publishers, 1959. 96 pp.

Bohme, Frederick G. "The Portuguese in California," *California Historical Society Quarterly,* vol. 35, Sept. 1956, pp. 233–52.

Das, Rajani Kanta. *Hindustani Workers on the Pacific Coast.* Berlin: Walter de Gruyter and Co., 1923. 126 pp.

Hedin, Elmer L. "Hindu Americans," *in* Francis J. Brown and Joseph Slabey Roucek, ed., *Our Racial and National Minorities: Their History, Contributions and Present Problems.* New York: Prentice-Hall, 1937. Pp. 450–62.

International Institute of Alameda County. *A Directory of the Foreign Communities of Alameda County.* [Oakland?] 1936. 27 pp.

Johnson, Annette Thackwell. "Rag Heads—a Picture of America's East Indians," *Independent,* vol. 109, Oct. 28, 1922, pp. 234–35.

Ken, Charles W. "Descendents of Captain Sutter's Kanakas," *Proceedings,* Second Annual Meeting of the Conference of California Historical Societies, June 21–23, 1956. Sonora, Calif.: Mother Lode Press. Pp. 87–102.

Kohs, Samuel C. "The Jewish Community of Los Angeles," *Jewish Review,* vol. 2, July–Oct. 1944. "Occupational Distribution," pp. 115–26.

Lévy, Daniel. *Les Français en Californie.* San Francisco: Gregoire, Tauzy et Cie., 1884. 373 pp.

L'Union Laborieuse Fondée à San Francisco (Californie) le 13 Août, 1868. *Constitution.* San Francisco: A. H. Rapp, 1869. 11 pp.

Mahakian, Charles. "History of the Armenians in California." Unpublished M.A. thesis. University of California, Berkeley, 1935. Chaps. 1–2, "Armenian Immigration to California," "Economic Life of Armenians in California," pp. 1–40.

Meler, Vjekoslav, ed. *The Slavonic Pioneers of California.* San Francisco, 1932. 101 pp.

Nicosia, Frances. *Italian Pioneers of California.* [San Francisco?] Italian American Chamber of Commerce of the Pacific Coast, 1960. [32] pp.

Niland, Billyanna. "Yugoslavs in San Pedro, California," *Sociology and Social Research,* vol. 26, Sept.–Oct., 1941, pp. 36–44.

Raup, H. F. "The Italian-Swiss in California," *California Historical Society Quarterly,* vol. 30, Dec. 1951, pp. 305–14.

Sestanovich, Stephen Nicholas, ed. *Slavs in California: An Historical, Social and Economic Survey of Slavic Progress in California Since Their Arrival*. Oakland: Slavonic Alliance of California, 1937. 136 pp.

UTOPIAN COLONIES

Hanna, Hugh A. "The Llano del Rio Cooperative Colony," *Monthly Labor Review,* vol. 2, Jan. 1916, pp. 19–23.

Describes life at the colony a year and a half after it had been established.

Haskell, Burnette G. "Kaweah, How and Why the Colony Died," *Out West,* vol. 17, Sept. 1902, pp. 300–22.

The first and only president of Kaweah explains why, in spite of the high ideals on which it was founded, the colony nevertheless failed. The reasons, he points out, were many, but human frailty was most prominent among them. The opposition of the press and the lumber monopoly as well as federal prosecution made failure the more certain.

Hine, Robert V. *California's Utopian Colonies, 1850–1950.* San Marino, Calif.: The Huntington Library, 1953. 209 pp.

Gives an account of the establishment and fortunes of the numerous utopian colonies which once dotted California. Only the cooperative colonies of Kaweah, Icaria Speranza, and Llano del Rio are indicated to have had any significant relationship to the California labor movement.

Hoffman, Abe. "A Look at Llano: Experiment in Economic Socialism," *California Historical Society Quarterly,* vol. 40, Sept. 1961, pp. 215–36.

"The years 1914 through 1918 witnessed the birth, existence, and death in California of the socialistic cooperative colony of Llano del Rio." Stating that Llano was the result of Job Harriman's desire for practical and applied socialism, this paper by a graduate student at Los Angeles State College describes the formation, erratic course, and early death of the colony, and in the process demonstrates that the experiment was somewhat less than practical and not quite socialist.

Lewis, Ruth R. "Kaweah: An Experiment in Cooperative Colonization," *Pacific Historical Review,* vol. 17, Nov. 1948, pp. 429–41.

Relates some of the brief history of the utopian colony: its beginnings, dissension among the colonists, difficulties with the Department of the Interior and the federal courts, and its dissolution in 1892.

Shinn, Charles Howard. *Coöperation on the Pacific Coast.* Johns Hopkins University Studies in Historical and Political Science, 6th series, nos. 9–10. Baltimore, 1888. Pp. 447–81.

Discusses a number of cooperative enterprises in California, including the Kaweah and the Italian-Swiss agricultural colonies, and the boot and shoe and watch repairing cooperatives. The author observes that, with the exception of the Kaweah colony, these enterprises were cooperative only in a limited sense. Also included is a brief discussion of cooperation among the Chinese in California.

Altruria Co-operative Union of Oakland, California. *Code of By-Laws.* Oakland, 1895. 16 pp.

Bauer, Patricia M. *Cooperative Colonies in California: A Bibliography Collected . . . in Bancroft Library and Doe Memorial Library (for Joseph Henry Jackson).* [Berkeley] n.d. [26] pp.

Berland, Oscar. "Giant Forest's Reservation: The Legend and the Mystery," *Sierra Club Bulletin,* vol. 47, Dec. 1962, pp. 68–82.

Clifton, A. R. "History of the Communistic Colony, Llano del Rio," Historical Society of Southern California, *Annual Publications,* vol. 11, pt. 1, 1918, pp. 80–90.

Hine, Robert V. "A California Utopia: 1885–1890," *Huntington Library Quarterly,* vol. 11, Aug. 1948, pp. 387–405.

Jones, William Carey. "The Kaweah Experiment in Co-operation," *Quarterly Journal of Economics,* vol. 6, Oct. 1891, pp. 47–75.

Kaweah Colony Association. *First Annual Report of the Executive Committee of the Kaweah Colony.* [Visalia, Calif.?] 1887. 8 pp.

Kaweah Co-operative Colony Company. *Pen Picture of the Kaweah Co-operative Colony.* Supplement to *The Commonwealth.* San Francisco, April 1889. 32 pp.

———. Eastern Group. *The Persecution of Kaweah: Story of a Great Injustice.* [New York] 1891. 44 + 5 pp.

———. San Francisco Committee. *The Crisis: To All Kaweah Colonists; A Statement of the Legal and Moral Position of the Colony at the Present Time.* [San Francisco, 1887] 22 + 7 pp. List of membership, pp. 1–7.

Kaweah, a Cooperative Commonwealth. [Visalia, Calif.] n.d. 16 pp.

McWilliams, Carey. *Factories in the Field: The Story of Migratory Farm Labor in California.* Boston: Little, Brown, 1939. "Kaweah," pp. 39–47.

Payne, Edward B. "Altruria," *American Magazine of Civics,* vol. 6, Feb. 1895, pp. 168–71.

Purdy, Will. *Kaweah: An Epic of the Old Colony.* [Poem] Visalia, Calif.: Tulare County Historical Society [1959?] 15+ pp.

Swift, Morrison. "Altruria," *Overland,* vol. 29, June 1897, pp. 643–45.

Turner, Alice Lee. "Communistic Colonies in California." Unpublished M.A. thesis. University of California, Berkeley, 1925. 113 pp.

U.S. Congress. Senate. Select Committee on Forest Reservations in California. *Report of the Committee.* 52d Cong., 2d sess., S. Rept. 1248. Washington, 1893. 82 pp.

Wooster, Ernest S. "Bread and Hyacinths," *Sunset,* vol. 53, Aug. 1924, pp. 21–23, 59–60.

———. *Communities of the Past and Present.* New Llano, La.: 1924. "Llano Co-operative Colony, 1914 to the Present Time," pp. 117–37.

———. "They Shared Equally," *Sunset,* vol. 53, July 1924, pp. 21–23, 80–82.

LABOR FICTION

Carey, Bernice. *The Beautiful Stranger*. Garden City: Doubleday, 1951. 192 pp.

The small California town of Conway with its mill, owned by Montgomery Street interests, the beautiful bride whom Jim McGowan, one of the mill's workers, brought home from San Francisco, a campaign by the CIO to organize an industrial union in the mill, and the murder of Lester Coleman, Conway's bachelor "wolf" and spy for the mill's management, make up the elements of this thriller. The mill management's measures to forestall organization of the mill, which include an attempt to implicate Jim McGowan in the murder of Coleman, fall through, and the CIO's efforts are presumably headed for success.

Chevalier, Haakon. *For Us the Living*. New York: Knopf, 1949. 400 pp.

A murder mystery is unfolded against a background of migrant labor-rancher strife in the San Joaquin Valley of California, the depression years of the 1930's, the second world war, and academic life at a university near San Francisco. Steve Callahan, manager of the Regan Ranch, largest in the valley, is murdered. In turn, his wife Germaine is tried for the murder and acquitted; four years later Larry Hellman, a liberal professor at the university, is tried for the crime and also acquitted; four years after Hellman's acquittal Angelo Parenti, leader of the agricultural workers, is charged with the murder. The story is climaxed by the disclosure that a secret antilabor operative for the Western Packers, and Nazi agent, was the actual murderer of Callahan.

Dooner, P. W. *Last Days of the Republic*. Illustrated by G. F. Keller. San Francisco: Alta California Publishing House, 1880. 258 pp.

A simulated history of the conquest of the United States by the Chinese. As part of a carefully preconceived plan, starting at the time of the California gold rush, the Chinese government gradually populates California, then other Pacific Coast states, and later New England and the South, with millions of coolies, the Six Chinese Companies acting as the secret subgovernment. These coolies eventually destroy the native working class and go on to take over commerce and industry, local and state governments, and militias. Then China openly invades the United States and after a number of bloody battles plants the dragon flag atop the national capitol.

Duncan, David. *The Serpent's Egg*. New York: Macmillan, 1950. 243 pp.

A minor but vital labor relations issue serves as the basis for a sometimes dramatic novel. John Duffy, a long-distance bus driver, is held up by the dispatcher for five hours between assignments. Duffy's union files an overtime claim for the five hours and a number of people are immediately affected: Brad Johnsen, the union's business agent, who is slated for a top job in the international and is for that reason in conflict with his wife, fearing what effect her membership in the Communist

Party might have on his appointment; Jim Kensington, who worked his way from a farm to top-flight labor arbitrator; Ann Cameron, secretary to the union's lawyer and wife of Kensington's closest friend. The arbitration case is fought fiercely by the bus company, which fears an industry precedent, and it sees its chance for victory when it discovers an indiscretion between Ann and Kensington. Everything, however, ends happily: Kensington sacrifices himself and saves the case for the union; Johnsen's wife drops out of the Communist Party, thus assuring her husband's career; and John Duffy gets his five hours' overtime.

Fisher, Anne B. *Cathedral in the Sun.* New York: Carlyle House, 1940. 408 pp.

A leisurely paced novel of life in Monterey and at the Carmel Mission under Spanish and later under Mexican and American rule, as seen through the eyes of the neophyte O-nes-e-mo and his daughter Loreta. A recurring theme is the exploitation of the native Indian. By implication, the mission padres are absolved of blame for this exploitation, and the Spanish and Mexican colonists held responsible.

Gallen, A.A. *The Wetback.* Boston: Bruce Humphries, 1961. 243 pp.

A story of the fortunes and conflicts of two Imperial Valley ranchers and their families. The migrant agricultural worker, the bracero, and "wetback" smuggling operations figure prominently in the novel as its action develops in a highly productive area of the valley, adjacent to the Mexican border.

Hardman, R. L. *No Other Harvest.* New York: Doubleday, 1962. 346 pp.

A novel set in the "Grapes of Wrath" country, at a time when agriculture is undergoing rapid mechanization. Involved in a complex plot is a rancher family, a contractor of agricultural labor, and some migrant agricultural workers.

Jackson, Helen Hunt. *Ramona.* Boston: Roberts Bros., 1884; Little, Brown, 1939. 424 pp.

Ramona is widely remembered because of its touching love story and its glamorous background. But it is known that Mrs. Jackson's purpose in writing the novel went beyond its romantic features. In November 1883 she wrote to her friends, the Coronels of Southern California: "I am going to write a novel, in which will be set forth some Indian experiences in a way to move people's hearts." Her concern was the condition of the California Indian who, dispossessed of his lands, was barely surviving as a ward of the federal government on a reservation or eking out a marginal existence as a farm laborer under conditions little removed from peonage.

London, Jack. "The Dream of Debs," *in* Philip S. Foner, *Jack London, American Rebel.* New York: Citadel Press, 1947. Pp. 240–57.

A San Francisco capitalist awakens an hour earlier than his usual time because of an unaccustomed silence that has fallen over the city. From his serving man he learns that the daily deliveries of bread, milk, and cream have not been made; only the morning paper has been delivered and from that he learns the reason for the strange state of affairs: the ILW has called a national general strike in retaliation for the open-shop drive of the employers. The rest of the story describes the strike as it progresses and tells how labor brings the employers to their knees.

————. "South of the Slot," *in* Foner, *Jack London, American Rebel*. Pp. 258–72.

A short story with a Dr. Jekyll and Mr. Hyde plot. Frederick Drummond, professor of sociology at the University of California at Berkeley, is continually writing books on labor with an antilabor slant. To get his material, he at times crosses San Francisco's "slot" into the labor ghetto and becomes Big Bill Botts, the loyal and militant union man. How his two identities come to clash, and how in the end Big Bill Botts marries both the working class and Mary Condon, president of Glove Makers Union No. 974, is told in the surprising and amusing climax of the story.

————. *The Valley of the Moon*. New York: Macmillan, 1913. 530 pp.

A novel of working-class life in Oakland shortly after the San Francisco earthquake. Railroad shopman Bert Wanhope and his wife Mary, and teamster Bill Roberts and his wife Saxon, both couples newly married, are friends and neighbors and live quietly, hopefully planning future families. But their plans are suddenly interrupted by fast developing labor-capital strife sparked by an employer drive to institute the open shop. Bert is killed in a clash with railroad shop strikebreakers, and Mary, rather than go back to her work in a laundry, turns to prostitution. After experiencing extreme poverty during a long and violent teamster strike, Bill and Saxon decide to seek a more satisfying life in the country. They wander through the countryside for three years, looking for their ideal—"The Valley of the Moon"—which they finally find in Sonoma County.

Mitchell, Ruth Comfort. *Of Human Kindness*. New York: Appleton-Century, 1940. 359 pp.

This novel suggests parallels to John Steinbeck's story about the problems of migrant agricultural labor in the 1930's, *The Grapes of Wrath*. The point of view, however, is reversed, the rancher Banner family changing symbolic places with the migrant Joad family. Ed Banner, his mother, wife, son, and daughter slowly build their modest inherited San Joaquin farm into sizable proportions. Then they are faced with the problems of the depression years: There is trouble with the migrant help; the daughter marries an Oklahoma migrant worker; the son joins "The Cause" of the left. But in the end everything rights itself. The Oklahoma migrant turns out to be the son of a well-to-do farmer; the son becomes disillusioned with "The Cause"; and the ranchers, with Ed Banner now leading them, solve the problem of the migrant workers in their own way.

Norris, Charles Gilman. *Flint*. Garden City, N.Y.: Doubleday, Doran, 1944. 354 pp.

"... this is a novel and does not describe actual happenings or portray real people living or dead." Despite the author's disclaimer, this story of conflict in the 1930's between the maritime workers on the Pacific Coast and their employers can be related to actual happenings. The shipowning family, the Rutherfords; Rory O'Brien, the left-wing longshoremen's leader; Mat Swenson, the blond leader of the sailors; and Caddie Welch, the woman who influenced waterfront affairs beyond her seeming importance, are all identifiable. The story, however, ends with a smashing climax which is not identifiable with actual events of the period.

Oakes, Vanya. *Footprints of the Dragon: A Story of the Chinese and the Pacific Railways*. Illustrated by Tyrus Wong. Philadelphia: Winston, 1949. 240 pp.

A fictional account of the labor and fortunes of a Chinese railroad crew, engaged in the construction of the Central Pacific Railroad (Southern Pacific) over the Sierras and the Nevada and Utah deserts.

Saxton, Alexander. *Bright Web in the Darkness*. New York: St. Martin's Press, 1958. 308 pp.

Discrimination against the Negro worker during World War II in a San Francisco Bay Area shipyard, by both his white fellow workers and their unions, is the immediate theme of this novel. But in a larger sense the injustice of the Negro's position, highlighted by a period of crisis, could be regarded as the theme. The two leaders of the Negro shipyard workers, Richard Crooks and Reverend Beezley, represent different approaches to meeting the problem of the Negro. The novel is peopled with bona fide working-class types.

Sinclair, Upton. *Co-op: A Novel of Living Together*. New York: Farrar & Rinehart, 1936. 426 pp.

Depicts the fortunes of one of the numerous self-help cooperatives that sprang up in California during the depression of the 1930's. Most of the devices of story-telling are used, including "boy meets girl." The cast of characters is varied and includes workers of all kinds and descriptions, capitalists, hard and soft, wobblies, communists, socialists, and also "epics," under whose banner the author unsuccessfully ran for governor of California in 1934.

Steinbeck, John. *The Grapes of Wrath*. New York: Viking, 1939. 619 pp.

The intense drama of the hundreds of thousands of midwestern and southwestern small farmers and sharecroppers displaced from their land by drought and the machine, symbolized in the trek of the patriarchal Joad family from Oklahoma to the cotton fields of California—to them the promised land. Their journey is an odyssey of death, hunger, and privation, and when they reach their goal it is only to share the destitution and degradation of the many thousands that had preceded them.

————. *In Dubious Battle*. New York: Covici-Friede, 1936. 349 pp.

An action-packed novel of a strike in the California apple country. The Growers' Association advertising has brought hundreds more pickers than are necessary to harvest the crop, and the picking price is cut. Nolan and McLeod, field Party organizers, appear on the scene and with the help of London and Dakin, the natural leaders among the workers, they get the pickers out on strike. The strike brings with it imported strikebreakers, intimidation, provocation, and armed deputy and vigilante violence. The action of the novel ends inconclusively but not before, in the view of McLeod, the broader aims of the Party are realized: giving the strikers a feeling of their united strength and a conviction of the implacable nature of their enemy.

Villarreal, Jose Antonio. *Pocho*. Garden City: Doubleday, 1959. 235 pp.

Juan Rubio had been one of Pancho Villa's devoted officers. When Villa was assassinated in 1923, Rubio thought of the Mexican revolution as lost and left Mexico, going on to California, where with his family, he first followed the crops and later settled in the Santa Clara Valley to work in the orchards. *Pocho* is the story of the Rubio family's struggle with their everyday problems in the context of this California Mexican-American community; but it is especially the story of the boyhood and youth of Rubio's only son, Richard.

MISCELLANEOUS

Alkaline Salt Workers, Local 414. *The Story of Trona: An American Fight for Economic Independence.* Trona, Calif.: Local 414, Mine, Mill and Smelter Workers Union [1941?] 14 pp.

Local 414 tells of its victory over its rival, a company-supported union, and of its attempt to negotiate wages, housing, preferential hiring, and other issues with the American Potash and Chemical Corporation, a British-owned company producing chemicals at a plant in Death Valley, California. Convinced that the negotiations would not succeed, the union called a strike to realize its demands.

Atherton, Gertrude. *My San Francisco: A Wayward Biography.* Indianapolis: Bobbs-Merrill, 1946. Chap. 10, "California Labor School," pp. 193–99.

An enthusiastic account of an adult education project for workers, organized in San Francisco during the early part of World War II by groups from local AFL and CIO unions. Tells of its growth from 100 students with classes in a loft to 2600 with classes in a five-story building, and from a teaching staff of a few trade-union officials to a large faculty including nationally famous instructors and lecturers.

Beatty, Bessie. "The Closing of the Line," in *The Bulletin Book.* San Francisco: *The Bulletin* [1917?] Pp. 75–78.

A reporter visits a "house" after a police shutdown and learns from the girls, former domestic servants and stenographers, how and why they had adopted their new way of life.

Bers, Melvin K. *Union Policy and the Older Worker.* Berkeley: Institute of Industrial Relations, University of California, 1957. 87 pp.

The study is based, in the main, on an examination of hiring and retirement practices of San Francisco Bay Area unions.

Cross, Ira B. *Financing an Empire: History of Banking in California.* San Francisco: S. J. Clarke Publishing Co., 1927. Vol. 2, chap. 23, "Labor Banks in California," pp. 869–81.

Describes the establishment of banks by the railroad brotherhoods and other unions in the mid-1920's in Los Angeles, San Bernardino, Bakersfield, and San Francisco.

Garbarino, Joseph W. "The Development of Health Insurance Plans," *Monthly Labor Review,* vol. 82, May 1959, pp. 572–78.

Sketches the development of health insurance plans, including vision and dental programs, on the west coast and shows how they compare with such plans nationally. The features of two union-negotiated plans, the Teamsters Security Fund and the Kaiser Foundation Health Plan, and several vision and dental care programs are examined in some detail.

Aaron, Benjamin. "The Use of Arbitration [on the West Coast]" *Monthly Labor Review,* vol. 82, May 1959, pp. 543–46.

Bennett, John E. "Is the West Discontented?" *Overland,* vol. 28, Oct. 1896, pp. 456–63.

California. Department of Industrial Relations. *Middle Aged and Older Workers.* Special Bull. no. 31. Sacramento, 1930. 35 pp.

———. Division of Labor Statistics and Research. *Arbitration Provisions in California Union Agreements.* San Francisco, 1951. 15 pp.

———. ———. *Handbook of California Labor Statistics, 1949–1950.* Sacramento, 1951. 104 pp.

———. ———. *Labor-Management Negotiated Health and Welfare Plans, Northern California.* San Francisco, 1954. 71 pp.

———. State Planning Board. *An Economic and Industrial Survey of the San Francisco Bay Area.* Sacramento, 1941. Parts 3–4, "Incomes and Planes of Living," "The Pattern of Economic Activities," pp. 74–131.

California Campaign Federation. *How Prohibition Affects Labor.* San Francisco, n.d. 8 pp.

California CIO Council. *The CIO Reports on the War.* Report of Executive Committee meeting, April 3–4, 1943. San Francisco, 1934. 22 pp.

Cleland, Robert Glass. *California Pageant: The Story of Four Centuries.* New York: Knopf, 1946. "Economic Unrest," pp. 203–12.

Committee of Forty-three. *The State of the City: A Report to the People of San Francisco on Industrial Relations.* San Francisco, 1938. 15 pp.

The Crockett Vigilantes (Hidden Fascism in a California Industrial Town). [Crockett, Calif.? 1937?] 7 pp.

Cross, Ira B. "Workmen's Compensation in California," *American Economic Review,* vol. 4, June 1914, pp. 454–59.

Golden, Clinton S., and Virginia D. Parker, eds. *Causes of Industrial Peace under Collective Bargaining.* New York: Harper, 1955. Part 2, Condensations of Thirteen Case Studies. "Crown Zellerbach Corporation and Two AFL Unions," by Clark Kerr and Roger Randall, pp. 57–81.

Hays, John. "A New View of the Labor Question," *Overland,* vol. 6, Feb. 1871, pp. 140–47.

Hopkins, C. T. "The Present Crisis in San Francisco," *Californian,* vol. 1, May 1880, pp. 407–12.

Kossoris, Max. Statement in *Proceedings,* Governor's Conference on Automation, Los Angeles, Nov. 27, 1961. [Sacramento? 1961?] Pp. 19–24.

Lewis, Austin. "The Drift in California," *International Socialist Review,* vol. 12, Nov. 1911, pp. 272–74.

Linsenmayer, Leonard R. "Postwar Developments in the Pacific Region," *Monthly Labor Review,* vol. 64, April 1947, pp. 610–26.

Malm, Theodore. "Hiring Procedures and Selection Standards in the San Francisco Bay Area," *Industrial and Labor Relations Review,* vol. 8, Jan. 1955, pp. 231–52.

Miller, Joaquin. "If I Were California," *Californian Illustrated,* vol. 5, Dec. 1893, pp. 88–91.

Minor, Robert. "The 'Epic' Mass Movement in California," *Communist,* vol. 13, Dec. 1934, pp. 1214–33.

Monaco, F. "San Francisco Shoe Workers' Strike," *International Socialist Review,* vol. 13, May 1913, pp. 818–19.

Nylander, Towne. "Activities of a Regional Labor Board of the Fifteenth District," *Sociology and Social Research,* vol. 19, March–April 1935, pp. 349–54.

Pagano, Reinaldo. "History of the Building Service Employees' International Union in San Francisco, 1902–1939." Unpublished M.A. thesis. University of California, Berkeley, 1948. 97 pp.

Princeton University. Department of Economics and Social Institutions. *Collective Bargaining in the West Coast Paper Industry.* Princeton, N.J., 1941. 24 pp.

Richmond, Al. *Ten Years: The Story of a People's Newspaper.* San Francisco: Daily People's World, 1948. 32 pp.

Ross, Arnold M. *Twenty-five Years of Building the West: The Story of Calaveras Cement from 1925–1950.* San Francisco: Calaveras Cement Co., 1950. 52+ pp.

San Francisco Labor Council. *Rules to Regulate Picketing.* San Francisco, 1938. [6] pp.

Shaeffer, John W. Address to the Cigar Makers of the International Union. San Francisco, 1886. 4 pp.

U.S. Congress. Joint Committee on Labor-Management Relations. *Hearings on the Operation of the Labor-Management Relations Act of 1947.* 80th Cong., 2d sess. Part 2. Washington, 1948. Testimony of Arthur W. Ford, California Packing Corp., pp. 825–47.

U.S. Department of Labor. Fact-Finding Board. *Report and Recommendations in the Dispute between the P. G. and E. and Utility Workers Union of America, C.I.O., Locals 133, 134, 135, 136, 137, 169, 236 and 241.* N.p., 1946. 41 pp.

AFL Papers. Inventory.

Strikes and Agreements File, 1898–1953. Series 7. Call no. U.S. MSS-117A. State Historical Society of Wisconsin. Correspondence, Telegrams, Reports and Other Miscellaneous Materials Exchanged Between Union Locals and the President of the AFL Concerning Negotiations with Management, Planned Strikes, and Copies of Agreements Made Between Local Unions and Management. 80 boxes.
Information and Research File. Series 10, File C. Call no. U.S. MSS-117A.
10C

Note: Copies of a check list of the above manuscript papers having reference to California unions have been deposited in the Bancroft Library and in the Institute of Industrial Relations Library at UCLA. The check list contains some 135 items abstracted from a national check list in the library of the State Historical Society of Wisconsin. The papers were not examined.

BIBLIOGRAPHICAL AIDS

American Council on Race Relations. *Discrimination in Employment: A Selected Bibliography*. Bibliographic Series no. 2. Chicago, 1949. 8 pp.

American Federation of Labor. Workers Education Bureau. *Labor's Library*. A bibliography for trade unionists, educators, writers, students, librarians. Washington, 1952. 109 pp.

Benjamin, Hazel C. *A Trade Union Library, 1949*. Princeton: Industrial Relations Section, Princeton University, 1949. 53 pp.

Bepler, Doris West. "Descriptive Catalogue of Materials for Western History in California Magazines, 1854–1890." Unpublished M.A. thesis. University of California, Berkeley, 1920. 299 pp.

Blum, Albert A., comp. "Research in Progress in American Labor History," *Labor History,* vol. 3, Spring 1962, pp. 218–25. [Includes some projects on California labor history]

Bogardus, Emory S. *The Mexican Immigrant: An Annotated Bibliography*. Los Angeles: Council on International Relations, 1929. 21 pp.

California. State Library. *Right to Work Laws: A Selected Bibliography*. Sacramento, 1958. 16 pp.

———. State Relief Administration. Division of Planning and Research. *List of References on Migrants and Related Subjects in the S.R.A. Library,* by Blanche H. Dalton. [Sacramento?] 1939. 34+ pp.

California Library Association. Committee on Local History. *California Local History: A Centennial Bibliography,* edited by Ethel Blumann and Mabell W. Thomas. Stanford: Stanford University Press, 1950. 576 pp.

Chapman, Charles E. *A History of California: The Spanish Period*. New York: Macmillan, 1930. Annotated bibliography, pp. 487–509.

Committee of University Industrial Relations Librarians. *American Labor Union Periodicals: A Guide to Their Location,* by Bernard G. Naas and Carmelita S. Sakr. Ithaca: Cornell University, 1956. 175 pp.

Cowan, Robert Ernest, and Robert Grannis Cowan. *A Bibliography of the History of California, 1510–1930*. San Francisco: John Henry Nash, 1933. 3 vols. 825 pp.

Cowan, Robert Ernest, and Boutwell Dunlap. *Bibliography of the Chinese Question in the United States.* San Francisco: A. M. Robertson, 1909. 68 pp.

Eaton, Allen, and Shelby M. Harrison. *A Bibliography of Social Surveys.* New York: Russell Sage Foundation, 1930. 467 pp.

Fenn, William Purviance. *Ah Sin and His Brethren in American Literature.* Delivered before the Convocation of the College of Chinese Studies, June 1933. Peiping (Peking): College of Chinese Studies, Cooperating with California College in China [1933?] 131 + xli pp. [*Note:* Bancroft Library also refers to this work as a Ph.D. dissertation, University of Iowa, 1932]

Gates, Francis. "Labor History Resources in the Libraries of the University of California, Berkeley," *Labor History,* vol. 1, Spring 1960, pp. 196–205.

———. *Reference Guides for Labor Research.* A selected bibliography of directories, bibliographies, handbooks and guides to special collections relating to American labor unions, employers and employer associations. Berkeley: University of California, 1957. 35 pp.

Greenwood, Robert, ed. *California Imprints, 1833–1862: A Bibliography.* Compiled by Seiko June Suzuki and Marjorie Pulliam. Los Gatos, Calif.: Talisman Press, 1961. 524 pp.

Hasse, Adelaide. *Index of Economic Material in Documents of the States of the United States: California, 1849–1904.* Publication no. 85. Washington: Carnegie Institute of Washington, 1908. 316 pp.

Kessler, Selma P. *Industry-Wide Collective Bargaining: An Annotated Bibliography.* Prepared for the Labor Relations Council of the Wharton School of Finance. Philadelphia: University of Pennsylvania Press, 1948. 50 pp.

Larson, Henrietta M. *Guide to Business History.* Cambridge: Harvard University Press, 1948. 1181 pp.

Magistretti, William. "A Bibliography of Historical Materials in the Japanese Language on the West Coast Japanese," *Pacific Historical Review,* vol. 12, March 1943, pp. 67–73.

Matthews, Miriam. "The Negro in California from 1781–1910." An annotated bibliography. Unpublished research project, University of California, Los Angeles, 1944.

Pan-American Union. Division of Labor and Social Information. *Mexicans in the United States: A Bibliography.* Bibliographic Series no. 27. Washington, 1942. 14 pp.

Powell, Lawrence Clark. "Resources of Western Libraries for Research in History," *Pacific Historical Review,* vol. 11, Sept. 1942, pp. 263–80.

Rand, Anne. "The Development of the Labor Movement in California Since 1900: A Guide to the Bibliographic Sources." Unpublished M.A. thesis. University of California, Berkeley, 1940. 53 pp.

Reynolds, Lloyd G., and Charles C. Killingsworth. *Trade Union Publications.* The official journals, convention proceedings and constitutions of international unions and federations, 1850–1941. 3 vols. Baltimore: Johns Hopkins Press, 1944. 1347 pp.

Rosenthal, Clarice A., M. Meeker, M. Ottenberg, and others. "Selected Bibliography on Civil Liberties in the United States," *in* George Seldes, *You Can't Do That.* New York: Modern Age Books, 1938. Pp. 255–301.

Social Science Research Council, Pacific Coast Regional Committee. *Agricultural Labor in the Pacific Coast States.* A bibliography and suggestions for research. N.p., 1938. 64 pp.

U.S. Children's Bureau. *List of References on Child Labor,* by H. H. B. Meyer and Laura A. Thompson. Bureau Publication no. 18, Industrial Series no. 3. Washington, 1916. 161 pp.

———. *List of References on Child Labor,* by Laura A. Thompson. Bureau Publication no. 147 (supplementary to no. 18, above). Washington, 1925. 153 pp.

U.S. Department of Agriculture. *Bibliography on the Japanese in American Agriculture,* by Helen E. Hennefrund and Orpha Cummings. Annotated. Bibliographical Bull. no. 3. Washington, 1944. 61 pp.

U.S. Library of Congress. Division of Bibliography. *Selected List of References on Chinese Immigration.* Washington, 1904. 31 pp.

U.S. Work Projects Administration. *History of Journalism in San Francisco.* 7 vols. San Francisco, 1939–40. Vol. 1, *History of Foreign Journalism in San Francisco.* 171 pp.

———. *Inventory of the County Archives of California.* No. 39, "The City and County of San Francisco." San Francisco, 1940. Items 740–748, "Labor Activity," pp. 138–39.

U.S. Works Progress Administration. *Catalogue: WPA Writers' Program Publications.* American Guide Series; American Life Series. Washington, 1942. 54 pp.

———. *Journals of the Bay Cities,* by E. T. H. Bunje, F. J. Schmits, and H. Penn. Berkeley, 1936. 93 pp.

Waters, Willard O. "California Bibliographies," *California Historical Society Quarterly,* vol. 3, July 1924, pp. 245–58.

AUTHOR–TITLE INDEX

(many titles have been abridged)